VBScript For D...

MW00345663

VBScript Statements

Statement	Action
Call	Transfers control to another procedure
Dim	Declares a variable or an array
Do Until...Loop	Loops
Do While...Loop	Loops
Do...Loop Until	Loops
Do...Loop While	Loops
End Function	Ends a function procedure
End Sub	Ends a subroutine procedure
Erase	Reinitializes an array
Err	Sets Err to a specified value
Error	Simulates a specific error condition
Exit Do	Exits a block of Do...Loop code
Exit For	Exits a block of Do...For code
Exit Function	Exits a function procedure
Exit Sub	Exits a subroutine procedure
For...Next	Loops
Function	Declares the name and arguments for a Function procedure
If...Then	Processes statements conditionally
If...Then...Else	Processes statements conditionally
Mid	Replaces characters in a string with other characters
Option Explicit	Forces declaration of all variables in a script block
Private	Declares a local array
Public	Declares a public array
Randomize	Initializes the random number generator
ReDim	Changes the dimensions of an array
Rem	Specifies a line of comments (same as an apostrophe)
Select Case	Processes statements conditionally
Set	Creates an object variable
Sub	Declares the name and arguments of a subroutine procedure
While...Wend	Loops

VBScript For Dummies®

COMPUTER BOOK SERIES FROM IDG

MsgBox Reference

The MsgBox function displays a message in a dialog box and can also return a value that represents which button the user clicked.

Syntax

```
MsgBox(prompt[,buttons][,title])
```

Values for the buttons argument

Value	Description
0	OK button only
1	OK and Cancel buttons
2	Abort, Retry, and Ignore buttons
3	Yes, No, and Cancel buttons
4	Yes and No buttons
5	Retry and Cancel buttons
16	Critical Message icon (bix X)
32	Warning Query icon (question mark)
48	Warning Message icon (exclamation)
64	Information Message icon (letter i)
0	First button is default
256	Second button is default
512	Third button is default

These values can be added together. The following statement displays a message box with Yes and No buttons and a question mark icon:

```
Ans=Msgbox ("Continue?", 4+32)
```

Msgbox Return Values

Value	Button Selected
1	OK
2	Cancel
3	Abort
4	Retry
5	Ignore
6	Yes
7	No

Important Web sites

Microsoft VBScript home page:

```
http://www.microsoft.com/vbscript/
```

Microsoft VBScript online documentation:

```
http://www.microsoft.com/vbscript/us/vbsmain/vbsdocs.htm
```

Microsoft Internet Explorer object model documentation:

```
http://www.microsoft.com/intdev/sdk/docs/scriptom/
```

Corrections and updates to this book:

```
http://www.j-walk.com/vbsbook/
```

...For Dummies: #1 Computer Book Series for Beginners

VBSCRIPT

FOR

DUMMIES®

VBSCRIPT FOR DUMMIES®

by John Walkenbach

IDG BOOKS WORLDWIDE

IDG Books Worldwide, Inc.
An International Data Group Company

Foster City, CA ♦ Chicago, IL ♦ Indianapolis, IN ♦ Southlake, TX

VBScript For Dummies®

Published by
IDG Books Worldwide, Inc.
An International Data Group Company
919 E. Hillsdale Blvd.
Suite 400
Foster City, CA 94404
www.idgbooks.com (IDG Books Worldwide Web Site)
http://www.dummies.com (Dummies Press Web Site)

Library of Congress Catalog Card No.: 96-77274

ISBN: 0-7645-0030-9

Printed in the United States of America

10 9 8 7 6 5 4 3 2 1

1B/RZ/RR/ZW/IN

Distributed in the United States by IDG Books Worldwide, Inc.

Distributed by Macmillan Canada for Canada; by Contemporanea de Ediciones for Venezuela; by Distribuidora Cuspide for Argentina; by CITEC for Brazil; by Ediciones ZETA S.C.R. Ltda. for Peru; by Editorial Limusa SA for Mexico; by Transworld Publishers Limited in the United Kingdom and Europe; by Academic Bookshop for Egypt; by Levant Distributors S.A.R.L. for Lebanon; by Al Jassim for Saudi Arabia; by Simron Pty. Ltd. for South Africa; by Pustak Mahal for India; by The Computer Bookshop for India; by Toppan Company Ltd. for Japan; by Addison Wesley Publishing Company for Korea; by Longman Singapore Publishers Ltd. for Singapore, Malaysia, Thailand, and Indonesia; by Unalis Corporation for Taiwan; by WS Computer Publishing Company, Inc. for the Philippines; by WoodsLane Pty. Ltd. for Australia; by WoodsLane Enterprises Ltd. for New Zealand. Authorized Sales Agent: Anthony Rudkin Associates for the Middle East and North Africa.

For general information on IDG Books Worldwide's books in the U.S., please call our Consumer Customer Service department at 800-762-2974. For reseller information, including discounts and premium sales, please call our Reseller Customer Service department at 800-434-3422.

For information on where to purchase IDG Books Worldwide's books outside the U.S., please contact our International Sales department at 415-655-3172 or fax 415-655-3295.

For information on foreign language translations, please contact our Foreign & Subsidiary Rights department at 415-655-3021 or fax 415-655-3281.

For sales inquiries and special prices for bulk quantities, please contact our Sales department at 415-655-3200 or write to the address above.

For information on using IDG Books Worldwide's books in the classroom or for ordering examination copies, please contact our Educational Sales department at 800-434-2086 or fax 817-251-8174.

For authorization to photocopy items for corporate, personal, or educational use, please contact Copyright Clearance Center, 222 Rosewood Drive, Danvers, MA 01923, or fax 508-750-4470.

is a trademark under exclusive license to IDG Books Worldwide, Inc., from International Data Group, Inc.

About the Author

John Walkenbach

John Walkenbach has been involved with computers for the past 25 years. He has written more than 250 articles and reviews for publications such as *PC World, Windows, PC/Computing,* and *InfoWorld.* In addition, he's the best-selling author of more than a dozen books, including *Excel For Windows 95 Power Programming With VBA* and *Excel Programming For Windows 95 For Dummies.* John holds a Ph.D. in experimental psychology from the University of Montana and has worked as an instructor, consultant, programmer, and market research manager for the largest S&L ever to fail (and he takes no responsibility for that). Currently, he heads JWalk and Associates, a small consulting firm in Southern California. John currently maintains two World Wide Web sites: The Spreadsheet Page and the VBScript/ActiveX Demo Page (you can access either site from http://www.j-walk.com). In his spare time, he likes to annoy his neighbors with loud blues guitar playing and weird sounds from his synthesizers.

ABOUT IDG BOOKS WORLDWIDE

Welcome to the world of IDG Books Worldwide.

IDG Books Worldwide, Inc., is a subsidiary of International Data Group, the world's largest publisher of computer-related information and the leading global provider of information services on information technology. IDG was founded more than 25 years ago and now employs more than 8,500 people worldwide. IDG publishes more than 275 computer publications in over 75 countries (see listing below). More than 60 million people read one or more IDG publications each month.

Launched in 1990, IDG Books Worldwide is today the #1 publisher of best-selling computer books in the United States. We are proud to have received eight awards from the Computer Press Association in recognition of editorial excellence and three from *Computer Currents'* First Annual Readers' Choice Awards. Our best-selling *...For Dummies*® series has more than 30 million copies in print with translations in 30 languages. IDG Books Worldwide, through a joint venture with IDG's Hi-Tech Beijing, became the first U.S. publisher to publish a computer book in the People's Republic of China. In record time, IDG Books Worldwide has become the first choice for millions of readers around the world who want to learn how to better manage their businesses.

Our mission is simple: Every one of our books is designed to bring extra value and skill-building instructions to the reader. Our books are written by experts who understand and care about our readers. The knowledge base of our editorial staff comes from years of experience in publishing, education, and journalism — experience we use to produce books for the '90s. In short, we care about books, so we attract the best people. We devote special attention to details such as audience, interior design, use of icons, and illustrations. And because we use an efficient process of authoring, editing, and desktop publishing our books electronically, we can spend more time ensuring superior content and spend less time on the technicalities of making books.

You can count on our commitment to deliver high-quality books at competitive prices on topics you want to read about. At IDG Books Worldwide, we continue in the IDG tradition of delivering quality for more than 25 years. You'll find no better book on a subject than one from IDG Books Worldwide.

John J. Kilcullen

John Kilcullen
President and CEO
IDG Books Worldwide, Inc.

Eighth Annual Computer Press Awards ≥1992

Ninth Annual Computer Press Awards ≥1993

Tenth Annual Computer Press Awards ≥1994

Eleventh Annual Computer Press Awards ≥1995

Dedication

This book is dedicated to VaRene, Dustin, Marisa, and K.C.

Author's Acknowledgments

Many people are responsible for getting a book like this into your hands, so I don't take all the blame — I mean credit. There's not room to acknowledge them all, so I'd like to thank a few folks who played a major role in the process. First, thanks to all the talented behind-the-scenes folks at IDG Books. Kelly Ewing, my project editor, did an excellent job helping me organize this book and coordinating the entire effort. Thanks also to Jill Brummett, my copy editor, who helped make this book much more readable. I'm also indebted to Garrett Pease, who provided a thorough technical review and set me straight on a few issues. I'd also like to acknowledge Rick Teale, an e-mail buddy who took the time to try out all of the sample files.

John Walkenbach

La Jolla, California

Publisher's Acknowledgments

We're proud of this book; please send us your comments about it by using the Reader Response Card at the back of the book or by e-mailing us at feedback/dummies@idgbooks.com. Some of the people who helped bring this book to market include the following:

Acquisitions, Development, and Editorial

Project Editor: Kelly Ewing

Acquisitions Editor: Tammy Goldfeld

Product Development Manager: Mary Bednarek

Permissions Editor: Joyce Pepple

Copy Editor: Jill Brummett

Technical Editor: Garrett Pease

Editorial Manager: Seta K. Frantz

Editorial Assistant: Michael D. Sullivan

Production

Project Coordinator: Regina Snyder

Layout and Graphics: Brett Black, Cameron Booker, Linda Boyer, J. Tyler Connor, Dominique DeFelice, Angela F. Hunckler, Todd Klemme, Jane Martin, Mark Owens, Michael Sullivan

Proofreaders: Joel Draper, Rachel Garvey, Robert Springer, Carrie Voorhis, Karen York

Indexer: Sherry Massey

Special Help: Stephanie Koutek, Proof Editor

General and Administrative

IDG Books Worldwide, Inc.: John Kilcullen, President and CEO; Steven Berkowitz, COO and Publisher

Dummies, Inc.: Milissa Koloski, Executive Vice President and Publisher

Dummies Technology Press and Dummies Editorial: Diane Graves Steele, Vice President and Associate Publisher; Judith A. Taylor, Brand Manager

Dummies Trade Press: Kathleen A. Welton, Vice President and Publisher; Stacy S. Collins, Brand Manager

IDG Books Production for Dummies Press: Beth Jenkins, Production Director; Cindy L. Phipps, Supervisor of Project Coordination; Kathie S. Schutte, Supervisor of Page Layout; Shelley Lea, Supervisor of Graphics and Design; Debbie J. Gates, Production Systems Specialist

Dummies Packaging and Book Design: Patti Sandez, Packaging Assistant; Kavish+Kavish, Cover Design

◆

The publisher would like to give special thanks to Patrick J. McGovern, without whom this book would not have been possible.

◆

Contents at a Glance

Introduction *1*

Part I: What's It All About? *11*
Chapter 1: What You Need and Where to Get It 13
Chapter 2: Your First VBScript Program (A Script-Tease) 23

Part II: How VBScript Works *33*
Chapter 3: Exploring the Explorer (Internet Explorer 3.0, That Is) 35
Chapter 4: Using Scripts in Your HTML Documents 45
Chapter 5: Introducing Objects and the Object Model 57
Chapter 6: All about Properties, Methods, and Events 69

Part III: Programming Concepts *79*
Chapter 7: All about Subroutines and Functions 81
Chapter 8: Using Variables and Arrays 95
Chapter 9: Controlling Program Flow and Decision-Making 111
Chapter 10: Getting Acquainted with Built-In Functions 131
Chapter 11: Correcting Errors and Exterminating Bugs 149

Part IV: Doing Useful Stuff *161*
Chapter 12: Working With the HTML Intrinsic Controls 163
Chapter 13: Working with Forms 185
Chapter 14: Working with Frames 205
Chapter 15: Useful Code Snippets That You Can Steal 227

Part V: Incorporating ActiveX Controls *239*
Chapter 16: ActiveX Controls: What, Where, and Why 241
Chapter 17: Using ActiveX Controls: The Gory Details 253
Chapter 18: The Coolest Control: The HTML Layout Control 279

Part VI: Putting It All Together *295*
Chapter 19: Creating Column Charts with VBScript 297
Chapter 20: Calculating Mortgage Payments 309
Chapter 21: Creating a Calendar Application 323
Chapter 22: Administering an Online Quiz 337

Part VII: The Part of Tens *345*
Chapter 23: Top Ten VBScript Questions and Answers 347
Chapter 24: Top Ten VBScript Resources on the Net 351
Chapter 25: Top Ten Ways to Become a VBScript Guru 355

Index *359*

Reader Response Card .... *Back of Book*

Cartoons at a Glance

By Rich Tennant • Fax: 508-546-7747 • E-mail: the5wave@tiac.net

"SO I SAID, 'WAITER! WAITER! THERE'S A BUG IN MY SOUP!' AND HE SAYS, 'SORRY, SIR, THE CHEF USED TO PROGRAM COMPUTERS.' AHH HAHA HAHA THANK YOU! THANK YOU!'"

page 79

"IT SAYS HERE IF I SUBSCRIBE TO THIS MAGAZINE, THEY'LL SEND ME A FREE DESK-TOP CALCULATOR. DESKTOP CALCULATOR?!! WHOOAA - WHERE HAVE I BEEN?!!"

page 295

"IT'S AMAZING HOW MUCH MORE SOME PEOPLE CAN GET OUT OF A PC THAN OTHERS."

page 11

"NAAAH - HE'S NOT THAT SMART. HE WON'T BACK UP HIS HARD DISK, FORGETS TO CONSISTENTLY NAME HIS FILES, AND DROOLS ALL OVER THE KEYBOARD."

page 345

Real Programmers do their best work between 1 and 5 a.m.

page 161

Real Programmers don't sleep - their systems just temporarily go down.

page 239

Real Programmers don't like to be bothered when they're working.

page 33

Table of Contents

· ·

Introduction 1

So, You Want to Be a Programmer 1
    What This Book Covers 2
    What This Book Doesn't Cover 3
How This Book Is Organized 3
    Part I: What's It All About? 3
    Part II: How VBScript Works 3
    Part III: Programming Concepts 4
    Part IV: Doing Useful Stuff 4
    Part V: Incorporating ActiveX Controls 4
    Part VI: Putting It All Together 4
    Part VII: The Part of Tens 4
Assumptions About You 5
VBScript: New Language, Old Friend 6
What You Can Do With VBScript 6
Marginal Icons 8
The Web Site On a Disk 8
    And More! 9
Wanna Reach Out? 9
Now What? 9

Part I: What's It All About? **11**

Chapter 1: What You Need and Where to Get It **13**

Your Basic Needs 13
Just Where Is VBScript? 14
Surfing for Downloads 15
    Internet Explorer 3.0 16
    ActiveX Control Pad 16
    ActiveX Controls 17
Ladies and Gentlemen . . . Choose Your Editor 17
    Windows Notepad 17
    Windows WordPad 17
    Microsoft Word, with Internet Assistant 18
    SitePad 18
    More HTML editors 19
Getting Ready to Script 19
A Sneak Preview 20

Chapter 2: Your First VBScript Program (A Script-Tease) **23**

What You Do 23
Create the HTML Document 24
Adding the Buttons 25
Inserting the Script 26
    Creating the basic subroutine 26
    Modifying the subroutine 27
    Adding the second subroutine 28
    The final document (Take 1) 28
    Testing the script 29
    Making changes (Take 2) 29
    Taking a closer look 30
    The problem 31
    Fixing the bug (Take 3) 31

Part II: How VBScript Works *33*

Chapter 3: Exploring the Explorer (Internet Explorer 3.0, That Is) **35**

Excursions Into Versions 35
Cool Browser . . . Very Cool 36
    Internet Explorer innovations 36
    What about compatibility? 38
Internet Explorer Features You May Have Missed 38
Parts of Internet Explorer 40
    Your window on the World (Wide Web) 40
    I've been framed! 40
    The well documented document 40
        Links 41
        Anchors 42
        Forms 42
    What's your location? 42
    Don't know much about history 43

Chapter 4: Using Scripts in Your HTML Documents **45**

Including VBScript in HTML Documents 45
    Direct execution of VBScript 45
    Deferred execution by using a VBScript procedure 47
Understanding the <SCRIPT> Tag 48
    Match 'em up 49
    How many script blocks? 49
    Where to put scripts 49
    The LANGUAGE attribute for <SCRIPT> 50
    What about older browsers? 50

Writing VBScript Code 51
    Using comments in VBScript code 51
    Upper- or lowercase? 52
    Indenting and spaces 53
    Splitting a statement into two or more lines 53
Hey! That's Private! 54
Compatibility Issues 54
    When to use VBScript 55
    When to avoid VBScript 55
VBScript versus JavaScript 55

Chapter 5: Introducing Objects and the Object Model 57

The Object Model Visualized 57
The Collection Plate 59
Referring to Objects 59
How Objects Relate to Internet Explorer Features 60
    A concrete example 60
    A way to conceptualize objects 62
    A family affair 62
Drilling Deeper into the Object Model 63
The Objects Described 65
    The Window object 66
    The Frame object and the Frames collection 66
    The History object 66
    The Navigator object 66
    The Location object 66
    The Script object 67
    The Document object 67
    The Link object and the Links collection 67
    The Anchor object and the Anchors collection 67
    The Form object and the Forms collection 67
    The Element object and the Elements collection 68

Chapter 6: All about Properties, Methods, and Events 69

Making Objects Useful 69
Examining Object Properties 70
    Referring to properties 70
    Looking at property values 70
    Changing property values 71
    Pointing to objects 71
    Seeing the Document object properties in action 73
Exploring Object Methods 73
Understanding Object Events 75
    Handling those events 76
    An event-handling example 76
Finding Out More about This Stuff 78

Part III: Programming Concepts 79

Chapter 7: All about Subroutines and Functions 81

Procedural Matters 81
  Looking at subroutines 82
  Looking at functions 83
Subroutine Examples 83
  An event handler example 84
  A subroutine with an argument 85
    How it works 86
    Another way to do it 87
Calling a Subroutine from Another Subroutine: Rules of the Road 87
  Calling a subroutine with no arguments 87
  Calling a subroutine with an argument 88
Function Examples 88
  A simple function example 89
  The ReverseText function 90
Where to Put Your Procedures 91
  A bad example 91
  A good example 92
Troubleshooting Subroutines and Functions 92

Chapter 8: Using Variables and Arrays 95

Introducing Variables 95
  Naming variables 95
  Bad variable names 96
Today's Assignment 96
  Express yourself 97
  Hello, Operator 98
    Common operators 98
    Logical operators 99
  What gets calculated first? 100
    Order of precedence 100
    Parentheses to the rescue 100
Array of Hope 101
  Well, I declare! 101
  Multidimensional arrays 102
  Dynamic arrays 103
  How many elements? 103
Scoping Variables and Arrays 104
  Broadening a variable's scope 105
  Declaring multiple variables 106
Object Variables: A Special Type 106
Forcing Variable Declaration 107
  How to force yourself to declare all variables 108
  Why force yourself to declare all variables? 108

Chapter 9: Controlling Program Flow and Decision-Making **111**

Go with the Flow, Dude 111
If-Then Structure 112
    Examples of conditions 113
    If-Then examples 114
    If-Then with multiple instructions 114
Supplying an Alternative: If-Then-Else 115
    If-Then-Else with multiple instructions 115
    Another option: If-Then-ElseIf 116
The Select Case Structure 117
    A Select Case example 118
    A catch-all case 119
    Nested Select Case structures 119
Looping de Loops 121
For-Next Loops 121
    A For-Next example 121
    A For-Next example with a step value 122
    Looping backwards 123
    For-Next and arrays 123
    A nested For-Next example 125
Do Until Loops 126
Do While Loops 127
Do-Loop Until Loops 128
Do-Loop While Loops 128
Cheat Sheet For Looping 129

Chapter 10: Getting Acquainted with Built-In Functions **131**

Using Functions in Your Code 131
Functions Galore 132
Function Examples 132
    Conversion functions 133
        The Chr function 133
        The Asc function 134
        The Hex function 135
        The Int and Fix functions 135
    Date and time functions 136
        Current date and time functions 136
        Nesting date and time functions 137
    Weekday function 137
    Math functions 138
        Trigonometric functions 138
        Random number functions 138
    String functions 140
        The Mid function 140
        The Left and Right functions 140
        The Lcase and Ucase functions 141
        The Len function 142
        The Instr function 142

Variant functions 143
    The IsDate function 143
    The IsNumeric function 144
User Interface functions 144
    MsgBox 144
    The InputBox function 147
Finding out More about Functions 148

Chapter 11: Correcting Errors and Exterminating Bugs **149**

Make an Error? Me? 149
Syntax Errors 150
    Anatomy of a syntax error message 150
    Avoiding syntax errors 151
Entomology 101: Program Bugs 151
    Runtime errors 152
    Logical flaws 153
Identifying Bugs 153
Avoiding Error Messages 154
Stomping Those Bugs 155
    Examining your code 155
    Using Alert statements 155
    Monitoring a variable 156
Bug Prevention Tips 157
    Develop your code in small bits 157
    Force variable declaration 157
    Use consistent indentation 158
    Remember a variable's scope 158
    Test extreme cases 158
    Let others test your code 159
    Test your code on the server 159

Part IV: Doing Useful Stuff *161*

Chapter 12: Working With the HTML Intrinsic Controls **163**

HTML Intrinsic Controls: What's Available? 163
Button Controls 165
    Displaying a message 166
    Changing a button caption 166
    Opening a new URL 167
    Simulating the Back and Forward buttons 167
Submit and Reset Controls 168
Text Controls 168
    Using a text control for input 169
    Using a text control for output 170
    Understanding the OnFocus and OnBlur events 171

Textarea Control 172
Password Control 173
Radio Button Controls 174
   Executing a subroutine when a radio button is clicked 176
   Determining which radio button is selected 177
Check Box Control 178
Select Control 179
   Which item is selected? 180
   Determining multiple selections 182
Hidden Control 183

Chapter 13: Working with Forms **185**
Read Me First! 185
HTML Forms: A Refresher Course 186
   Defining a form 187
   Adding form controls 188
   Validating a form 188
VBScript and HTML Forms: A Winning Combination 189
Referring To Controls 189
   Referring to a control by its position in the form 190
   Referring to a control by name 190
   An example 191
   Using object variables 192
Generating Forms and Controls With VBScript 193
   Generating alphabet radio buttons 193
   Generating a list of numbers 194
   Generating a list of dates for the current month 195
Client-Side Data Validation 196
   What gets validated? 196
   The OnSubmit event 197
   Validating a form: Example one 198
   Validating a form: Example two 200
Using Form Controls For a Link List 202

Chapter 14: Working with Frames **205**
Frames: Not Just For Pictures Anymore 205
A Frame Example 206
   Referring to a different frame 208
   Other ways to refer to a frame 209
   Still confused? 209
Another Frame Example 210
   Using a button to load a URL into a different frame 212
   Loading a URL into a different frame using a hyperlink .. 213
   Changing the colors in a different frame 213

More Ways to Load Documents 214
    Loading a document in another frame 215
    Loading a new document in the current frame 215
    Loading a document in the browser's full window 216
    Loading a document in a new browser window 216
Floating Frames 217
    Updating a page dynamically with a floating frame 217
        The HTML document 218
        How it works 219
    A more sophisticated borderless frame example 220
Fun With Floating Frames 221
    Simple animation effects 221
    A VBScript message flasher 222
        Message flasher code 222
        Customizing the message flasher 224
    Frame animation — big time! 225

Chapter 15: Useful Code Snippets That You Can Steal 227

Number Formatting Functions 227
    Formatting dollars and cents 227
    Formatting percentages 228
    Spelling out numeric values 229
Displaying a Friendly Date and Time 230
Converting Hex to Decimal 232
Detecting a VBScript-Compatible Browser 232
Audio Greeting Based on the Time of Day 233
Validating a Credit Card Number 233
A Scrolling Status Bar Message 234
Special FX 235
    Background fade-in 235
Sorting an Array 236
Choosing Lottery Numbers 237

Part V: Incorporating ActiveX Controls *239*

Chapter 16: ActiveX Controls: What, Where, and Why 241

Okay, So What Is an ActiveX Control? 241
    Two quick examples 242
        An ActiveX Label control 242
        An ActiveX ScrollBar control 242
Where Do You Get ActiveX Controls? 243
    Types of controls 244
    ActiveX controls from Microsoft 245
        Microsoft Forms 2.0 controls 245
        Other Microsoft ActiveX controls 246
    Other sources for ActiveX controls 247

The Technology Behind the Magic 247
    Downloading a control 248
    Security for controls 249
Using ActiveX Controls: Pros and Cons 250
    The Pros 251
    The cons 251

Chapter 17: Using ActiveX Controls: The Gory Details 253

The <OBJECT> Tag: It Gets Ugly 254
    An example <OBJECT> tag 254
    The <OBJECT> tag attributes 254
    The <PARAM> tags 255
Introducing the ActiveX Control Pad 256
    HTML text editor 256
    ActiveX Control editor 257
    Script Wizard 258
    HTML Layout editor 258
Hands-On: Using the ActiveX Control Pad 259
    Creating a new document 259
    Inserting an ActiveX Label control 260
    Changing Label control properties 261
    Inserting an ActiveX SpinButton control 262
    Adding HTML 263
    Viewing the document 263
    Using the Script Wizard 264
    Testing the script 266
More about the Script Wizard 267
Discovering Properties and Methods 267
ActiveX Examples 268
    The ActiveX Marquee control 269
    The ActiveX PopUp Menu control 269
    The ActiveX ButtonMenu control 271
    The ActiveX Timer control 273
    Another ActiveX Timer control example 273
    Yet another ActiveX Timer control example 275
    Using ActiveX controls in HTML forms 277

Chapter 18: The Coolest Control: The HTML Layout Control 279

The HTML Layout control 279
    The upside of the HTML Layout control 279
    The downside of the HTML Layout control 280
An Introductory Example 280
    Using the example 281
    Looking at the <OBJECT> tag 281
    About ALX files 281

Hands-On: Creating a Layout 283
    1. Creating the HTML File 283
    2. Inserting a Layout control 284
    3. Saving the HTML file 284
    4. Editing the HTML Layout 285
    5. Adding the Image control 285
    6. Adding a Label control 287
    7. Adding a HotSpot control 288
    8. Writing the VBScript 288
    9. Testing the subroutine 290
    10. Finishing off the subroutine 290
Discovering More about the HTML Layout Control 290
Layout Control Examples 291
    Watch the bouncing balls 291
    Rolling the dice 292
    Using ListBox controls 293

Part VI: Putting It All Together 295

Chapter 19: Creating Column Charts with VBScript 297

What is a Column Chart? 297
    Using graphic files 297
    A cool chart-making technique 298
Creating a Chart with VBScript 299
    The code behind the magic 300
    How the code works 301
Creating a Chart in a Frame 301
    Creating the floating frame 301
    Creating the chart 302
    Trying out the chart example 303
    Scaling the chart 303
Getting Even Fancier 304
    Declaring the variables 305
    Generating the select controls 306
    Generating the chart 307
Adapting These Techniques 308

Chapter 20: Calculating Mortgage Payments 309

Project Goals 309
The Game Plan 310
Creating the Forms 310
    The data input form 311
    The results form 312

Calculating the Results 313
    The On_Click subroutine 313
    How the subroutine works 314
    Calculating the monthly payment 314
    Formatting the numbers 315
Amortizing the Loan 317
    Inserting a floating frame 317
    Adding another button 318
    Calculating the amortization schedule 319
        The Amortize_OnClick subroutine 319
        How the subroutine works 320
    Testing the subroutine 321
    A change of plans 322

Chapter 21: Creating a Calendar Application **323**

Project Background 323
The Game Plan 324
Specifying a Month and Year 324
    Inserting the ActiveX controls 324
    Creating an array of month names 325
    Adding a Window_OnLoad subroutine 325
    The event handlers 326
    Testing the controls 327
Developing the Calendar 327
    Adding a floating frame 328
    Sending HTML to the frame 329
    Calling the GenerateCalendar subroutine 331
    Testing it again 331
Adding the Links 332
    Creating an array 332
    Displaying the tour information 333
    Creating the links 333
    Trying out the code 334
Making It Look Good 335

Chapter 22: Administering an Online Quiz **337**

Project Goals 337
The Game Plan 338
Project Components 338
Storing the Data 338
Presenting the Items 339
How the Application Works 341
Creating Your Own Quiz 344

Part VII: The Part of Tens 345

Chapter 23: Top Ten VBScript Questions and Answers 347

Is VBScript the same as Visual Basic? 347
Where can I get a copy of the VBScript
     programming language? 348
What are the typical uses for VBScript? 348
If I use VBScript in my Web document, is the number
     of people who can access my site limited? 348
If a user accesses my Web site with a VBScript
     compatible browser, can the browser automatically
     load a different VBScript enhanced page? 349
I use VBScript on my Web site to perform proprietary
     calculations. How can I prevent my competitors from
     viewing my VBScript code? 349
When a user loads my page, how do I execute a program
     that's on the user's local drive? 349
When I visit a site that uses VBScript, I like to look at the
     source code. But if the site uses frames, I find that the
     View⇨Source command only shows the top level frame.
     What gives? 349
Can I set up a Web page hit counter using VBScript? 349

Chapter 24: Top Ten VBScript Resources on the Net 351

The Microsoft VBScript Site 351
The VBScript Mailing List 352
VBScript Newsgroups 352
VBScript Central 353
The VBScript / ActiveX Demo Page 353
Scribe: The VBScript Writers Resource 353
ActiveX Journal for HTML Writers 353
ActiveX Resource Center 354
ACTIVEX.COM 354
Web search engines 354

Chapter 25: Top Ten Ways to Become a VBScript Guru 355

Browse the Web 355
Look at a Lot of VBScript Code 355
Communicate with Others 355
Borrow and Adapt Others' Ideas 356
Study the Documentation 356
Study the Examples in this Book 356
Think like a Web Site Visitor, Not a Designer 356
Think Modular 357
Experiment 357
Experiment More 357

Introduction

Greetings, prospective Visual Basic Script programmer, and welcome to *VBScript For Dummies*.

You and I already have a lot in common — an interest in the World Wide Web (WWW) and a desire to produce more interesting Web pages. I don't have to tell you that the WWW is the most exciting thing happening these days in the world of computing. In fact, the Web reaches well beyond the computer community and has become a pervasive force in society. URLs are commonly listed in TV commercials, magazine ads, and even billboards.

Not too long ago, the WWW was a pretty boring place visually. All Web pages looked pretty much alike, and you had very few surprises when you loaded a page into your browser. But things are changing rapidly, thanks to a new generation of Web browsers — and a new generation of Web page development tools. One of the most exciting new tools is Visual Basic Script, which is actually a programming language that can add pizzazz to your Web pages and make them perform feats that are otherwise impossible.

VBScript is appealing because, as programming languages go, it's very easy to learn and use. In other words, you don't have to have a degree in computer science and spend months in the classroom in order to do meaningful things with VBScript.

Unlike most programming books, this one has an unusual twist: It's written in plain English, and even normal people can understand it. It's filled with "just the facts, ma'am" type of information — and very little technobabble that you might need once every third lifetime. Even better: It has lots of great examples that you can easily adapt to your own needs.

So, You Want to Be a Programmer. . . .

If you're like most computer users, the very word *programmer* probably conjures up an image of someone who looks and behaves nothing like yourself. Perhaps words like *nerd, geek,* and *dweeb* come to mind.

Fact is, times have changed. Computer programming has gotten much easier, and now even so-called normal people engage in this activity. *Programming* simply means developing instructions that are carried out automatically by the

Why I wrote this book

Two years ago, I didn't know the difference between HTML and a hot tamale. Sure, I browsed around a bit with my Web browser, but I had no idea what was going on behind the scenes. Then one day it occurred to me that, for the first time in my adult life, I was getting left behind in the world of computers. People were talking about the Web, and I realized that I didn't understand what they were talking about. So I took it upon myself to learn more about the Web and HTML.

I always find that the best way to master a new topic is to have a particular goal in mind. Therefore, I decided to create my very own Web site devoted to spreadsheets (which happens to be my specialty area). I bought a few books, studied dozens (or probably hundreds) of pages of HTML, and spent many hours writing and experimenting with HTML.

Within a few weeks, I posted the result of my efforts ("The Spreadsheet Page," at `http://www.j-walk.com/ss/`). The more I worked with HTML, the more I became engrossed in it. My Web site expanded rapidly, and before long I considered myself fairly adept at HTML.

And then, in spring 1996, the world changed. Microsoft released the first beta of its Internet Explorer 3.0 browser. I was very curious about a feature called VBScript. I studied a few examples at the Microsoft Web site and liked what I saw. Before long I was hooked big-time. I spent far too many hours experimenting with VBScript to see what it could do — in spite of documentation that was either nonexistent, very sparse, or completely wrong. I could have really used a book like *Visual Basic Script For Dummies.*

By the time the second beta of Internet Explorer hit the scene, I had developed another Web site (just for fun), which housed a few dozen interesting and useful VBScript demos. I was amazed at the number of visitors to this site — more than my *real* Web site! I received feedback from dozens of visitors who thanked me profusely for demonstrating what VBScript was all about.

After a few weeks playing around with VBScript, I decided that I wanted to write a book. IDG Books took me up on my offer, and you're holding the result in your hand right now.

computer. VBScript programming consists of embedding instructions in your Web pages that can perform things that are well beyond the powers of plain old HTML. Because you already know HTML, you should be able to pick up on VBScript in no time (well, it'll take *some* time).

What This Book Covers

In a nutshell, this book is about VBScript, Microsoft's new programming language for Web documents. In the pages that follow, I introduce you to VBScript, provide you with the basic knowledge you need to write scripts in that language, and give you the tools you need to advance even further, if you so desire. And in the process, you're exposed to *lots* of examples that clarify concepts and give you something to start with when you go out on your own. In fact, you can use many of the examples without making any changes.

Notice that the title of this book isn't *The Complete Guide to VBScript Programming*. I don't cover every aspect of VBScript programming — but then again you probably don't want to *know* everything about this topic. Suffice it to say that this book will definitely get you started and provide you with a firm foundation so that you can proceed as far as you want. Actually, most readers will probably find that this book is all they really need to use VBScript in their Web pages.

What This Book Doesn't Cover

Before you jump into this book, you need to know how to write HTML. As you see, VBScript is embedded in your HTML document, so you need to know HTML before you can add VBScript to your Web pages. This book does not teach you how to write HTML.

Let me say it again: This book does not cover HTML. Plenty of books are devoted to HTML, and this is not one of them. Okay? If you want to know about HTML, pick up a copy of *HTML For Dummies,* 2nd Edition, by Ed Tittel and Steve James (published by IDG Books Worldwide, Inc.).

How This Book Is Organized

This book started out as an outline in a Microsoft Word document. The outline went through several modifications and eventually turned into what is now the table of contents. Following is a quick synopsis of the book's major parts.

Part I: What's It All About?

This part is the official "introduction and background" section in which I discuss the origins of VBScript and describe what you need to use this book (and where to get the required software). The final chapter in this part is designed to get your feet wet right away. It's a step-by-step hands-on example in which you develop an actual Web page that uses VBScript.

Part II: How VBScript Works

Like it or not, you can't just jump into this stuff and expect to get results immediately. You need some basic knowledge. That's the purpose of the four chapters in this part. These chapters provide the foundation for virtually everything else that follows. In other words, if you're going to skip chapters, these are not the ones to skip.

Part III: Programming Concepts

The five chapters in Part III are all about programming. You'll learn the difference between subroutines and functions, and you'll be on familiar terms with concepts such as variables, arrays, operators, and expressions. I introduce you to the notion of program flow, VBScript built-in functions, and even delve into the wonderful world of debugging.

Part IV: Doing Useful Stuff

The chapters in this part get into the meat of things so that you can begin doing useful work with VBScript. I provide lots of examples that cover the HTML intrinsic controls, forms, frames, and an entire chapter is chock full of useful VBScript code examples that you can use as they are or modify for your own use.

Part V: Incorporating ActiveX Controls

VBScript and ActiveX controls go together like chocolate and peanut butter (but the software combination is slightly less messy on warm days). For the uninitiated, I introduce ActiveX controls and explain where to get them. Then I present many examples of using these controls with VBScript. The final chapter in this part covers the mother of all controls — the HTML Layout Control.

Part VI: Putting It All Together

Part VI consists of four chapters that tie everything together. In each chapter, I present a complete Web page and explain exactly what's going on and how I put it together. Again, these chapters contain useful, real-life examples, not just page filler.

Part VII: The Part of Tens

The ...*For Dummies* series include short chapters with useful lists of ten or so things in each one. This book is no exception, and you'll find these chapters collected together in Part VII. And if you're like most people, you'll turn to these chapters first.

Assumptions about You

Because you bought this book — or perhaps you're standing in a book store trying to decide whether to buy it — it's a safe bet that you're somehow interested in VBScript. Well, my friend, read on to see whether this book really *is* for you.

Whenever I write a book, I tend to have a target reader in mind. In this case, my target reader is a conglomerate of dozens of people that I've been in touch with over the past few years (most of whom are faceless e-mail correspondents). The following points more or less describe my target reader (probably even *you*):

- ✔ You're familiar with computers and know the ropes when it comes to editing files, managing directories, and downloading and uploading files.

- ✔ You've spent a fair amount of time browsing the Web, and you even have several URLs committed to memory.

- ✔ You may have developed (or tried to develop) some Web pages and (sort of) know your way around HTML (*Hypertext Markup Language*).

- ✔ You understand the basic concept of HTML forms (or you may have seen some cool ones on your Web travels), but you may or may not have actually worked with this feature.

- ✔ You understand how frames work — but you may or may not have actually used these creatures.

- ✔ Your programming experience is limited or nonexistent. You may have dabbled with some form of Basic, but you definitely do not consider yourself a programmer.

- ✔ You have a strong desire to create exciting and dynamic (in the literal sense of the word) Web pages.

- ✔ You have a reasonable sense of humor and prefer to be entertained while you learn.

- ✔ You learn more by seeing a well-thought-out example than by reading pages of technical details.

If you don't feel comfortable with these items, you can check out the following books, published by IDG Books Worldwide, Inc: *PCs For Dummies,* 4th Edition, by Dan Gookin; *Internet For Dummies,* 3rd Edition, by John R. Levine and Margaret Levine Young; *Creating Web Pages For Dummies,* by Bud Smith and Arthur Bebak; and *HTML For Dummies,* 2nd Edition, by Ed Tittel and Steve James.

VBScript: New Language, Old Friend

VBScript is new — *very* new. So new, in fact, that as I was writing this book, only a handful of WWW sites had yet incorporated VBScript. But that situation is changing rapidly, and more sites are coming online each day. By the time this book hits the stores, a Web search for "VBScript" will turn up thousands of sites.

Although VBScript is new, millions of programmers know how to use it already. That's because VBScript is based on Microsoft's popular Visual Basic (VB) programming language. Technically, VBScript is a subset of Visual Basic. You can think of VBScript as a "light" version of VB.

Newcomers to the fold are often confused about the world of Visual Basic — which isn't surprising, because it can be confusing. Currently, Visual Basic comes in three flavors:

- **Visual Basic (VB)**: A stand-alone programming language that produces executable files (EXEs). VB is a retail product from Microsoft that comes in several different versions. It is wildly popular, and your hard drive probably contains several programs that were written in VB (and you may not even know it).

- **Visual Basic for Applications (VBA)**: A programming language that's included with Microsoft Office applications, such as Excel and Access (and, eventually, all the other Office apps). VBA is used to automate operations; for example, you can create automated procedures that work within Excel. VBA is very similar to VB, but it doesn't produce stand-alone programs.

- **Visual Basic Scripting (VBScript)**: A subset of VB that works exclusively with Web pages (at least for now). The language is built into Microsoft Explorer 3.0 and will probably be licensed to other Web browser manufacturers.

Bottom line? Visual Basic (in all of its incarnations) is a relatively easy language to learn. So if you are already familiar with VB or VBA, using VBScript will be easy; similarly, after you know VBScript, adding the others to your repertoire is a piece of cake.

What You Can Do with VBScript

I'm tempted to write something like, *the uses for VBScript are limited only by your imagination*. But I'll spare you from such a trite statement. Truth is, VBScript has simply scads of potential uses. Here's a brief list of the spiffy things that you can do (all are described in this book).

✔ **Get input from users without using a form.** The VBScript built-in InputBox function makes displaying a dialog box and getting a response from the user very easy. See Chapter 10.

✔ **Display messages.** Using several different methods, you can display attention-grabbing messages in a small dialog box. See Chapter 10.

✔ **Perform client-side validation of forms input.** In the past, a CGI (*Common Gateway Interface*) program on the server normally performed forms validation. With VBScript, you can verify input before it's sent to the server — saving time and bandwidth. See Chapter 13.

✔ **Perform calculations.** A common use for scripting languages is to do calculations without having to interact with the server. For example, if you work for a mortgage company, you can write VBScript to calculate a potential borrower's monthly loan payment. Chapter 20 presents an example.

✔ **Create client-side image maps.** You know, the maps that let your users click part of an image and jump to a new location? In the past, this sort of feat usually required a CGI program. With VBScript, image maps are fast, efficient, and relatively easy to do. Chapter 15 has an example of an image map.

✔ **Create highly interactive Web pages by writing information to frames.** Your VBScript code can respond to user input and display new information without having to load another HTML document. I use this technique in many examples in this book.

✔ **Read and write cookies.** A *cookie* is a technique that lets you save information between user visits to your site. For example, you can store a user's name in a cookie so that you can greet him or her personally on the next visit to your site. Chapter 15 has an example of using a cookie.

✔ **Program the behavior of ActiveX controls.** Dealing with ActiveX controls can be tricky because hundreds of ActiveX controls are available — some are purely cosmetic, and others are highly useful. VBScript is what makes these controls so cool. I discuss ActiveX controls in Part V.

✔ **Create HTML code on the fly.** One very handy use of VBScript is to write HTML code and send it directly to the document as it loads. Several examples in this book use this technique.

✔ **Take control of the browser.** With VBScript, you can determine how a link is handled: displayed in the current window, in a frame, or even in a new instance of the browser. Refer to Chapter 14 for examples.

✔ **Create special effects.** You can use VBScript to create special effects such as multicolor text, fading text, or backgrounds that change color. Chapter 15 contains examples of these techniques.

✔ **Create games.** Yep. VBScript is an excellent tool to create some very slick interactive games.

✔ **Blah-blah-blah.** You can do lots more with VBScript, but this list is long enough — and I think you catch my drift.

Margin Icons

Somewhere along the line, a market research company must have shown that computer books sell more copies if they have icons stuck inside their margins. Icons are those little pictures that are supposed to draw your attention to various features or help you decide whether something is worth reading. I don't know if this research is valid, but I'm not taking any chances. So here are the icons that you encounter in your travels from front cover to back cover:

This icon flags material that might be considered technical in nature. You may find this information interesting, but you can safely skip it if you're in a hurry.

Don't skip these paragraphs. These icons mark shortcuts that can save you lots of time.

This icon tells you when you need to store information away in the deep recesses of your cortex for later use.

Read these paragraphs. Otherwise, you may blow up your computer, inadvertently shut down the Internet, cause a nuclear meltdown — or maybe even ruin your whole day.

This icon alerts you that the example is contained on the companion diskette so that you can try it out in the privacy of your own Web browser.

The Web Site on a Disk

I developed an entire Web site only for readers of this book (gee, don't you feel special?). The site contains all the examples I use in this book, so you won't have to waste your time typing them. As you'll see, these are not your typical wimpy examples — my goal was to make them interesting and useful.

But — unlike your typical Web site — this book's Web site is contained on the diskette attached to the inside back cover of this book. You'll need to install this disk to your hard drive. The installation instructions are on the last page.

After you install the diskette, you can access the files using Microsoft Internet Explorer 3.0. You'll find that these files are organized much like this book. The opening page has links that point to other documents — one for each chapter.

Each chapter document, in turn, has links that direct you to a particular example. In short, you shouldn't have any trouble finding what you're looking for.

Note: You are free to use and adapt any of the examples on the disk.

I round out the disk with three appendixes that you'll probably refer to frequently: The Internet Explorer Object Model, VBScript Function Reference, and a Glossary of terms.

Wanna Reach Out?

I enjoy hearing from readers, so please don't hesitate to get in touch with me with your questions, comments, or suggestions. The best way to contact me is by electronic mail. My e-mail address is

```
VBSauthor@j-walk.com
```

I get tons of e-mail, and I really appreciate it when my correspondents take the time to make their questions clear and concise. I'll make every effort to get back to you in a timely manner.

Now What?

If you're a programming virgin, I strongly suggest that you start with Chapter 1 and progress in chapter number order until you master the basics. Chapter 2 gives you immediate hands-on experience, so you have the illusion that you're making quick progress.

But America is a free country (at least it was when I wrote these words), so I won't sic the Computer Book Police on you if you opt to thumb through the book randomly and read whatever strikes your fancy. After all, *...For Dummies* books are designed to be a reference tool.

I hope you have as much fun reading this book as I did writing it.

Part I
What's It All About?

"IT'S AMAZING HOW MUCH MORE SOME PEOPLE CAN GET OUT OF A PC THAN OTHERS."

In this part . . .

*E*very book must start somewhere. This one starts by introducing you to VBScript (and I'm sure you two will become very good friends over the course of a few dozen chapters). Chapter 1 describes where to get the software you need (don't worry, it's all free), and Chapter 2 walks you through a real-live VBScript programming session so that you can see what you've gotten yourself into.

Chapter 1

What You Need and Where to Get It

● ●

In This Chapter

▶ Where to get VBScript

▶ Where to get Microsoft Explorer 3.0

▶ Other software that will make your job easier

● ●

*A*s the old song goes, "The best things in life are free." That certainly holds true for VBScript. Many people are surprised to find out that everything you need to become a VBScript developer — with the exception of this book — is completely free (no charge, nada, zip). This chapter explains how to "get" VBScript as well as the other tools that you need to begin your quest to become a VBScript developer.

Your Basic Needs

To use this book, you need:

✔ A copy of Microsoft Internet Explorer 3.0 or later and a PC with Windows 95 to run it

✔ A text editor of your choice

✔ The Microsoft HTML Control Pad (optional, but it makes working with ActiveX controls *much* easier) — I discuss this topic in Part V

✔ ActiveX controls (optional, but these things can *really* make your Web page sing!) — this topic is also covered in Part V

The good news: You can get all these items without leaving your home or office — and you don't have to spend a cent for anything.

A few words about learning VBScript

People vary quite a bit in how they learn things such as a programming language. Some people like to be exposed to it very methodically, and others prefer a more haphazard approach — picking up tidbits here and there, hoping that eventually it will all come together.

In this book, I combine these two approaches and (hopefully) strike a happy medium. True to the *...For Dummies* tradition, this book is certainly not a boring technical document. But, when necessary, I list technical details that you need to know. On the other hand, I'm a true believer in learning by example. Because of that, you can find lots of examples in the book — which are also available on the companion diskette.

If you want to master VBScript, here are some things to keep in mind:

✔ **Understand the object model.** It's tempting to jump right in and start writing VBScript programs. But — trust me — you'll be better off if you take some time to learn the VBScript object model. I cover this topic in Chapter 5.

✔ **VBScript samples are available for the taking.** Every time you browse a Web site that uses VBScript, you can look at the code. After loading the page, use the Internet Explorer View⇨Source command to look at the HTML document (which has the VBScript code embedded in it). It's amazing how much you can learn by reading other people's code.

✔ **Be willing to experiment.** When I write scripts, I often start out by writing small (usually trivial) routines to test ideas. After I understand how a particular feature works, then I can confidently incorporate the code into my main applications.

✔ **Test your code frequently.** When you're developing your scripts, frequently testing the code that you write is vitally important. As I point out in Chapter 11, VBScript debugging tools are virtually nonexistent. Therefore, you're only wasting your time if you write a huge block of code and then discover that it doesn't work.

✔ **Do your testing on a local system.** Internet Explorer can read HTML files directly from your local hard drive. In other words, you don't need to be connected via a modem, and the files that you produce don't have to reside on a server (I'm surprised at how many people don't realize this fact).

✔ **Let your imagination run wild.** The more I use VBScript, the more I realize the great potential of this tool. At first, you'll want to copy the ideas of others, but eventually your best work will come from ideas of your own.

Just Where Is VBScript?

Here's the weird thing: VBScript doesn't really exist as a product. You can go to any software store, and the shelves are chock full of boxes that contain programming languages such as Visual Basic, C++, Delphi, and so on. But you can search the shelves all day, and you won't find a box that's labeled VBScript.

VBScript: The technical details

For those of you who care about such things, the guts of VBScript are contained in a file named VBSCRIPT.DLL, which is copied to your WINDOWS/SYSTEM folder when you install Internet Explorer 3.0. Microsoft has arranged things such that developers can incorporate VBScript into their own applications. For example, if you're a C programmer who is developing a Windows application, you can incorporate VBScript into your app — which allows end users to develop scripts that work with your app. This process is known as *hosting* VBScript. Once again, you can host VBScript without paying any royalties to Microsoft. Check out the Microsoft Web site for details.

With a normal programming language, you buy the package, install the disks, and then execute the file that loads the programming language's development environment. The development environment is what you use to write your code, debug it, and do all the other programming language things.

With VBScript, on the other hand, you use any old text editor to write your code. But here's the difference: Your VBScript code must be embedded in an HTML document. Then, the code springs to life when the HTML document is loaded into a browser that can understand VBScript.

Note: As I write this book, Microsoft Internet Explorer 3.0 is the only browser in the world that can interpret VBScript. I suspect that this situation will change soon, and it's a safe bet that an upcoming version of Netscape Navigator also will support VBScript.

Surfing for Downloads

Nowadays, an amazing amount of software is available via the Internet — and you can download this software directly from your Web browser. In this section, I describe where to get the software you need to use this book. Most of the software comes to you courtesy of Microsoft.

Note: As you probably know, the WWW is a dynamic entity — which is another way of saying that things change a lot. The URLs reported in this book worked just fine when I was writing this chapter. But, there are no guarantees that these URLs will still be valid tomorrow. If any of these are dead-end URLs, don't despair. The Microsoft Web site has a very powerful search capability that lets you locate the information you need.

Who's winning the browser war?

Even the most casual Web surfer knows that a battle is being waged. The key players are Microsoft Corporation versus Netscape Corporation. The battle involves the Web browser market. Netscape Navigator has long been the market share leader — by a huge margin.

One day, the big guys at Microsoft woke up and discovered that the whole world was becoming infatuated with the Internet (more specifically, the infatuation is with the WWW). These Microsofties also realized that a major software category existed — namely, Web browsers — in which Microsoft's market share was (to put it

bluntly) pitifully poor. All of a sudden, Microsoft pumped millions of dollars into Internet-related efforts. Its goal, of course, is to become the leading supplier of Internet products (including Web browsers).

Whether Microsoft succeeds remains to be seen. Clearly, Netscape's share of the browser market will decline now that Microsoft has a competitive product available. However, most observers (including myself) agree that the real winner of this battle will be the users, because both companies will continue to improve their products.

The companion disk includes a document that has ready-to-click hyperlinks to all these URLs.

Internet Explorer 3.0

To download the latest version of Microsoft's Internet Explorer, point your browser to

```
http://www.microsoft.com/ie/
```

You'll probably be offered several different configurations. For the best results, download the configuration that has the most goodies.

ActiveX Control Pad

In Chapter 17, I cover the Microsoft ActiveX Control Pad, which is an application that makes incorporating ActiveX controls in your HTML documents very easy. You can download a copy of the ActiveX Control Pad from

```
http://www.microsoft.com/workshop/author/cpad/cpad.htm
```

ActiveX Controls

When you install Internet Explorer 3.0, you have access to several ActiveX controls. If you're hungry for more, you can download them from the Microsoft site. The URL is

```
http://www.microsoft.com/activex/gallery/
```

Ladies and Gentlemen . . .
Choose Your Editor

Because VBScript code is embedded in HTML documents, you can use your favorite text editing software to write and edit your VBScript programs. If you already have a favorite HTML editor, you need to determine whether it's appropriate for writing VBScript. Most HTML editors will do just fine — provided that they let you work with the actual HTML source. A "hands-off the HTML" editor that doesn't display the actual HTML code doesn't work for writing VBScript.

Choosing an HTML editor is a matter of personal choice. Here, I offer a few words of wisdom — which you can accept as gospel or take with a grain of salt.

Windows Notepad

Every copy of Windows comes with a free text editor called Notepad. Although Notepad will do in a pinch, I don't recommend it because it can only handle one file at a time. Often, you'll want to work on more than one HTML document at a time (copying and pasting between documents plays a big role in writing VBScript). You can, of course, open multiple instances of Notepad, but that quickly gets messy and confusing. Another problem is that Notepad (at least the Windows 95 version) chokes when your file exceeds 64K — but if your HTML page gets that big, you're probably doing something wrong. But worst of all, Notepad does not have a search-and-replace feature — an absolute necessity as far as I'm concerned.

Windows WordPad

WordPad is another editor that comes with Windows. I don't recommend this one, either. WordPad is slow to load and (like Notepad) doesn't support multiple documents. But at least WordPad has a good search-and-replace capability. If you do resort to using WordPad, make sure that you use a fixed-width font, such as Courier New. Doing so makes your code (HTML and VBScript) much easier to work with.

Add an HTML editor to your toolbar

You may have noticed the Edit button on the Internet Explorer toolbar. Chances are, that button is lifeless. Here's how to set things up so that clicking the Edit button loads the current document into your favorite editor.

1. **In Windows, open any folder and choose the View⇨Options command.**

2. **In the Options dialog box, click the File Types tab.**

3. **Scroll down the list of file types and select the item labeled Internet Document (HTML).**

4. **Click the Edit button.**

5. **In the Edit File Type dialog box, click the New button.**

6. **In the New Action dialog box, type** Edit **as the action.**

7. **In the New Action dialog box, click the Browse button and locate the executable (EXE) file for your editor.**

8. **When you're finished, keep clicking OK and Close buttons to close the various dialog boxes.**

The next time you start Internet Explorer, clicking the Edit toolbar button (or choosing the Edit⇨Current Page command) launches your editor and opens the current browser page for viewing or editing.

Microsoft Word, with Internet Assistant

When I first started writing HTML documents, I relied heavily on Internet Assistant — an add-in for Microsoft Word that lets you develop HTML documents in a WYSIWYG (what you see is what you get) environment. It took me a few months to realize that the main advantage of this product (easy to use) did not exceed the disadvantages (poorly written HTML code and some nasty bugs). And, when it comes to incorporating VBScript, Internet Assistant is completely useless because it pretty much forces you to work in a WYSIWYG mode. In other words, you don't work with the actual HTML code. So you can forget about this one.

SitePad

Currently, my favorite editor for writing VBScript is SitePad, from ModelWorks Software. You can download a trial copy of SitePad from

```
http://www.modelworks.com/express
```

The trial copy is full-featured, but limits the file size to 2,500 characters. If you like the product, you can obtain the full version for $39.

SitePad is great for writing VBScript because it can identify some problems for you automatically. Figure 1-1 shows SitePad in action.

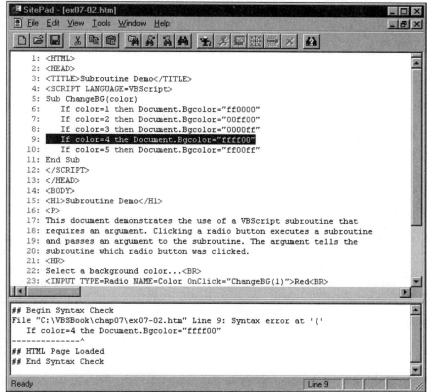

Figure 1-1:
SitePad,
from
ModelWorks
Software, is
an HTML
editor worth
checking
out.

More HTML editors

As I was writing this chapter, I found a Web site that lists and describes just
about every HTML editor known to mankind. If you're searching for a new
editor, here's a good place to start:

```
http://www.magpage.com/~cwagner/htmldex.html?
```

Getting Ready to Script

After you decide what you want to accomplish with your Web page, it's just a
matter of writing the script, inserting it into your HTML document, and loading
the file onto your server for the world to enjoy, right? Wrong.

Writing VBScript code can be a long and tedious process. In general, you need to take several steps:

1. **Enter the HTML and VBScript code in your text editor.**
2. **Save the file to disk.**
3. **Activate your browser.**
4. **Load the document into the browser (or simply press F5 to reload the document, if it's already there).**
5. **Test it.**
6. **If the code does not work correctly, switch back to your editor.**
7. **Make your corrections or additions.**
8. **Go back to Step 2**

Repeating these steps dozens or even hundreds of times while working on a particular document is not uncommon. The sequence of saving your document, switching to the browser, and reloading the modified document may be familiar to you because it's the same sequence that you use to write standard HTML documents. However, you'll probably find that you'll be saving and testing a lot more frequently when VBScript enters the picture.

Therefore, becoming thoroughly familiar with your editor and the procedures for switching among windows is in your best interest. And having your windows arranged optimally to facilitate this constant switching helps, too.

A Sneak Preview

Without further ado, I'm going to present VBScript so that this discussion isn't so abstract.

The following listing is a complete (albeit short) HTML document that contains simple VBScript code. You should recognize most of the HTML elements in this document. What might be new to you are the `<SCRIPT>` and `</SCRIPT>` tags — and the stuff in between them.

```
<HTML>
<HEAD></HEAD>
<BODY>
<H1>Introductory Example</H1>
This example demonstrates how to use VBScript to write
text to a document as it is being loaded by the browser.
```

```
<HR>
<SCRIPT LANGUAGE=VBScript>
Document.Write "Hello reader...<BR>"
Document.Write "Today is " & Now()
</SCRIPT>
</BODY>
</HTML>
```

Figure 1-2 shows what this page looks like when it is opened by Internet Explorer. If you try this example, your page will look different because the VBScript code inserts the actual date and time. In other words, this "active" document looks different every time it loads.

In the preceding example, the VBScript consists of the two statements between the `<SCRIPT>` and the `</SCRIPT>` tags. These two statements write text directly to the document as the document is loaded by the browser. The second statement uses the Now function — which is one of many functions built into VBScript.

If none of this makes sense yet, don't worry. Remember, you're only in Chapter 1.

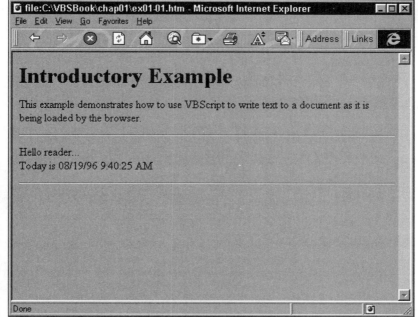

Figure 1-2:
A simple
HTML
document
that
contains
some
VBScript
code.

Chapter 2

Your First VBScript Program
(A Script-Tease)

In This Chapter

▶ Developing an HTML document that incorporates VBScript

▶ Testing and developing the code

▶ Making changes to the code

1'm not much of a swimmer, but I have learned that the best way to get into a cold body of water is to jump right in — no sense prolonging the agony. If you wade through this chapter, you'll get your feet wet immediately and you'll probably feel better about this whole programming business. The chapter consists of a step-by-step demonstration of developing a simple, but useful, HTML document that contains VBScript.

Note: You're not expected to understand everything in this chapter. The point is not to find out the specific details. Rather, it's to give you early hands-on experience — and a bit of instant gratification.

What You Do

In this chapter, you create an HTML document with the following elements:

✔ A level 1 header and text (so far, so good)

✔ Two buttons that are added by using the <INPUT> tag (still on familiar territory?)

✔ Scripts that execute when buttons are clicked

If you've never programmed before

If you've never done any type of computer programming, you may be surprised at how easily you can get up to speed with VBScript. It's important to understand that VBScript is a simple language, and it isn't suitable for writing huge applications, such as an accounting system.

VBScript has quite a few limitations that aren't found in other languages. For example, you can't use VBScript to read or write files from a user's hard disk. Many limitations in VBScript are for security purposes. (You wouldn't really want to access a Web page that contains code to read the files on your hard drive, right?)

Because you're an experienced HTML writer (or at least familiar with HTML), you already understand basic programming concepts (perhaps without even realizing it). Programming really boils down to providing a sequence of instructions in a highly structured format. As you've undoubtedly discovered by now, a computer simply follows these instructions blindly. If you've ever omitted a </H1> tag in an HTML document, you discovered that the browser displays all the subsequent text in the larger heading font. In other words, it's simply following your instructions.

VBScript works the same way. It will do exactly what you tell it to do. But first you must find out how to provide the instructions according to the rules VBScript can understand.

Create the HTML Document

Start by firing up the editor and then creating the following document. So far, the document consists of pure HTML, with no VBScript:

```
<HTML>
<HEAD></HEAD>
<BODY>
<H1>My First VBScript Example</H1>
<H2>Take 1</H2>
<P>
This is an example of an HTML page that uses VBScript.
Clicking a button executes a subroutine that randomly
changes the background or foreground color of this page.
<HR>
</BODY>
</HTML>
```

Save the file and load it into Internet Explorer. You can use the File⇔Open command (with the Browse button), or you can drag the document's icon into the Internet Explorer window. After the file loads, you see a rather drab-looking document that uses the default colors.

Adding the Buttons

The next step involves adding the two buttons. Activate the editor and then insert the following lines directly below the `<HR>` tag:

```
<INPUT TYPE=Button NAME=btnFG VALUE="Foreground">
<INPUT TYPE=Button NAME=btnBG VALUE="Background">
```

Save the file again and then reload the document into Internet Explorer (pressing F5 is a fast way to reload the document). Your screen now resembles Figure 2-1.

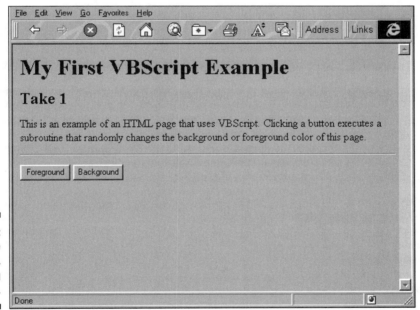

Figure 2-1:
The sample document, after adding two buttons.

The `<INPUT>` tag is standard HTML that generates an *intrinsic* control (see Chapter 12 for details). The tag's parameters define the type of control, its name, and a value (which is the text that appears on the button).

Inserting the Script

Now comes the fun part. In this section, you create a subroutine that executes when the first button, named btnFG, is clicked. A subroutine, which I explain in detail in Chapter 7, holds the script. You start with this button and then work on the subroutine for the second button (named btnBG) later.

Creating the basic subroutine

Enter the following lines of text directly below the two <INPUT> tags:

```
<SCRIPT LANGUAGE=VBScript>
Sub btnFG_OnClick()
    Alert "Hello from btnFG"
End Sub
</SCRIPT>
```

This subroutine executes when the first button is clicked. So far the subroutine doesn't do much — it simply displays a message in an alert box. However, displaying this message is a good way to make sure that everything is working.

Save the file again and then reload into Internet Explorer. Click the first button, and you see the alert box appear, as shown in Figure 2-2.

Figure 2-2:
This alert
box means
that the
button is
working.

In the previous listing, notice that the name of the subroutine (btnFG_OnClick) consists of the button's name, followed by an underscore, and the word OnClick. This is how the subroutine is connected to the button.

VBScript code writing tips

Here are a few words of wisdom. You may find one or two of these tips helpful.

✔ **Test frequently as you work.** I can't over-state how important testing is. Finding the source of a VBScript error can sometimes be challenging. The best approach is to write a small snippet of code and then test it immediately. You can isolate errors much easier when you've only written a few new lines of code.

✔ **Use the highest screen resolution that is legible to your eyes.** 1024 x 768 works very well. 800 x 600 is okay. 640 x 480 is pretty much unacceptable.

✔ **Keep the number of open windows to a minimum.** When I'm writing VBScript (or simply writing HTML, for that matter), I like to close down everything except my editor, my browser, and one Windows Explorer window.

✔ **Use an editor that supports drag-and-drop for opening files.** I avoid the File⇨Open command in my editor. Rather, I load files into my editor by dragging them from the Windows Explorer window to the editor window (not all editors support this feature) — this method is much more efficient. The same goes for opening files in Internet Explorer. Dragging is much faster than using the Internet Explorer File⇨Open command.

✔ **Use the shortcut key for saving your file.** In the vast majority of text editors, Ctrl+S saves the file. Get in the habit of using that key sequence. It's faster than using the mouse.

✔ **Use Alt+Tab to switch among windows.** This method is the fastest way to jump between your editor and your browser for testing.

✔ **Use F5 to reload the current document in Internet Explorer.** This key is faster than using the View⇨Refresh command and even faster than clicking the Refresh toolbar button.

Note: These keystrokes will eventually become burned in your muscle memory and will seem like a single event: Ctrl+S, Alt+Tab, F5.

Modifying the subroutine

Now that you know that the button is executing the subroutine, you can change the subroutine so that it actually does something more useful. You can edit the subroutine to change the document's foreground and background color in a random manner. Replace the Alert statement with these two statements:

```
Color = Hex(Rnd()* 16777215)
Document.Fgcolor = Color
```

What are these statements all about? The first statement calculates a random number between 0 and 16,777,215 and then converts this number to *hexadecimal* (which is the system used for HTML colors). The random number is assigned to a variable named Color. The next statement assigns this color to the document's foreground color. Technically, the second statement is changing the Fgcolor property of the Document object — but I'm getting ahead of myself.

Save the file and then reload it into Internet Explorer. Clicking the button now changes the text (foreground) color of the document. The actual color that appears is one of 16,777,216 possible colors. Where does that number come from? That number is the decimal representation of the hexadecimal number FFFFFF (see the sidebar "What the hex is going on?" for a refresher course in hex arithmetic).

Note: If you're running in 256-color mode, you aren't able to see the full range of colors.

Adding the second subroutine

Because the first subroutine seems to be doing its job, creating the second subroutine — the one that changes the background color — is a simple matter. Insert the following code directly below the End Sub statement:

```
Sub btnBG_OnClick()
    Color = Hex(Rnd()* 16777215)
    Document.Bgcolor = Color
End Sub
```

This subroutine, btnBG_OnClick, is similar to the btnFG_OnClick subroutine. It has a different name, of course, and changes the document's Bgcolor property — the background color.

When you need to type something that's similar to something you've already typed, you can probably save time by copying the original text, pasting it to a new location, and then editing the copied text.

The final document (Take 1)

Here's the complete listing of the HTML document:

```
<HTML>
<HEAD></HEAD>
<BODY>
<H1>My First VBScript Example</H1>
<P>
```

(continued)

```
This is an example of an HTML page that uses VBScript.
Clicking a button executes a subroutine that randomly
changes the background or foreground color of this page.
<HR>
<INPUT TYPE=Button Name=btnFG Value="Foreground">
<INPUT TYPE=Button Name=btnBG Value="Background">
<SCRIPT LANGUAGE=VBScript>
Sub btnFG_OnClick()
    Color = Hex(Rnd()* 16777215)
    Document.Fgcolor = Color
End Sub
Sub btnBG_OnClick()
    Color = Hex(Rnd()* 16777215)
    Document.Bgcolor = Color
End Sub
</SCRIPT>

</BODY>
</HTML>
```

Like HTML, VBScript is not at all picky about capitalizing, indenting, or adding extra spaces or blank lines.

Testing the script

Save your document again and then reload it into Internet Explorer. Click away to see whether everything is working correctly. If it's not, check to make sure that the code in your document matches the preceding code.

Making changes (Take 2)

Most HTML authors are never satisfied with their pages. The pages always seem to need tweaking. VBScript code often needs tweaks as well. For example, wouldn't it be nice to be able to see the actual color values that are generated randomly? That way, if you come up with a particularly attractive color combination, you can note the colors and use them in a real Web page.

Fortunately, this particular tweak is fairly easy. The tough part is figuring out how to display the values. One option is to display the values using the Alert statement. But clicking that pop-up dialog box gets old very quickly. A better solution is to change the text displayed on the buttons themselves. Doing so requires only two more lines of code.

What the hex is going on?

If you're an old hand at HTML, you're probably intimately familiar with the RGB (Red-Green-Blue) color model. An RGB color value consists of six hexadecimal digits: two for the red value, two for the green value, and two for the blue value. FF0000 is pure red, 00FF00 is pure green, and 0000FF is pure blue.

The normal decimal number system uses 10 digits (0 through 9). The hexadecimal number system uses 16 digits: 0 through 9, followed by the letters A, B, C, D E, and F. In hexadecimal, the number that follows 09 is 0A (which is decimal 10). OF is decimal 15, and 10 is decimal 16. Work your way up, and you discover that FF (the maximum two-digit hex number) is equal to decimal 255. When you consider that a value also can be 0, then 256 values are between 00 and FF.

If you relate the hexadecimal number system to the RGB color system, then 256 levels of red (00 through FF), 256 levels of green, and 256 levels of blue exist. Put another way, $256 \times 256 \times 256 = 16{,}777{,}216$ possible color values.

Because 16,777,216 possible foreground colors and the same number of possible background colors exist, you can have approximately 2.8×10^{14} possible combinations of foreground and background colors. So if you use the VBScript example in this chapter to view one combination every second, examining them all would take you nearly nine million years — even longer, if you break for lunch.

1. **Add the following statement to the btnFG_OnClick subroutine, directly before the End Sub statement:**

```
btnFG.Value = Color
```

2. **Add the following statement to the btnBG_OnClick subroutine, directly before the End Sub statement:**

```
btnBG.Value = Color
```

These two statements change the button's Value property to the contents of the variable Color (which holds the random hex color value). The button's Value property is the text that's displayed on the button.

Save your document and reload it in Internet Explorer. Click a button, and the hex color code is displayed right on the button face.

Taking a closer look

Play around with your new creation and see if you notice anything unusual. Okay, time's up.

The problem

This script has a subtle problem that isn't apparent until the actual hex color codes are displayed in the buttons.

Click the buttons a few times, and eventually you come up with a color value that is fewer than six digits long. For example, you may have a color value of FA782. You may think Internet Explorer is interpreting this color value as 0FA782 (that is, tacking on a leading zero). Internet Explorer actually interprets such a color value as FA7820 (it adds a trailing zero), which means the random number generation isn't working like it should. Some numbers will never be chosen! In other words, your very first VBScript program has a bug.

Fixing the bug (Take 3)

The code needs to be modified such that random color codes with fewer than six digits have leading zeros appended to them. You're not expected to know how to make this modification, of course. Here's the modified btnFG_OnClick subroutine:

```
Sub btnFG_OnClick()
    Color = Hex(Rnd()* 16777215)
    If Len(Color) = 5 Then Color = "0" & Color
    If Len(Color) = 4 Then Color = "00" & Color
    If Len(Color) = 3 Then Color = "000" & Color
    If Len(Color) = 2 Then Color = "0000" & Color
    If Len(Color) = 1 Then Color = "00000" & Color
    Document.Fgcolor = Color
    btnFG.Value = Color
End Sub
```

The modification looks more complicated than it is. This code uses the VBScript Len function to determine the length of the value stored in Color. Then it uses several If-Then statements to perform various actions. If the length is 5, it adds one zero to the left of the value. If the length is 4, it adds two zeros and so on. The ampersand (&) is the VBScript concatenation operator used to combine text strings.

For more information about the Len function (as well as other useful functions), refer to Chapter 10. I discuss If-Then statements in Chapter 9.

You can add these same five statements to the btnBG_OnClick subroutine.

Part II
How VBScript Works

The 5th Wave

Real Programmers don't like to be bothered when they're working.

In this part . . .

The chapters in this part get into the real meat of things. I start off with key information about the Internet Explorer browser (some of it may be old hat, but then again . . .). Subsequent chapters cover topics such as scripts, objects, properties, methods, and events. Some terms may be a bit fuzzy (or a *lot* fuzzy) at this point, but I guarantee that they'll make more sense in the near future.

Chapter 3

Exploring the Explorer (Internet Explorer 3.0, That Is)

- -

In This Chapter

▶ Key facts about Microsoft Internet Explorer 3.0

▶ How Microsoft Internet Explorer 3.0 uses objects

▶ Cool features you may have overlooked

- -

*B*ecause, at least for the moment, Microsoft Internet Explorer 3.0 is the only Web browser that supports VBScript, understanding how this product works is important. As you probably know, the VBScript code that you develop isn't worth a hill of beans until it is interpreted by a Web browser.

You may already be quite comfortable using Internet Explorer. Even if that's the case, some of the information in this chapter paves the way for other information that *will* be new to you.

Excursions into Versions

When I talk about Microsoft Internet Explorer in this book, I mean Version 3.0 or later. Previous versions of this browser do not support VBScript and are therefore useless if your goal is to use VBScript. In fact, you can just forget that pre-3.0 versions even exist.

To find out which version of Internet Explorer you're using, choose the Help➪About Internet Explorer command. A dialog box appears, like the one in Figure 3-1, that tells you, among other things, which version you're using. The numbers in parentheses indicate the *build* of the version. Microsoft periodically makes improvements to the product without changing the actual version number. Therefore, different subversions are identified by a build number.

Figure 3-1:
Figuring out
which
version of
Internet
Explorer
you're using.

If the version you're using isn't at least 3.0, you need to upgrade. You can get the latest version from the Microsoft Web page:

```
http://www.microsoft.com/ie/
```

Note: At this writing, Microsoft was working on Version 4.0 of Internet Explorer. Version 4.0, of course, supports VBScript, so if you're using this later version of the browser, all the better. Version 4.0 is more tightly integrated into Windows. In fact, it's actually a complete user interface for Windows, and you can use it to browse the files on your disk as well as files on the WWW.

Cool Browser . . . Very Cool

Microsoft's goal in designing Internet Explorer 3.0 was to match the features found in market leader Netscape Navigator and then add a slew of new features to boot. This section briefly discusses the innovative features of my favorite Web browser.

Internet Explorer innovations

Following is a list of innovative features in Internet Explorer 3.0.

  ✔ **Cascading style sheets.** This feature makes creating a standard design for multiple Web pages easy. Plus, you have control over margins, line spacing, colors, fonts, and point sizes. Desktop publishing on the Web? You got it. Figure 3-2 shows a modest example of a Web page that uses a style sheet to generate a special effect (the page looks much better in color).

Style sheets are so slick, I included a few modest examples on the companion diskette. Check 'em out!

✔ **Floating frames:** Frames aren't new, but Internet Explorer lets you insert them anywhere you want in the document (not just along an edge). Better yet, You can insert a floating frame without a border so that it blends into your main document Your VBScript can write HTML code and send it to a floating frame, making it look like the document is being updated interactively.

✔ **New table features:** The new features give you lots of control over the appearance of your tables. For example, you can specify background colors and images. You also have minute control over individual cell borders.

✔ **ActiveX support:** The ability to insert controls directly into your Web page is indeed exciting — so exciting that this book devotes a few chapters to that very topic (see Part V).

✔ **Improved multimedia:** Your pages can use inline sound and video and also display text as a scrolling marquee.

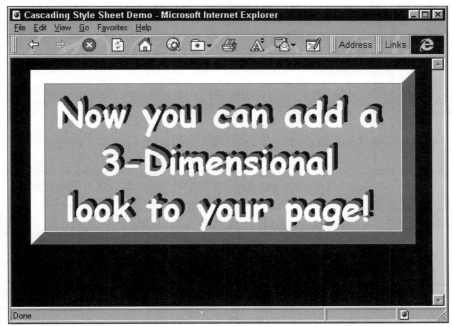

Figure 3-2:
A style sheet produces these text effects.

- ✔ **Security features:** In this age of viruses, downloading files from strangers can be dangerous. Internet Explorer provides several features that help you practice safe browsing.

- ✔ **Smooth multitasking:** Internet Explorer is a 32-bit multithreading application. In plain English, *multitasking* means you can work on other stuff while Internet Explorer is doing something else (downloading a huge file, for example).

- ✔ **Fast text and progressive rendering:** Internet Explorer displays text first and then displays images as they are being loaded. Because you're not staring at a completely blank screen, the page appears to be loading faster.

- ✔ **VBScript support:** This feature is so slick that I wrote an entire book about it.

What about compatibility?

Netscape Navigator is a good browser, no doubt about it. But one key criticism about the product, besides the frequent crashes, is that Netscape Navigator uses too many nonstandard HTML tags. In other words, Netscape developers took too many liberties with its features. Although Internet Explorer 3.0 also runs that risk, Microsoft appears to be a bit more conservative when it comes to extending the HTML standards.

Actually, Microsoft claims to be working closely with Internet standard-setting organizations. Hopefully, this collaboration means that any HTML extensions supported by Internet Explorer will not be unique to Internet Explorer.

Internet Explorer Features You May Have Missed

Most people don't spend a whole lot of time investigating every nook and cranny of Internet Explorer. But I did. This section lists features you may not know about.

- ✔ **Shortcut menus:** Right-click in the document window, and you get a shortcut menu of common commands. Figure 3-3 shows what this shortcut menu looks like.

- ✔ **Open a document in a new window.** If you right-click on a hyperlink, you get a shortcut menu that includes a very useful command: Open in New Window. Select this command, and the linked document is opened in a new instance of Internet Explorer.

Figure 3-3:
Right-click
the
document
window to
get a
shortcut
menu.

Save Background As...
Set as Wallpaper

Copy Background

Select All

Create Shortcut
Add to Favorites...
View Source

Refresh

Properties

✔ **Toolbars:** You have a great deal of control over how the toolbars look. To move a toolbar, move the mouse pointer to the border that separates the document window from the toolbars. When the mouse pointer changes to a vertical bar with an arrow, click and drag. You also can change the size of the toolbar by dragging the Address bar or the Quick Links button up or down or to the left or right to remove or display these toolbar buttons. Changing the size of the toolbar is easier to do than to describe, so play around to discover how easily you can change the toolbars.

✔ **Drag-and-drop to the desktop:** If you run across a cool graphic during your browsing, click it and drag it to your desktop to snag a copy. And if you encounter a hyperlink that you'd like to come back to, drag that, too — you end up with a shortcut stored right on your desktop.

✔ **Find a site:** You've probably used one or more of the popular Web search engines such as AltaVista or Lycos. You can do a quick Yahoo! search simply by typing the text in Explorer's address box and pressing Enter. If the search text consists of only one word, precede it with the word *Find*. For example, to search for sites that deal with modems, type **Find modem** and press Enter.

✔ **Full-screen mode:** Not many people know it, but you can start Internet Explorer in full-screen, or *kiosk*, mode. The browser fills the entire screen, and its size cannot be changed. You don't see a menu, status bar, or toolbars. To start up in full-screen mode, use the following command:

```
iexplore -k
```

Unfortunately, toggling between full-screen and normal mode is impossible, so you have to restart Internet Explorer.

✔ **Mouse not required:** Internet Explorer 3.0 makes good use of a mouse, but you can do practically everything without taking your hands from the keyboard. Take a look at the online Help file for a complete list (search for "keyboard shortcuts" in the Help file's index).

Speaking of mice, Microsoft's new IntelliMouse works particularly well with Internet Explorer. This new mouse features a small wheel in between the two buttons. Roll the wheel to scroll vertically. Press the wheel and drag for ultra-smooth scrolling.

Parts of Internet Explorer

In this section, I briefly point out various parts of Internet Explorer. In describing these parts, I also describe the Internet Explorer *object model*. The object model becomes important when you start writing VBScript. In Chapter 5, things click when you understand how VBScript can access all these browser parts (that is, objects) — and do some very interesting things with them.

Your window on the World (Wide Web)

When you use Internet Explorer, everything takes place in the Internet Explorer window. This window is just like any other window used in Windows. For example, if you're using your word processor, it runs in a window. If you're looking at a list of files, those files appear in a My Computer window (or maybe a Windows Explorer window — which, by the way, has nothing to do with Internet Explorer). Like most windows, the Internet Explorer window can be moved, resized, minimized, and maximized.

I've been framed!

At any time, the information that you're viewing is contained in one or more frames. For example, you can access a URL that displays information to you using two or three frames, which is not at all uncommon. Figure 3-4 shows a typical site with three frames. The top frame displays an advertising banner, the left frame displays a menu of links, and the right frame displays the main content. (Some people hate frames with a passion, but that's another issue.)

The well documented document

Every frame that appears in the Internet Explorer window holds a document. By document, I'm referring to an HTML file that was retrieved from a server or your hard drive. An HTML document can contain a wide variety of textual and graphical information. The way information is displayed depends on the HTML tags that are included in the Web document.

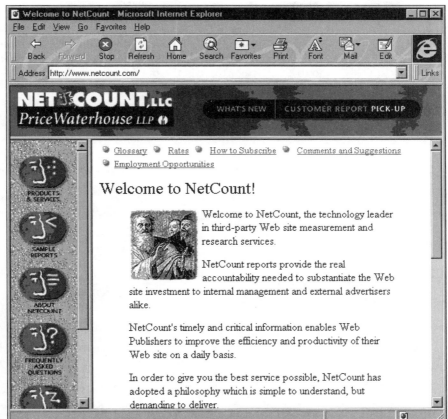

Figure 3-4:
This Web
site is set up
to display
in three
frames.

Three parts of a document (all optional) are relevant:

- ✔ Links
- ✔ Anchors
- ✔ Forms

Links

Links, in an HTML document, are largely responsible for the "Web" part of the WWW. *Links* take you to other places in the world and make these sites interconnected. Here's an example of a link defined in HTML:

```
<A HREF="http://www.microsoft.com">Microsoft's Site</A>
```

Anchors

An anchor is identified in an HTML document by an <A> tag. An *anchor* is similar to a link, but the link is internal to the document. Anchors are most commonly found in longer HTML documents because they make it easy to quickly jump to a particular topic in the document. Here's an example of an anchor defined in HTML:

```
<A NAME="SearchEngines"></A>
```

Forms

You've undoubtedly encountered Web sites that use forms, and you may have even created forms yourself. A *form* consists of one or more controls (such as buttons, check boxes, text boxes, and so on) enclosed within <FORM> and </FORM> tags. A single document can have any number of separate forms, and each form can have a name.

Here's an example of a simple form defined in HTML:

```
<FORM NAME=Form1>
 What is Your Name?
 <BR>
 <INPUT TYPE=Text NAME=YourName>
 <P>
 What Sex Are You?
 <BR>
 <INPUT TYPE=Radio NAME=Gender>Male<BR>
 <INPUT TYPE=Radio NAME=Gender>Female<BR>
</FORM>
```

Figure 3-5 shows how this form appears in a browser.

The controls within a form are called *elements*. After the user supplies the information, the values of the elements are usually processed in some way. For example, the values can be sent back to the server, or manipulated with VBScript.

What's your location?

Although a window can display a number of different HTML documents in separate frames, at any given time Internet Explorer references only one *location*. This URL appears in the Address box in the toolbar.

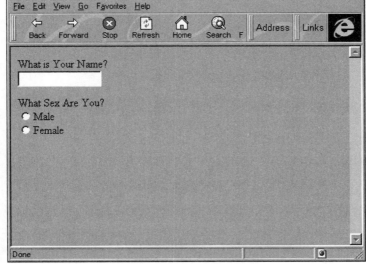

Figure 3-5:
A simple
form with a
text control
and two
radio
controls.

Don't know much about history. . . .

Internet Explorer also records history. In this case, history refers to the sites
that you've visited previously in the current Web surfing session. When you
click the Back and Forward icons, Internet Explorer uses its history list to
determine where to send you and which document to load next.

Chapter 4

Using Scripts in Your HTML Documents

In This Chapter

▶ Three ways to include VBScript in your Web page

▶ Everything you need to know about the `<SCRIPT>` tag

▶ The mechanics of entering VBScript code

▶ Compatibility issues: When to use VBScript and when to avoid using it

▶ How to protect your code from prying eyes — not!

▶ What happens when you load an HTML document into Internet Explorer

*W*hen you write VBScript, the code is inserted, or *embedded*, directly into an HTML document. This chapter discusses the mechanics involved in embedding scripts into HTML documents.

Including VBScript in HTML Documents

VBScript can be included in your Web page in two ways:

✔ Directly (an *immediate* script)

✔ As a subroutine or function procedure (a *deferred* script)

Direct execution of VBScript

One way to include VBScript in your document is to insert it directly into your HTML code. The script must be embedded between a `<SCRIPT>` and a `</SCRIPT>` tag. When the document is loading, Internet Explorer executes the script and follows your instructions.

The following example is an HTML document with embedded VBScript code:

```
<HTML>
<HEAD>
</HEAD>
<BODY>
<H1>Sample Document</H1>
Hello, and thanks for dropping by.
<P>
In case you're wondering, this HTML document was last
updated on
<SCRIPT LANGUAGE=VBScript>
Document.Write Document.LastModified
Document.Write "."
</SCRIPT>
<HR>
Please visit again!
</BODY>
</HTML>
```

Figure 4-1 shows how the document looks in the browser.

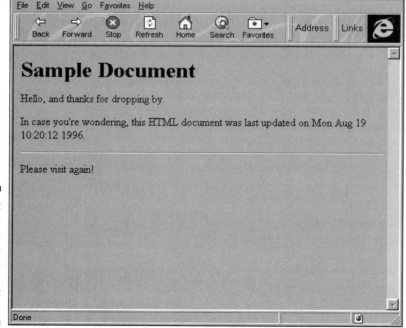

Figure 4-1:
Use
VBScript to
write the
date and
time into a
document
as it loads.

This example is a standard HTML file. The only unusual part is the text between the <SCRIPT> and </SCRIPT> tags. That text, as you've probably deduced by now, is VBScript code.

When the browser loads this document, it encounters the <SCRIPT> tag and switches over to the VBScript interpreter, which executes the statements. In this case, the statements write text directly to the document. The text consists of the date and time the document was modified (first line of code) and a period (second line of code). Then, the </SCRIPT> tag signals the end of the script, and the browser finishes displaying the document.

Note: At this juncture, you don't need to understand the code. The point is to demonstrate various ways of inserting VBScript into a document.

This type of script is sometimes called an *immediate* script because it is executed immediately as the page is being loaded and interpreted by the browser. Such scripts are useful because they can create dynamic content. For example, you can use an immediate script to include the current date and time, display the contents of a cookie, or generate special text effects.

These immediate scripts execute only once, when the page loads, and cannot be executed by other events, such as button clicks. If you need to execute VBScript code more than once, it must be placed in a procedure (which I discuss in the next section).

Deferred execution by using a VBScript procedure

In the previous section, I discuss immediate scripts, which is one way to insert VBScript into a Web document. The second way to insert VBScript into your documents is to use a *procedure*. VBScript procedures come in two types: subroutines and functions (see Chapter 7, if you're unsure of the difference between the two).

The following example is an HTML document that has VBScript coded as a subroutine. The subroutine is named MyButton_OnClick, and it consists of a single line of code:

```
<HTML>
<HEAD>
</HEAD>
<BODY>
<H1>Sample Document</H1>
Hello, and thanks for dropping by. Click the button to
find out
```

(continued)

(continued)

```
when this document was last updated.
<P>
<INPUT TYPE=Button NAME=MyButton VALUE="Click Me">
<HR>
Please visit again!
<SCRIPT LANGUAGE=VBScript>
Sub MyButton_OnClick ()
    Alert Document.LastModified
End Sub
</SCRIPT>
</BODY>
</HTML>
```

Figure 4-2 shows how this page looks when displayed in a browser. When you click the button, a small dialog box displays the date and time when the document was last modified.

Figure 4-2:
This
VBScript is
stored in a
subroutine.

Unlike the previous example, this script does not execute when the document loads. This type of script is sometimes known as a *deferred* script. The only way this script executes is when a particular event calls it. In this case, clicking the button is the event that calls the subroutine. And, this subroutine can be called any number of times.

Understanding the <SCRIPT> Tag

As you know, HTML uses tags to specify how the browser handles the document's content. In this section, I tell you everything you need to know about the soon-to-be-important <SCRIPT> tag.

Match 'em up

In HTML, tags usually surround the text they affect, which means that the tags must be paired up properly. For example, every <H1> tag requires a corresponding </H1> tag.

The <SCRIPT> tag is no exception. Every time you insert a <SCRIPT> tag, make sure that you add a matching </SCRIPT> tag. Failure to do so causes Internet Explorer to simply ignore everything after the <SCRIPT> tag — and the script won't execute. The VBScript that's inserted between the <SCRIPT> and </SCRIPT> tag is referred to as a *script block*.

How many script blocks?

A single HTML document can include as many script blocks as needed. If you insert VBScript code that will be executed as the document is being loaded, you simply insert the scripts where they are needed in the document. Each script block has its own <SCRIPT> and </SCRIPT> tags.

If you're using VBScript subroutines or functions, placing them all within a single set of <SCRIPT></SCRIPT> tags is usually a good idea because it keeps them together in one place. But this placement isn't a requirement; you can arrange things any way you like.

Where to put scripts

As far as I know, no hard-and-fast rules govern where in the document scripts should be placed. Here are a few guidelines.

- ✔ If you're using an immediate script that generates content, the script goes in its appropriate place within the <BODY> section — the location in which you want the content to appear. However, the script can't refer to objects that are defined later in the document.

- ✔ Subroutines and functions can go anywhere, but placing them in the <HEAD> section is often a good idea. By doing so, if the page loading stops before it finishes, you have a better chance that the scripts will have already loaded.

The LANGUAGE attribute for <SCRIPT>

Many HTML tags include *attributes*. Think of an attribute as supplying further instructions to the browser. The following HTML tag uses the WIDTH attribute to specify the width of a table:

```
<TABLE WIDTH=300>
```

The <SCRIPT> tag has only one attribute: LANGUAGE

For your purposes, the LANGUAGE attribute's value will always be "VBScript." Including this attribute is necessary because VBScript is not the only scripting language. (JavaScript is the only other language, for now.)

Note: Although you may be able to omit the LANGUAGE attribute in some cases, practice using it all the time. If this attribute is omitted, Internet Explorer assumes that the script is written in the most recently used scripting language it encountered.

What about older browsers?

You may be curious about what happens if someone accesses your Web page using an older browser — one that has no concept of the <SCRIPT> tag. Most browsers simply ignore tags that they don't understand. However, the VBScript code in between the <SCRIPT> and </SCRIPT> tags is interpreted as plain text and displayed as is. Although this treatment probably doesn't ruin anyone's day, it does make your Web site look like it's broken (or at least seriously wounded).

To avoid an injured Web page, get into the habit of hiding your VBScript code inside of HTML comment tags. HTML comment tags are

<!-- The tag that begins the comment

--> The tag that ends the comment

Here's an example of a comment in HTML:

```
<!--The order form begins here -->
```

Here's an example of using comment tags to hide VBScript from older browsers:

```
<SCRIPT LANGUAGE=VBScript>
<!--
Alert "If you see this message, your browser supports VBScript!"
-->
</SCRIPT>
```

Newer, script-aware browsers (including Netscape Navigator) are programmed to ignore comment tags that fall in between <SCRIPT> and <SCRIPT> tags.

To save space — and because I *know* that everyone using these examples does have a VBScript-compatible browser — most examples in this book do not enclose the VBScript code in between HTML comment tags. In general, any page you produce for public consumption should include comment tags. To add comment tags to scripts, insert the following HTML begin comment tag after every occurrence of a <SCRIPT> tag:

```
<!--
```

And, insert the following HTML end comment tag before every occurrence of the </SCRIPT> tag:

```
-->
```

Writing VBScript Code

In this section, I provide some additional information about the mechanics of writing VBScript code. I cover the following topics:

- ✔ Using comments in your code
- ✔ Using upper- and lowercase
- ✔ Using spaces and tabs to provide indentation
- ✔ Splitting a VBScript statement into two or more lines

Using comments in VBScript code

In the previous section, I discuss HTML comment tags. In case you're wondering, VBScript has its own way of handling comments. You may want to include comments in your code to describe what the code does or to identify yourself as the author. Because VBScript isn't HTML, you use the comment indicator for the VBScript language — which happens to be an apostrophe. Whenever VBScript encounters an apostrophe, everything else on that line is simply ignored. The only exception is when the apostrophe falls within a pair of quotes. Here's an example of a VBScript subroutine that uses three comments. The comment lines begin with an apostrophe:

```
<SCRIPT LANGUAGE="VBScript">
<!--
Sub ShowMessage()
'  This subroutine was written by Mike Jones
'  Display the current date
   Alert Date()
'  Next, show the time of day
   Alert Time()
End Sub
-->
</SCRIPT>
```

Upper- or lowercase?

The VBScript language is not case-sensitive. In other words, whether you use uppercase or lowercase in your scripts doesn't matter at all. The following VBScript statements are all equivalent as far as Internet Explorer is concerned.

```
Document.Write Document.LastModified
```

```
DOCUMENT.WRITE DOCUMENT.LASTMODIFIED
```

```
document.write document.lastmodified
```

```
DoCuMeNt.WrItE dOcUmEnT.lAsTmOdIfIeD
```

Although Internet Explorer doesn't care about upper- or lowercase, you may want to develop your own style. For example, some programmers prefer to use lowercase for everything. Other programmers like to use "proper" case — they use uppercase for the first letter and lowercase for other letters.

Note: The exception to the "anything goes" rule for capitalization occurs with information within quote marks. Text within quotes is always interpreted literally, and Internet Explorer does not change such text. The following statements each display the exact message that's within quotes:

```
Alert "HELLO USER"
```

```
Alert "Hello User"
```

```
Alert "hello user"
```

```
Alert "HeLlO uSeR"
```

Indenting and spaces

When you write VBScript, you may find it helpful to indent your code to indicate the structure of the code. Here's an example of a simple VBScript subroutine that uses indentations:

```
Sub ShowMessage()
    Alert Date()
    Alert Time()
End Sub
```

Following is the same subroutine without indentation:

```
Sub ShowMessage()
Alert Date()
Alert Time()
End Sub
```

Internet Explorer is completely oblivious to the number of spaces (or tabs) that you use in your VBScript code. However, getting into the habit of using indentation to make your code more readable is a good idea.

Note: The importance of using indentation in your code is most apparent when you use For-Next loops, If-Then statements, and other such structures (see Chapter 9).

Splitting a statement into two or more lines

When you're writing HTML code, you can make the lines of text as long as you want. The same is true for writing VBScript code. Many programmers, however, prefer to break lengthy lines of code into two or more separate lines. To split a line of VBScript code, use the standard line continuation character sequence: a space followed by an underscore.

Here's an example of a VBScript statement that appears on one line.

```
Document.Write "This was modified on " & Document.LastModified
```

And here's the same statement, split into two lines.

```
Document.Write "This was modified on " _
    & Document.LastModified
```

You need to decide when (if ever) to use line continuation character sequence. The only thing to keep in mind is that you cannot break a line inside of a quoted string. For example, the following is not a correct line break because the break occurs inside of the quoted text:

```
Document.Write "This was modified _
    on " & Document.LastModified
```

Hey! That's Private!

Because your VBScript code is embedded directly in an HTML document, you may think that anyone who loads your page can look at your VBScript code. You're right. Anyone who sees your document can use the Internet Explorer View⇨Source command to see every byte of your code.

Compatibility Issues

You need to understand that VBScript is not supported by all browsers. In fact, currently it's supported by exactly one browser: Internet Explorer 3.0. You need to keep this fact in mind — especially because Netscape Navigator is (at least for now) the market share leader in the Web browser department.

A plug-in, which allows you to use VBScript with Netscape Navigator, is available. You can get this plug-in from the following Web site:

```
http://www.ncompasslabs.com/
```

When to use VBScript

In general, using VBScript under the following conditions is safe:

- ✔ **You know that almost everyone who will load your Web document is using Internet Explorer 3.0 or later.** This condition may be true in the case of a corporate Intranet or for sites that cater to a particular class of visitors.

- ✔ **The features for which you're using VBScript are not critical to the Web page.** If you're using VBScript to add snazzy effects, those who don't have a compatible browser aren't missing out on anything critical.

- ✔ **You provide a screening page that lets the user determine whether to load the VBScript-enhanced version of your page or the boring generic version that works for all browsers.**

In Chapter 15, I present a method that automatically determines whether the user's browser is VBScript-compatible.

When to avoid VBScript

If you don't know which browser your visitors will be using, you'll generally want to avoid using VBScript for critical aspects of your site. For example, you probably won't want to rely on VBScript to generate an order form for a product. Doing so eliminates a good chunk of potential customers (those whose browsers don't support VBScript).

More browsers will likely support VBScript in the not-so-distant future. But for the time being, you need to carefully evaluate the ramifications of using VBScript for critical components of your site.

VBScript versus JavaScript

You've probably heard of JavaScript — and I've even referred to it several times already. JavaScript, like VBScript, is a scripting language that is used for programming Web pages. Both languages use code that is embedded directly within HTML documents.

So what's the difference? I've attempted to summarize these two languages in Table 4-1. As you see, both languages have their advantages and disadvantages (so what else is new?).

Table 4-1	VBScript versus JavaScript	
	VBScript	*JavaScript*
Developer	Microsoft	Sun Microsystems
Easy to learn	Yes	Not really
Easy to read	Yes	Not really
Supported by MS Internet Explorer	Yes	Yes
Supported by Netscape Navigator	No*	Yes
In widespread use	Not yet	Yes
*It's quite likely that a future version of Navigator will support VBScript.		

Both of these scripting languages are pretty much capable of doing the same sorts of things. But the real advantages of VBScript (at least to me) is that it is *much* easier to learn and to use. And if your primary objective is to produce slick Web pages with minimal fuss, ease of use can be a very important consideration.

To demonstrate how different these scripting languages are, I developed a simple example programmed in both JavaScript and VBScript. When you load the HTML document, you see two buttons — one executes the VBScript code, and the other executes the JavaScript code. You might want to view the source document to see how the two languages differ. (I think you'll find that the VBScript code is *much* easier to understand.)

Clicking a button presents you with a dialog box asking for a number. Enter a number, and another dialog box displays the square root of the number. Figure 4-3 shows an example of how the result is displayed.

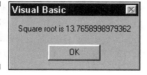

Figure 4-3:
Displaying
the result.

Note: This example also demonstrates that these two scripting languages can coexist quite peacefully in a single HTML document.

Chapter 5

Introducing Objects and the Object Model

In This Chapter

▶ What the object model is and why it is important

▶ How to refer to objects using dot notation

▶ Understanding which objects make up collections

▶ How objects relate to Internet Explorer features

▶ Familiar examples and how the objects concept relates

▶ A description of each and every object in the object model

*E*veryone's familiar with the word *object*. The *American Heritage Dictionary* defines it as:

> **ob·ject** (ŏb'jĭkt, -jĕkt´) *noun.* Something perceptible by one or more of the senses, especially by vision or touch; a material thing.

Well, folks, forget this definition. In the world of programming, *object* has a new meaning. It's often used as part of an expression: *object-oriented programming,* or OOP, for short. OOP is based on the idea that software consists of distinct objects, which have attributes (or properties), that it can be manipulated, and that it can respond to events. These objects are not material things. Rather, they exist in the form of bits and bytes.

In this chapter, I introduce you to the Internet Explorer object model so that you can see how it relates to the features in the browser.

The Object Model Visualized

Because a picture is worth 1K words, start out by examining Figure 5-1 — a graphical depiction of the Internet Explorer object model.

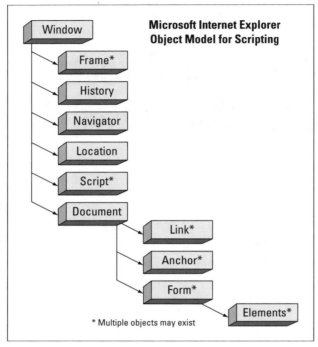

**Microsoft Internet Explorer
Object Model for Scripting**

Window
Frame*
History
Navigator
Location
Script*
Document
Link*
Anchor*
Form*
Elements*

* Multiple objects may exist

Figure 5-1:
The Internet
Explorer
object
model. Now
does it all
make
sense?

The objects in this model are arranged in a *hierarchy,* which means that objects are contained within other objects. At the very top of the object model is the Window object. Think of the Window object as the mother of all objects. In fact, notice that all the other objects are contained in the Window object. This containment should be easy to grasp, because everything that happens in your Web browser takes place in a single window.

When you get down to the Document object, things start getting a bit more interesting. The Document object can contain three additional objects (Link, Anchor, and Form). And, as you can see, the Form object can contain Element objects.

Note: As object models go, the one in Figure 5-1 isn't really complex. If exploring complex object models is your thing, pick up an advanced programming book for Microsoft Excel or Word and check out the object models for these products. Now those are major league object models.

There are objects ... and there are objects

I'll be the first to admit it: Dealing with objects can sometimes be confusing. To add to the confusion, realize that the object model that I discuss in this chapter is just part of the story. Another type of object rears its head in Chapters 16 through 18: the ActiveX object.

If you're thumbing through this book, trying to figure out the relationship between ActiveX objects and VBScript, you're in the wrong chapter. ActiveX objects are completely different and aren't part of the Internet Explorer object model. But Internet Explorer does use ActiveX objects. So for now, simply keep that factoid in mind and stay tuned. Or, you can skip ahead to Part V and get the lowdown on ActiveX objects right now.

The Collection Plate

Some objects can appear more than once. Looking again at the object model diagram in Figure 5-1, consider the Link object. A Link object is a hyperlink contained in a Document object. Click a link, and a new document usually loads in the browser window.

An HTML document can contain several (even hundreds) of hypertext links. So, a Document object can contain more than one Link object. A group of like objects is sometimes called a *collection,* and all the links in a particular document are called the Links collection (notice that *Links* is plural).

In fact, several objects in the object model can be collections:

- **Frames:** The Window can display several frames.
- **Links:** A Document can have multiple links.
- **Anchors:** A Document can have multiple anchors.
- **Forms:** A Document can have multiple forms.
- **Elements:** A Form can have multiple elements.

Referring to Objects

The object of the preceding section (pun intended) was to prepare you for the next concept: how to refer to objects in your VBScript code. Here's an example of VBScript that references the Document object contained in the Window object:

```
Window.Document
```

Notice that I connect the two objects with a dot, which is standard procedure for VBScript as well as all other variations of Visual Basic.

To refer to a particular link in a document within a window, you simply extend this *dot notation* to include the collection of Links, as follows:

```
Window.Document.Links(0)
```

Because Links is a collection of objects, you need to identify the exact link to which you're referring. The preceding example refers to the first Link object in the Links collection contained in the document in the window.

If you've been around computers for long, you may have noticed that computer numbering systems often begin with 0 instead of 1. So the first Link in the Links collection is actually link 0, not link 1. The numbering is weird, but you just have to get used to it.

Simply referring to objects doesn't do anything (except generate an error message). To do anything useful with objects, you must manipulate their properties, methods, and events — topics covered in the next chapter.

How Objects Relate to Internet Explorer Features

In Chapter 3, I describe the key features in Internet Explorer. You may want to check out that chapter, if you haven't already, so that the following sections make sense.

A concrete example

Enough theory. Time to get real. Figure 5-2 shows a screen shot of Internet Explorer. The browser's window is showing two frames.

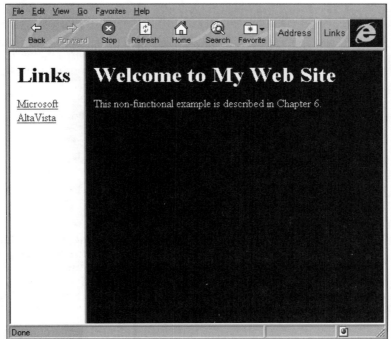

Figure 5-2:
Two frames
displayed in
the Internet
Explorer
window.

Although only two documents are visible, three HTML documents are actually involved in Figure 5-2:

- ✔ **makeframe.htm:** The Document object directly below the Window object
- ✔ **links.htm:** The Document object that's displayed in the left frame
- ✔ **main.htm:** The Document object that's displayed in the right frame

The following is a listing of the entire contents of the makeframes.htm document. This document simply uses the HTML `<FRAMESET>` tag to create two frames. The frame named LeftFrame displays the links.htm document, and the frame named RightFrame displays the main.htm document. Notice that the document in the left frame also includes two links:

```
<HTML>
<BODY>
<FRAMESET COLS="20%,80%">
    <FRAME SRC="links.htm" NAME="LeftFrame">
    <FRAME SRC="main.htm" NAME="RightFrame">
</FRAMESET>
</BODY>
</HTML>
```

A way to conceptualize objects

Here's how to conceptualize what's going on in terms of objects. Notice that I use indentation to indicate how these objects are *nested* in the object hierarchy. (A nested object is an object that's contained within another object.)

```
The Window object — the top-most object
  Document object (makeframes.htm)
    Frame object #1 (LeftFrame)
      Document object (links.htm)
        Link object #1
        Link object #2
    Frame object #2 (RightFrame)
      Document object (main.htm)
```

What this script means, in semi-plain English, is that the Window object holds a Document object. That document is not actually visible because it holds two Frame objects that take up the entire window. Each Frame object contains another Document object — and you're seeing those documents on-screen. The document in the left frame contains two additional objects (Link objects in the Links collection).

Chances are, you've seen or even created Web sites that use this sort of arrangement. But maybe you've never thought about it in terms of objects.

A family affair

If you're not comfortable with the concept of objects inside of objects that contain other objects, here's yet another way to look at the preceding example.

This time, start in the middle of the script and work your way out. The inner-most object is one of the Link objects in the document in the left frame. The parent of these link objects is the containing Document object. That Document object's parent is a Frame object. That Frame object's parent is a Document object. That Document object's parent is the Window object.

Taken from another perspective, the Window object has one child (a Document object). That Document object has two children (both Frame objects). The first Frame object has one child, and that child has two children. Unlike normal parent-child relationships, a weekly allowance does not enter into the picture.

Note: You may think that this parent-child stuff sounds rather strange. But this terminology is common in the world of object-oriented programming! One property is even called Parent.

Frame = Window?

You may have noticed that a Frame object seems to be just like a Window object, because both contain a Document object.

By and large, a Frame object works very much like a Window object. There are a few differences, however. A document contains only one Window object but can have many Frame objects. The Frame and Window objects also share many properties, methods, and events, but a Frame object doesn't have all the properties and methods that the Window object has.

In case you're wondering, the Document object contained in a Frame object also can contain other Frame objects. You've probably seen examples of this during your Web surfing excursions. Sometimes, your browser window gets so loaded with frames you can hardly see a thing.

Frames play an increasingly important role in the World Wide Web. In Chapter 14, you can find out all about working with frames using VBScript.

Drilling Deeper into the Object Model

Figure 5-3 also illustrates the concept of nesting objects. This example is similar to the one in Figure 5-2, but this time the main.htm document was modified to include a *floating frame*.

Note: The floating frame is one of the new features introduced in Internet Explorer 3.0. Unlike a normal frame, a floating frame can appear anywhere in a document. You create a floating frame using the <IFRAME> tag.

Here's the HTML code that generates the floating frame:

```
<IFRAME HEIGHT=200 WIDTH=300 SRC=survey.htm><IFRAME>
```

The floating frame contains a Document object (survey.htm), the Document object contains a Form object, and the Form object contains four Elements. Here's the listing of survey.htm:

```
<HTML>
<BODY>
<H2>Please fill out this brief survey.</H2>
<FORM NAME=Survey>
 Name: <INPUT TYPE=Text NAME=UserName>
<P>
```

(continued)

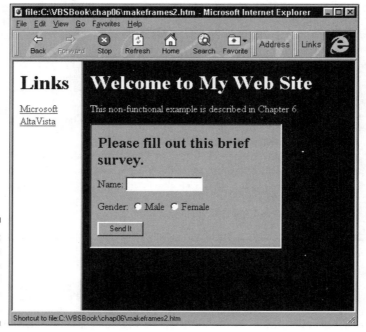

Figure 5-3:
Now, the
objects are
nested
even more
deeply.

(continued)

```
Gender:
 <INPUT TYPE=Radio NAME=Gender>Male
 <INPUT TYPE=Radio NAME=Gender>Female
 <P>
 <INPUT TYPE=Submit NAME=SendIt Value="Send It">
</FORM>
</BODY>
</HTML>
```

In the following, I use indentations to help conceptualize how the objects fit together:

```
The Window object — the top-most object
  Document object (makeframes.htm)
    Frame object #1
      Document object (links.htm)
        Link object #1
        Link object #2
    Frame object #2
      Document object (main.htm)
        Frame object (floating)
```

```
Document object (survey.htm)
    Form object
        Elements #1 (textbox)
        Elements #2 (radio button)
        Elements #3 (radio button)
        Elements #4 (submit button)
```

As you can see, each element in the form is contained in the Form object. The Form object is contained in the Document object (survey.htm), which is contained in a Frame object, which is contained in a Document object (main.htm), which is contained in a Frame object, which is contained in a Document object (makeframe.htm), which is contained in the Window object. Objects within objects may be a bit complicated, but I think you'll agree that it is all quite logical.

Note: In Chapter 13, I discuss the ins and outs of working with forms.

The Objects Described

You probably have a pretty good feel for objects and have a basic understanding of how the object model fits together. If not, the first part of this chapter can set you straight. In this section, I briefly describe the objects you'll be working on and set the stage for actually writing VBScript code.

How much of this object stuff is actually important?

Good question. The answer is, it depends on what you're doing.

As you know, you can have simple Web pages, complicated Web pages, and Web pages that fall somewhere in between. The same goes for VBScript. Some people are quite happy to use a few simple VBScript routines in their page. Others like to go all out and take full advantage of the power of VBScript.

For simple VBScript applications, you don't need to get too involved with the object model. In fact, you can probably just snag code snippets from this book and make simple adaptations. But for more complex applications, such as working with frames and forms, a good understanding of the object model makes your job easier. You can look at it from another perspective. If you take the time to become well-acquainted with the object model, you will most definitely get new ideas regarding Web site design.

This book takes a middle-ground approach when it comes to Web pages. In subsequent chapters, you can find many Web page examples designed to illustrate common solutions.

The Window object

The Window object is the *top-level* object. Every other object that you use is contained in the Window object. The Window object can hold only one Document object, but that Document object may contain Frame objects that hold other Document objects.

The Frame object and the Frames collection

The Window object contains the Frame object. A Frame object is also a member of the Frames collection. Frames(0) is the first frame, Frames(1) is the second frame, and so on.

The Frame object is much like a Window object in that it can hold only one Document object. But a Document object in a Frame can contain other frames that hold other Document objects.

The History object

The History object is rather unusual. Its sole purpose in life is to provide a means to navigate through history using VBScript. History, in this context, refers to the list of pages that you've viewed. You can access the History object manually by clicking the Forward and Back icons in your browser. Or, you can use VBScript code to go backward or forward though history.

The Navigator object

The Navigator object is also a strange one. This object provides information about the browser application itself. If you ever need to know which browser (or even which version of the browser) is being used by a visitor to your Web site, your VBScript code can find out by accessing the Navigator object.

Note: This object is included primarily to make Internet Explorer compatible with Netscape Navigator.

The Location object

The Location object is one level below the Window object, and it represents information about the URL of the document currently open. Much of this URL information is rather technical. For example, you can access the Location object to find out the protocol, hostname, port, and other details.

The Script object

Yet another unusual object, a Script object is simply a script block in your document that is enclosed between a `<SCRIPT>` and a `</SCRIPT>` tag.

The Document object

The Document object can lie just below the Window object and just below a Frame object.

This object is one of the most important because it is what the user sees when the Web page is loaded into the browser. The Document object contains other objects, such as Links, Anchors, and Forms.

The Link object and the Links collection

The Link object represents a hypertext link in a Document object. Because a document can have multiple links, your VBScript code can refer to the Links collection.

The Anchor object and the Anchors collection

An Anchor object represents an anchor in a Document object. An anchor tag, `<A>`, identifies an item. Anchor objects are used in lengthy documents to allow the viewer to jump to a particular location on the page. Because a document can have multiple anchors, your VBScript code can refer to the Anchors collection.

The Form object and the Forms collection

A Form object represents a form in a Document object. Forms are commonly used as a way to obtain information from a user. Information collected in a form is sent back to the server and processed. Because a document can have multiple forms, your VBScript code can refer to the Forms collection.

The Element object and the Elements collection

An Element object represents an item displayed in a document using the
<INPUT> tag. Because a document can have multiple Elements, your VBScript
code can refer to the Elements collection. Refer to "Internet Explorer Objects,
Properties, Methods, and Events" on the disk for a list of the element types.

Chapter 6

All about Properties, Methods, and Events

● ●

In This Chapter

▶ An introduction to properties, methods, and events

▶ Finding out the value of properties and changing their values

▶ Using methods to make things happen

▶ How to spring your VBScript into life when a particular event occurs

● ●

*I*f you're coming to this chapter after reading Chapter 5, you probably realize that objects in and of themselves aren't all that exciting. To add excitement to the picture, you need to know how to *do something* with those objects. And now I'm about to let you in on a little secret:

Programming in VBScript really boils down to manipulating objects. It's as simple as that.

Making Objects Useful

Objects have properties, methods, and events (I define these terms a bit later in this chapter). In order to do anything useful with an object, you must

✔ Read or modify an object's *properties.*

✔ Specify a *method* of action to be used with an object.

✔ Create VBScript code to handle an *event* that occurs.

You may be confused because each object has its own unique set of properties and its own set of methods, and each object responds to specific events. And some objects have no methods, and other objects don't respond to any events. Yikes! What have you gotten yourself into?

I can assure you that this state of confusion is only temporary. Only a few properties, methods, and objects are really important.

Note: "Internet Explorer Objects, Properties, Methods, and Events," located on the companion disk, contains a quick reference to all the objects, properties, methods, and events. Take a minute or so to look at it to get a feel for what you can do using VBScript.

In the following sections, I answer questions you probably have regarding properties, methods, and events. And I probably answer some questions you haven't thought of yet.

Examining Object Properties

Every object has properties. Think of a property as an attribute that describes the object. An object's properties determine how it looks, how it behaves, and whether it's visible. Using VBScript, you can do two things with an object's properties:

✔ You can examine the current setting for a property and then take action based on what you find.

✔ You can change the property to make it look or act differently.

Referring to properties

To refer to a property for an object, connect the object and the property with a dot. This is the same technique used to refer to a nested object (see Chapter 5 for an explanation of referring to objects).

One property of the Document object is Bgcolor. The Bgcolor property holds the hex value of the background color of the document. (See Chapter 2 for more information on hex values.) You can refer to the Bgcolor property of the Document object like this:

```
Document.Bgcolor
```

Looking at property values

Simply referring to the property in your VBScript code doesn't do anything (actually, it generates an error message). You need to examine the property's value or change it. The following line of VBScript displays an alert box that shows the current value of the Bgcolor property for the Document object:

```
Alert Document.Bgcolor
```

Figure 6-1 shows the alert box that appears when the document's background color is pure red (FF0000 is the hex code for red).

Figure 6-1:
Displaying
the value
of the
Document
object's
Bgcolor
property.

Here's another example: The following statement displays the document's title in an alert box. In official terminology, the statement displays the value of the Title property of the Document object:

```
Alert Document.Title
```

Changing property values

Besides looking at a property value, you also can write VBScript to change a property value. You use the equal sign operator (=) to change a property value. The following statement changes the document's background color to yellow (FFFF00 is the hex code for the color yellow). When this statement executes, the document's background color changes:

```
Document.Bgcolor = "FFFF00"
```

Some properties are *read-only*. Read-only means that you can look at the property value, but you can't change it by using VBScript. An example of a read-only property is the LastModifed property of the Document object which holds the date and time that the document was last saved. That particular property only changes when the document is saved.

Pointing to objects

Okay, here's where it gets a bit tricky: In addition, properties can return a pointer to another object. For example, if you look at the official list of properties for the Window object (see Appendix A), you'll find that the Windows object has a Document property.

The following statement returns a reference to the Document object:

```
Window.Document
```

Note: A property that returns an object is sometimes called an *accessor*. The Window object includes the following accessors: Frame, History, Navigator, Location, or Document. Take a look at the object model presented in Chapter 5, and you can see that these properties all return objects contained in the Window object.

You can extend this referencing stuff one step further and access a property as well — all in a single VBScript statement. In the following statement, the alert box displays the value of the Fgcolor property of the Document object:

```
Alert Window.Document.Fgcolor
```

Here's another way to look at this: The preceding statement contains a *fully qualified* reference that includes the Document object *and* its containing object (the Window object). You get exactly the same result by using the following statement:

```
Alert Document.Fgcolor
```

In fact, I present the preceding statement earlier in this chapter. VBScript doesn't require you to fully qualify your references. In this case, VBScript assumes that the Document object is contained in the Window object. This assumption makes your coding easier — you don't have to fully qualify your references.

Here's another example that may help. The Location object has a property called Href, which holds the current URL. This example displays the Href property of the Location object:

```
Alert Window.Location.Href
```

Again, the preceding statement contains a fully qualified reference. The Location property of the Window object is an accessor that returns the Location object. You get exactly the same result by referring to the Location object directly:

```
Alert Location.Href
```

Figure 6-2 shows the message that appears when this statement executes. In this case, the browser has opened a file on a local drive. If the document is located on a Web server, the alert box displays a normal URL, such as `http://www.Website.com`.

Figure 6-2:
The Href
property of
the Location
object.

Seeing the Document object properties in action

The companion disk for this book includes a document that uses VBScript to write the current value for every property of the Document object. Figure 6-3 shows part of this document. By the way, Write is a method of the Document object (I cover methods in the next section).

The document uses immediate script (script that executes as the document loads) and consists of a series of Document.Write statements to write the information directly to the document. Note that you need three lines of VBScript code to generate one line of text in the browser. For each line generated in the browser, the code:

✔ Writes the name of the property being examined (within `<B>` and `</B>` tags to make it bold).

✔ Writes the property's value.

✔ Writes a `<BR>` tag to skip to the next line.

Exploring Object Methods

Besides properties, objects also have methods. I should say *most* objects have them, because Navigator, Link, and Anchor objects don't have any methods at all.

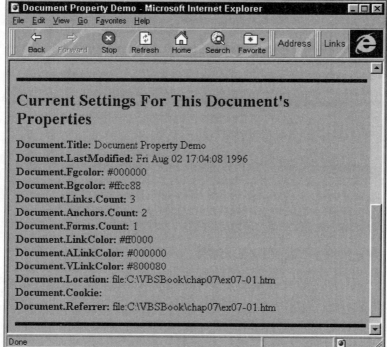

A *method* is an action that you perform with an object or on an object. A method also can change an object's properties or make the object do something. In the previous section, I demonstrate using the Write method of the Document object. The Write method writes a string of text to the document. The following statement, when executed, writes "Hello User" to the document:

```
Document.Write "Hello User"
```

The Window object has quite a few useful methods. The Alert method is a handy method that I've used previously in this chapter (and in other chapters).

```
Alert "Hello user"
```

Yes, Alert is a method of the Window object that displays a message in a small dialog box. You can accomplish the same effect by using this statement:

```
Window.Alert "Hello"
```

Qualifying the Alert method with the Window object isn't necessary, so "Window" is usually omitted.

Here's another example (again, I omit the reference to the Window object because it is assumed):

```
Confirm "Do you want to load this URL?"
```

The Confirm method is similar to the Alert method, but it displays two buttons (OK and Cancel) instead of only an OK button. Figure 6-4 shows what this dialog box looks like.

Figure 6-4:
The Confirm
method
displays a
dialog box.

Here's an example of using the Back method of the History object. When the following statement executes, the browser loads the previous page, just as if the user clicked the Back button:

```
History.Back
```

Understanding Object Events

An *event* is something that may cause an object to do something. For example, one of the events for the Window object is OnLoad. Loading a window is an event. You can specify what happens when this event occurs by writing VBScript code.

Earlier in this chapter, I describe how to specify properties and methods by using the dot operator. You connect the object with the property by using a dot, as follows:

```
Document.Bgcolor = "FF0000"
```

You also specify a method by connecting the object with the method using a dot, like this:

```
Document.Write
```

When it comes to events, you don't use the dot operator because objects respond to events — they don't create events. I clarify this concept in the next section.

Handling those events

Specifying an event works differently than working with properties and methods. An event requires a subroutine to serve as the event handler. Here's a simple example that displays a message after the window is loaded into the browser:

```
Sub Window_onLoad()
    Alert "Welcome to my Web site!"
End Sub
```

You specify an event handler for an object by creating a subroutine. The subroutine's name consists of the object, an underscore character, and the name of the event.

Most objects don't respond to any events. The Element object has events because Element objects are *controls* — buttons, check boxes, and the like. These objects respond to events such as being clicked (the OnClick event), having values changed (the OnChange event), or being selected by the user (the OnSelect event).

An event-handling example

The following list is a complete HTML document that demonstrates the concept of an event. In this case, the event of interest is a button click. Figure 6-5 shows how the document appears in the browser.

The document uses the <INPUT> tag to display a button named MyButton. When the user clicks the button, the button click generates an OnClick event. A subroutine named MyButton_onClick handles this event. The subroutine changes the foreground and background colors by modifying the Fgcolor and Bgcolor properties of the Document object:

```
<HTML>
<HEAD>
<TITLE>Sample Document</TITLE>
</HEAD>
<BODY TEXT=000000 BGCOLOR=FFFFFF>
<H1>Welcome to my Web site</H1>
<P>
Click the button below to reverse the foreground and
background colors.
<HR>
<INPUT TYPE=Button NAME=MyButton Value="Click Me">
<SCRIPT LANGUAGE="VBScript">
Sub MyButton_onClick()
    If Document.Bgcolor="#ffffff" then
        Document.Fgcolor="#ffffff"
        Document.Bgcolor="#000000"
        Exit Sub
```

(continued)

Figure 6-5:
Clicking
the button
triggers
an event.

(continued)

```
    End If
    If Document.Bgcolor="#000000" then
        Document.Fgcolor="#000000"
        Document.Bgcolor="#ffffff"
    End If
End Sub
</SCRIPT>
</BODY>
</HTML>
```

This subroutine uses two programming concepts, that I discuss in Chapter 9. It uses If-Then to execute code conditionally. In plain English, if the background color is white, the code changes the background color to black and the foreground color to white. The second If-Then code does the opposite.

The first If-Then code uses an Exit Sub statement, which simply causes the subroutine to stop executing. If this statement is omitted, the next If-Then code executes, and the color changes back to the original color. In effect, nothing noticeable happens.

Finding Out More about This Stuff

This chapter may leave you feeling sort of stranded. I only touch on a few properties, methods, and events, but there are plenty more where those came from. Rather than spend a few dozen pages explaining every boring detail, I present just the basics in this chapter. Later chapters contain useful examples that involve properties, methods, and events. If you want to see an exhaustive list, refer to "Internet Explorer Objects, Properties, Methods, and Events," located on the companion disk.

Part III
Programming Concepts

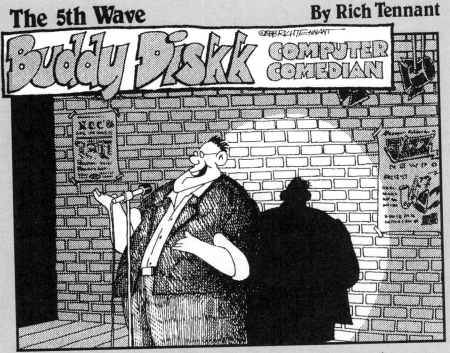

The 5th Wave   By Rich Tennant

Buddy Diskk COMPUTER COMEDIAN

©1998 RICH TENNANT

"SO I SAID, 'WAITER! WAITER! THERE'S A BUG IN MY SOUP!' AND HE SAYS, 'SORRY, SIR, THE CHEF USED TO PROGRAM COMPUTERS.' AHH HAHA HAHA THANK YOU! THANK YOU!"

In this part . . .

The chapters in this part deal with actual programming. You know, the cryptic thing people use to create software, which actually makes a computer useful. In this case, of course, the programming language is VBScript. Topics include subroutines and functions, variables and arrays, program flow, built-in functions, and (yikes!) bug extermination techniques.

Chapter 7

All about Subroutines and Functions

In This Chapter

▶ How to tell the difference between subroutines and functions

▶ How to execute subroutines and call functions

▶ Where to put your VBScript procedures

▶ How to troubleshoot subroutines and functions

In Chapter 4, I discuss the two different ways to include VBScript in your HTML documents. *Immediate scripts* execute as the document loads. *Deferred scripts* execute when they are needed or when a particular event occurs.

Another term for a deferred script is a *procedure*. In fact, there are two types of procedures: subroutines and functions. And subroutines and functions just happen to be the topic of this chapter.

Procedural Matters

You've probably heard the term *subroutine* and *function*, but these concepts may not be perfectly clear. In this chapter, I clear up any confusion you may have about these two terms. First, the definitions:

✔ **Subroutine:** A group of VBScript statements that perform an action or actions.

✔ **Function:** A group of VBScript statements that perform a calculation and return a single value.

VBScript has simple rules about how you create subroutines and functions. I let you in on these rules in the following sections.

What shall we name it?

As with human beings and pets, every subroutine and function procedure must have a name. When coming up with a name, you must adhere to a few rules:

✔ You can use alphabetic characters, numbers, and some punctuation characters, but the first character must be alphabetic.

✔ You cannot use any spaces or periods in the name.

✔ VBScript does not distinguish between upper- and lowercase. You can mix and match all you want.

✔ The following characters cannot be embedded in a name: #, $, -, %, &, or !.

✔ Names can be no longer than 254 characters. But no one in his right mind makes a variable name this long — excessively long variable names are too easy to misspell.

✔ You can't use any of VBScript's reserved words. And VBScript has quite a few of these words (refer to Chapter 9 for a complete list of reserved words). You can tell whether you use a reserved word because you get an error message. The message may say, "Expected identifier," "Expected statement," "Cannot assign to a variable," or something equally uninformative.

If the procedure is an event handler, the object and the event determines the procedure's name. For example, a subroutine that executes when a button, named MyButton, is clicked is named MyButton_OnClick.

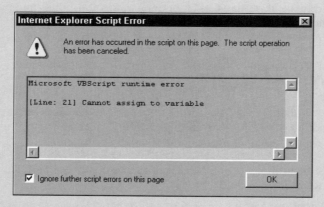

Looking at subroutines

Every subroutine procedure starts out with the keyword Sub and ends with an End Sub statement. Here's an example:

```
Sub LoadNewFrame()
   [VBScript code goes here]
End Sub
```

In this case, the subroutine is named LoadNewFrame. A set of parentheses follows the subroutine name. Most of the time, these parentheses are empty. If the parentheses are empty, you can even omit them, if you'd like to save a few keystrokes. However, you also can pass *arguments* (a value that is used in the subroutine) to subroutines — in which case, you list the argument(s) in the parentheses. (More about arguments later in the upcoming section "Subroutine Examples.")

Looking at functions

Every function procedure starts out with the keyword `Function` and ends with an `End Function` statement. Here's an example:

```
Function CubeRoot(number)
   [VBScript code goes here]
End Function
```

This function, named CubeRoot, takes one argument, named number, which is enclosed in parentheses. Most of the time, function procedures have at least one argument, but some functions don't have any arguments. If a function has more than one argument, commas separate the argument names. When the function executes, it returns a single value.

Note: VBScript is kind enough to provide quite a few built-in functions. These functions are always available, and you can use them freely in your code. Built-in functions is the topic of Chapter 10.

Subroutine Examples

This section provides all the additional information you need to create subroutines in your documents. Well, you're still missing some essential programming concepts, but those come in Chapters 8 and 9.

Subroutines essentially serve two purposes in life, and they can be classified into two categories:

✔ **Event handlers:** Subroutines that do something when an event occurs. Examples of events include clicking a button, loading a document, and submitting a form.

> ✔ **Other subroutines:** This rather broad classification includes all subrou-
> tines that aren't event handlers. These types of subroutines are always
> *called,* or executed, by another subroutine.

Note: In Chapter 13, I describe everything you need to know about the important events that can occur.

An event handler example

To get the ball rolling, look at the following HTML document listing:

```
<HTML>
<HEAD>
<TITLE>Subroutine Demo</TITLE>
<SCRIPT LANGUAGE=VBScript>
Sub GetName_OnClick()
    UserName = InputBox ("Enter your full name")
    Msg = "Hello " & UserName & ". Welcome to my site."
    Alert Msg
End Sub
</SCRIPT>
</HEAD>
<BODY>
<H1>Subroutine Demo</H1>
<P>
This document demonstrates the use of VBScript subroutines.
</P>
<HR>
<INPUT TYPE=Button NAME=GetName Value="Tell me your name">
</BODY>
</HTML>
```

This document contains one VBScript procedure — a subroutine named
GetName_OnClick.

Clicking the button (the event) executes the subroutine (the event handler).
The subroutine displays a dialog box that asks for the user's name. The name
that's entered is assigned to a *variable* named UserName. (I discuss the concept
of variables in Chapter 8.) The next statement creates a message and stores it in
another variable, Msg. The third statement displays an alert box with the
message. Figure 7-1 shows an example of this message.

Figure 7-1:
Displaying a
message
by using
information
entered by
the user.

Here are a few factoids about the GetName_OnClick subroutine.

- ✓ **This subroutine is an event handler for a button.** Clicking the button is the event that executes the subroutine. The subroutine's name is determined by the button's name and the event it will handle, separated by an underscore character.

- ✓ **The subroutine is placed in the document's** `<HEAD>` **section.** You could put it anywhere in the document.

- ✓ **The subroutine is enclosed between the** `<SCRIPT>` **and** `</SCRIPT>` **tags.** You can place additional procedures within either the same set of `<SCRIPT>` and `</SCRIPT>` tags or in a different set of `<SCRIPT>` and `</SCRIPT>` tags.

- ✓ **The subroutine doesn't use any arguments.** The parentheses after the subroutine name are empty, and I could have omitted the parentheses altogether.

- ✓ **The subroutine consists of three statements that execute one after another.**

- ✓ **The End Sub statement signals the end of the subroutine.**

A subroutine with an argument

The following example is just a bit more sophisticated than the previous example. The ChangeBG subroutine (listed in the following code) takes an argument. Figure 7-2 shows a document with five radio buttons. Clicking any of these buttons executes the event handler subroutine that changes the background color of the document.

The complete listing for the document follows.

```
<HTML>
<HEAD>
<TITLE>Subroutine Demo</TITLE>
```

(continued)

(continued)

```
<SCRIPT LANGUAGE=VBScript>
Sub ChangeBG(color)
    If color=1 Then Document.Bgcolor="ff0000"
    If color=2 Then Document.Bgcolor="00ff00"
    If color=3 Then Document.Bgcolor="0000ff"
    If color=4 Then Document.Bgcolor="ffff00"
    If color=5 Then Document.Bgcolor="ff00ff"
End Sub
</SCRIPT>
</HEAD>
<BODY>
<H1>Subroutine Demo</H1>
<P>
This document demonstrates the use of VBScript subroutines.
<HR>
Select a background color...<BR>
<INPUT TYPE=Radio NAME=Color OnClick="ChangeBG(1)">Red<BR>
<INPUT TYPE=Radio NAME=Color OnClick="ChangeBG(2)">Green<BR>
<INPUT TYPE=Radio NAME=Color OnClick="ChangeBG(3)">Blue<BR>
<INPUT TYPE=Radio NAME=Color OnClick="ChangeBG(4)">Yellow<BR>
<INPUT TYPE=Radio NAME=Color OnClick="ChangeBG(5)">Purple<BR>
<P>
</BODY>
</HTML>
```

How it works

The argument that is passed to the ChangeBG subroutine determines exactly what the subroutine does. The color variable represents the argument passed to the subroutine. The subroutine uses that argument to determine what to do by using a series of If-Then statements to change the Bgcolor property of the Document object. Without the argument, the subroutine doesn't know what to do.

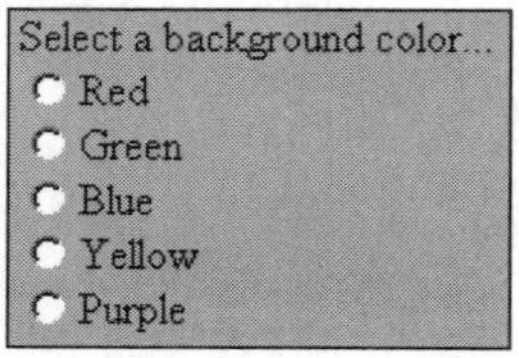

Figure 7-2:
Clicking a
radio button
executes a
subroutine
that uses an
argument.

Select a background color...
- Red
- Green
- Blue
- Yellow
- Purple

Notice that each `<INPUT>` tag has an OnClick attribute. For example, the first one is

```
OnClick="ChangeBG(1)"
```

The OnClick parameter specifies the subroutine to execute when the radio button is clicked and also passes an argument to the subroutine, in parentheses. Each `<INPUT>` tag calls the same subroutine (ChangeBG), but passes a different argument to it.

Another way to do it

You can accomplish the same effect *without* using arguments. However, each `<INPUT>` tag needs to have a different OnClick attribute to call a different subroutine. In other words, if you don't use an argument, you need five subroutines rather than one.

Bottom line? Using arguments in subroutines makes them more versatile. In this case, one subroutine does the work of five subroutines.

Calling a Subroutine from Another Subroutine: Rules of the Road

The previous subroutine examples in this chapter are event handler subroutines. An event, such as a button click, makes the subroutine kick into action. You also can *call* a subroutine from another subroutine. Calling a subroutine is the same as executing a subroutine.

Calling a subroutine with no arguments

Here are a few examples of VBScript statements that call a subroutine that doesn't have any arguments:

```
Call ChangeBackground()
Call ChangeBackground
ChangeBackground()
ChangeBackground
```

These four statements all produce exactly the same result: They execute the ChangeBackground subroutine. Notice that using an empty set of parentheses is optional, and using the Call keyword is also optional. VBScript is pretty flexible, don't you agree?

Using the Call *keyword* is usually a good idea, even though it's not required. Using the Call keyword makes it perfectly clear that the statement is calling a subroutine. As long as you're at it, get into the habit of including a set of empty parentheses. That way, there will be no question that the statement is indeed calling a subroutine.

Calling a subroutine with an argument

Here are examples of calling a subroutine that requires an argument.

```
Call ChangeBackground("ff00ff")
ChangeBackground "ff00ff"
```

In the second example, the argument is supplied without parentheses — which works just fine, although it's definitely not as clear as the first example. VBScript's flexibility has limits, however. If you use the Call keyword, you *must* enclose the argument(s) in parentheses. The following statement generates an error:

```
Call ChangeBackground "00ff00"
```

The following statement is an example of a statement that calls a subroutine that uses two arguments. The arguments are separated by a comma and enclosed in parentheses.

```
Call ChangeColors("ffffff","000000")
```

The ChangeColors subroutine may be something like this:

```
Sub ChangeColors(fg,bg)
    Document.FGcolor=fg
    Document.Bgcolor=bg
End Sub
```

Function Examples

A function is the other type of VBScript procedure. A function can be very useful because it:

- ✔ Eliminates the need to duplicate code.
- ✔ Simplifies your coding.
- ✔ Can often be re-used in other documents.

What's in that box? Who cares?

Think of a function as a black box. You put something into the black box, it does some mysterious things, and then you get something else in return. In the case of a function, you supply the function (the black box) with one or more arguments, and the function manipulates or calculates and gives you a single value in return.

The nice thing about black boxes is that you don't need to understand what goes on inside them. All you need to be concerned with is what you put into the black box (the arguments) and what comes out (the result of the function). For example, VBScript has a built-in function called Hex. The Hex function takes one argument (a number) and returns the hexadecimal equivalent of that number. The following statement displays an alert box that displays DB920E.

```
Alert Hex(14389774)
```

At this point, how the Hex function works doesn't matter. All that matters is that the Hex function returns the correct value for the argument you provide.

You also can consider VBScript functions that you, or someone else, create to be black boxes. In many cases, you can simply copy a function that someone else has written and then use it in your own page. You can use the function even if you don't understand how it works.

A function is very similar to a subroutine, with one exception: A function returns a value when it finishes executing.

A simple function example

Here's a simple VBScript function to start things off:

```
Function CalcRoot(number,root)
    CalcRoot = number ^ (1 / root)
End Function
```

The CalcRoot function returns a root of a number. For example, it can calculate square roots, cube roots, and any other root you can come up with. The mathematically inclined know that calculating a root involves raising a number to the 1/nth power, where n is the root. That's exactly what the CalcRoot function does.

This function takes two arguments: the number and the root. If you want to calculate and display the cube root of 65, you can use a statement like this to display the result:

```
Alert CalcRoot(65,3)
```

Figure 7-3 shows that this function does indeed work.

As functions go, the CalcRoot function is simple — only one statement. But, rest assured, VBScript functions can get as complicated as you like.

Figure 7-3:
Using the
CalcRoot
function to
perform a
calculation.

The ReverseText function

Here's another, slightly more complex function. The ReverseText function accepts one argument and then returns the argument backwards. For example, if the argument is *Evian,* the function returns *naivE.*

```
Function ReverseText(text)
    TextLength = Len(text)
    ReverseText=""
    For i = TextLength to 1 Step -1
        ReverseText = ReverseText & Mid(text,i,1)
    Next
End Function
```

Note: The ReverseText function uses programming concepts that are covered in later chapters of the book. So don't be too concerned if you don't understand the inner workings of the function. However, even if you don't understand how the ReverseText function works, you can still use this function any time you want. (See the sidebar, "What's in that box? Who cares?")

By the way, the ReverseText function uses two VBScript built-in functions: Len, which returns the length of its argument, and Mid, which returns a character inside of a text string. I describe both these functions in Chapter 10.

The companion disk includes an example that uses the ReverseText function. Figure 7-4 shows an example.

Figure 7-4:
The
ReverseText
function
returns text
backwards.

Where to Put Your Procedures

A common question is *Where in the HTML document should I put my subroutines and functions?* Good question.

You can put your procedures anywhere you like, as long as a `<SCRIPT>` and a `</SCRIPT>` tag enclose them. Many people like to put their procedures in the `<HEAD>` section to improve the chance that the code will be loaded if the user clicks the Stop button before the page finishes loading.

There is one exception to the "put it anywhere" rule: If your code uses immediate script that calls a procedure, the procedure must be placed before the immediate script, or at least within the same `<SCRIPT></SCRIPT>` block. *Immediate* script executes immediately as the document loads. If the immediate script tries to use a subroutine or function that appears later in the document, the browser isn't able to find the procedure. As long as the referenced procedure appears earlier in the document or within the same `<SCRIPT></SCRIPT>` block, things work okay.

A bad example

Here's an example that *doesn't* work. The immediate script, the Document.Write statement, calls a function that hasn't been defined yet.

```
<SCRIPT LANGUAGE=VBScript>
Document.Write "Hello. The year is " & GetYear()
</SCRIPT>

<H1>Welcome to my Web Site</H1>
<SCRIPT LANGUAGE=VBScript>
Function GetToday()
    GetYear =Year(Now())
End Function
</SCRIPT>
```

When this page loads, you're greeted with the message shown in Figure 7-5.

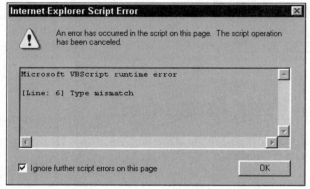

Figure 7-5:
Type
mismatch?
That's
VBScript's
way of
telling you
that it
doesn't
recognize a
procedure
name.

A good example

The following code works just fine because the immediate script calls a previously defined function.

```
<SCRIPT LANGUAGE=VBScript>
Function GetYear()
    GetYear =Year(Now())
End function
</SCRIPT>
<H1>Welcome to my Web Site</H1>
<SCRIPT LANGUAGE=VBScript>
Document.Write "Hello. The year is " & GetYear()
</SCRIPT>
```

Troubleshooting Subroutines and Functions

I close this chapter with a list of things to keep in mind when you're working with subroutine and function procedures.

- ✔ **Make sure that every subroutine has an End Sub statement and every function has an End Function statement.**

- ✔ **Make sure that your procedure name is not one of VBScript's reserved words.**

✔ **Your procedures must be enclosed between the** `<SCRIPT>` **and** `</SCRIPT>` **tags.**

You can put as many procedures as you want within a single set of these tags. Or, your document can have multiple `<SCRIPT>` and `</SCRIPT>` tags.

✔ **When you call a subroutine or function that uses arguments, make sure that you supply the correct number of arguments and that they are in the correct order.**

✔ **The argument passed to a procedure doesn't need the same variable name as the variable specified in the procedure's argument list.**

✔ **You can end a procedure prematurely by using an** `Exit Sub` **or an** `Exit Function` **statement.**

This statement is almost always used in conjunction with an If-Then statement. (I cover If-Then statements in Chapter 9.)

✔ **If you call a procedure from an immediate script (a nonprocedure script that executes as the document loads), the procedure must be located in the document before the script that calls it.**

✔ **The result of a function must always be assigned to the function's name.**

If the function is named MyFunction, the function must assign a value to MyFunction before it ends.

✔ **Variables used in a procedure are normally valid only in that procedure.**

If you assign a value to a variable in procedure A, the variable does not have that value in procedure B. Put another way, two procedures can use the same variable name, but they are considered two different variables. Refer to Chapter 8 for details about *variable scoping*.

Chapter 8

Using Variables and Arrays

In This Chapter

▶ Understanding variables: What they are and how to use them

▶ Knowing which variable names to avoid

▶ Creating expressions and assigning them to variables

▶ Introducing arrays: One-dimensional and multidimensional

▶ Scoping variables and arrays

▶ Declaring variables and arrays

▶ Introducing object variables

This chapter covers two important concepts: variables and arrays. Although you can write simple scripts without using variables or arrays, these critters are absolutely essential for anything other than the most trivial VBScript projects.

Introducing Variables

A *variable* is simply a named storage location in your computer's memory. This storage location holds data: a number, a text string, an object, or whatever.

Naming variables

You have lots of flexibility in naming your variables, so making variable names as descriptive as possible is a good idea. VBScript enforces a few rules regarding variable names (the rules are very similar to those for procedure names, which I cover in Chapter 7):

  ✔ You can use alphabetic characters, numbers, and some punctuation characters, but the first character must be alphabetic.

✔ You cannot use any spaces or periods, and you can't use any of the following characters: #, $, -, %, &, or !.

✔ VBScript does not distinguish between upper- and lowercase. So a variable named userpassword is the same as UserPassword, which is the same as USERPASSWORD, which is the same as uSeRpAsSwOrD.

✔ Variable names can be no longer than 254 characters. Keep names short, but not necessarily sweet.

To make variable names more readable, programmers often use mixed case (for example, VisitorName) or the underscore character (for example, Visitor_Name).

Bad variable names

VBScript has quite a few reserved words that cannot be used for variable names or procedure names. These reserved words are built-in functions or keywords that are part of the language. If you attempt to use one of these names as a variable, you get an error message.

Reserved words can make good variable names, but you get an error if you try to use any of them. For example, the reserved word *Year* (which is a built-in function) often makes a descriptive variable name. However, the following statement generates a syntax error:

```
Year = 1997
```

The statement produces an error that reads, *Cannot assign to a variable.* Unfortunately, the error message isn't all that descriptive. Actually it's down-right misleading. So if a statement produces a strange error, check the reserved words list.

You can get around this reserved word business by using a variation on a reserved word. For example, you can use TheYear or CurrentYear as your variable name.

Today's Assignment . . .

An *assignment statement* is a VBScript statement that assigns the result of an expression to a variable or an object. In other words, an assignment statement is what you use to give a value to a variable.

A few words about data types

When you use other variations of Visual Basic, you often need to be concerned about *data types*. For example, you can declare a variable to be used for a particular data type: a string, an integer, an object, and so on.

VBScript keeps things very simple by handling data types automatically. Technically, all variables in VBScript are *variants,* which means that the data type can vary depending on what you assign to the variable. For example, you can use a statement like the following to assign a text string to a variable:

```
MyVariable="Hello and good day."
```

Somewhere else in the same script, you can assign a number to that same variable, like this:

```
MyVariable=154.89
```

This sort of thing causes major havoc in some programming languages, but it works just fine in VBScript, because VBScript changes the data type for you automatically. However, using a single variable for all sorts of different data is usually not a good idea because it just confuses things for you.

Express yourself

Here's how Microsoft defines the term *expression* in the Visual Basic online Help system:

"*. . . a combination of keywords, operators, variables, and values that yield a string, number, or object. An expression can perform a calculation, manipulate characters, or test data.*"

I couldn't have said it better myself. An expression can be as simple as a single value, or it can be very complex. Much of the work you do in VBScript is developing (and debugging) expressions that you assign to variables.

Here are a few examples of assignment statements that use expressions. The expressions are to the right of the equal sign, and the variable names are on the left of the equal sign:

```
x = 1
x = x + 1
x = (y * 2) / (z * 2)
VisitedBefore = True
ReplyTo.Checked = Not ReplyTo.Checked
LastYear = ThisYear - 1
```

Often, your expressions use functions — either VBScript built-in functions (see Chapter 10) or functions that you develop yourself in VBScript (see Chapter 7).

Here's an example of an expression that uses the VBScript Rnd function, a function that returns a random number between 0 and 1:

```
RandomNumber = Rnd()
```

Here's a more complex expression that uses the VBScript Sqr (square root) function and Abs (absolute value) function. You may recognize this expression as the Pythagorean theorem:

```
Distance=Sqr((Abs(x1 - x2) ^ 2)+(Abs(y1 - y2) ^ 2))
```

Hello, Operator . . .

Operators are the symbols that represent mathematical operations. As you may have figured out, operators play a major role in creating VBScript expressions.

Common operators

Table 8-1 lists the operators that VBScript recognizes.

Table 8-1	VBScript Operators
Operator	*What It Does*
+	Addition
-	Subtraction
*	Multiplication
/	Division
^	Exponentiation
&	String concatenation
\	Integer division
Mod	Modulo arithmetic

The Mod operator (short for Modulo) is a bit unusual because it's a word rather than a symbol. Mod returns the remainder of a division operation. For example, after executing the following statement, x has a value of 2, because 2 is the remainder when you divide 14 by 3:

```
X = 14 Mod 3
```

Adding text

Most newcomers to programming don't have any problem with common mathematical operators such as +, -, and /. But the & operator is often a stumper. The & operator simply joins text strings together and is used quite a bit in VBScript. Here's an example:

```
Today = Now()
Msg = "Today is " & Today & ". Welcome to my Web site."
Alert Msg
```

When this code executes, it displays an alert box like the one shown in the accompanying figure. The Today variable holds the current date and time. The Msg variable is constructed by joining three pieces of text. An alert box displays the result. Notice that the first text string has a trailing space. If you omit this space, the date butts up directly against the word *is*.

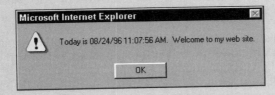

Logical operators

VBScript also provides a full set of *logical* operators. The And, Or, and Not operators are commonly used (and are quite useful); the others are used primarily by heavy-duty programmer types. Table 8-2 briefly describes all the logical operators.

Table 8-2	VBScript Logical Operators
Operator	*Description*
And	Performs a logical conjunction on two expressions
Or	Performs a logical disjunction on two expressions
Not	Performs a logical negation on an expression
XoR	Performs a logical exclusion on two expressions
Eqv	Performs a logical equivalence on two expressions
Imp	Performs a logical implication on two expressions

Note: You use logical operators the most with If-Then statements. See Chapter 9 for code examples that use these operators.

What gets calculated first?

When you use operators in your expressions, you need to be aware of a few rules that determine the order in which the operations execute. If you don't understand why the calculation order is important, consider the following assignment statement:

```
x = 6 + 9 / 3
```

What value is assigned to the variable x? Well, 6 plus 9 is 15, and 15 divided by 3 is 5, which means x is equal to 15, right? Wrong. Actually, x has a value of 9 after this statement executes. To find out why, keep reading.

Order of precedence

Division has a higher precedence than addition. Therefore, VBScript evaluates this previous expression as follows: 9 divided by 3 is 3, and 6 plus 3 is 9. Therefore, x gets a value of 9.

Table 8-3 lists the official order of precedence for the common operators. Operators with lower precedence numbers are performed first, and those with equal precedence numbers are performed from left to right. In other words, VBScript always performs the exponentiation (^) operator first, then it performs multiplication and division, and finally it performs addition and subtraction.

Table 8-3	Operator Order of Precedence	
Operator	*Description*	*Precedence*
^	Exponentiation	1
*	Multiplication	2
/	Division	2
+	Addition	3
-	Subtraction	3

Parentheses to the rescue

You can use parentheses to control the order in which calculations occur. Here's that same assignment statement I presented previously, rewritten to use parentheses:

```
x = (6 + 9) / 3
```

When you use parentheses, VBScript evaluates the items within parentheses first. Therefore, x has a value of 5.

You can use as many parentheses as you want, but make sure that each left parenthesis has a matching right parenthesis.

Don't be afraid to "overparenthesize" your expressions. I can never remember all of that order of precedence business, so I tend to use more parentheses than necessary. Often, I use parentheses even when they aren't necessary, just so I'm clear on how the expression is evaluated. The following statements both return the same value, but you'll probably agree that the one using parentheses is much easier to interpret.

```
x = 21 * 14 + 31 / 9^2 - 4 * 2
x = (21 * 14) + (31 / 9^2) - (4 * 2)
```

Array of Hope

Every programming language that I know of supports arrays (I think some sort of international law requires it). And, VBScript is no exception.

What is an array? An *array* is a group of variables that can be referred to with a common name using an index number. For example, you may have an array of 12 string variables to hold the names of each month of the year. If the array is named MonthNames, you can refer to the first element of the array as MonthNames(1), the second element as MonthNames(2), and so on.

Here's an example of how to assign values to three elements of an array:

```
MonthNames(1) = "January"
MonthNames(2) = "February"
MonthNames(3) = "March"
```

Well, I declare!

Before you can use an array in your VBScript code, you must *declare* it. Declaring an array simply means that you are telling VBScript how many elements the array will have.

You declare an array with a Dim statement and put the number of elements in the array, in parentheses. Here's an example of how to declare an array that can hold 101 items:

```
Dim MyArray(100)
```

The first item in an array is item 0. Therefore, the previous example can hold 101 items, numbered 0 through 100.

You may be wondering why the word *Dim* is used to declare an array. Dim is a shortened form of *Dimension*. So by using the word Dim, you're telling VBScript all about the dimensions of the array. The use of the word *Dim* makes more sense when you understand multidimensional arrays in the next section.

Multidimensional arrays

The array example in the previous section was a one-dimensional array. Arrays in VBScript can have up to 60 dimensions, although needing more than three dimensions in an array is rare. Here's an example of declaring an array with two dimensions:

```
Dim MyArray(9, 9)
```

This array consists of 100 items. You can think of this array as occupying a 10x10 matrix — sort of like an enlarged chessboard. When you refer to a specific element in this array, you need to specify two index numbers. Here's an example of how you can assign a value to an element in this array:

```
MyArray(4, 3) = 125
```

You can think of a two-dimensional array as a chessboard-like arrangement, and you can picture a three-dimensional array as a cube. But after you get beyond three dimensions, it gets pretty difficult to visualize the data layout of an array.

A multidimensional array may sound confusing, but it has lots of practical uses. For example, say you have a Web page that has several links. Each link has two parts that you want to keep track of: a description of the linked site and its URL. Here's how to set up a two dimensional array that holds the information for three links. The URLs are all fictitious, I think:

```
Dim LinkArray(3,2)
LinkArray(1,1) = "A cool music site"
LinkArray(1,2) = "http://www.acoolmusicplace.com"
LinkArray(2,1) = "VBScript demos"
LinkArray(2,2) = "http://www.vbsdemosite.com"
LinkArray(3,1) = "Groucho Marx home page"
LinkArray(3,2) = "http://www.grouchomarxhome.com"
```

Note: The preceding array actually consists of 12 items (remember, array numbering starts with 0). However, I chose to ignore the 0 elements and to start with 1. Personally, I find that it's much easier to keep track of things starting with the number 1 rather than 0. It really doesn't do any harm to ignore the 0 element in an array and start with 1. You're just "wasting" a tiny bit of memory.

After the array is declared and values are assigned to its elements, you can easily refer to any element in the array. This concept becomes much clearer in the next chapter when I discuss *looping* — a very common activity where arrays are involved.

Dynamic arrays

You also can create *dynamic* arrays. A dynamic array doesn't have a preset number of elements — the actual number of elements is determined when your procedure executes. You declare a dynamic array with an empty set of parentheses, like this:

```
Dim MyArray()
```

Before you can actually use this array, you must use the ReDim statement to specify how many elements the array has. You can use the ReDim statement any number of times, changing the array's size as often as you need to.

Here's code that declares a dynamic array and then redimensions it. The InputBox function asks the user for a value, which is assigned to the NumValues variable. The ReDim statement uses this variable to redimension the array:

```
Dim UserValues()
NumValues=InputBox("How many values do you want to enter?")
ReDim UserValues(NumValues)
```

When you use ReDim to redimension an array, the values in the array, if any, get wiped out. You can avoid this occurrence by using the Preserve keyword.

Here's an example of how to preserve an array's values when you redimension the array:

```
ReDim Preserve MyArray(200)
```

The topic of arrays comes up again in Chapter 10, when I discuss looping.

How many elements?

VBScript offers a handy built-in function that tells you how many elements are in an array. The Ubound function returns the upper bound of an array. Here's an example using the Ubound function:

```
Dim UserValues()
NumValues=InputBox("How many values do you want to enter?")
ReDim UserValues(NumValues)
Alert Ubound(UserValues)
```

When this script executes, the alert box displays the same value that was entered in the input box.

Scoping Variables and Arrays

This section deals with scoping variables and arrays. A variable's scope (or an array's scope) determines the extent to which the variable (or array) is valid in a particular Web document.

Take a look at this simple example:

```
<SCRIPT LANGUAGE=VBScript>
Sub Button1_OnClick()
    x = InputBox("Enter a value for x")
End Sub
Sub Button2_OnClick()
    Alert "x =" & x
End Sub
</SCRIPT>
<INPUT TYPE=button NAME=Button1 VALUE="Assign Value">
<INPUT TYPE=button NAME=Button2 VALUE="Show Value">
```

This code consists of event handlers for two buttons (Button1 and Button2). If you click Button1, an input box appears that lets you enter a value, which is assigned to the variable x (see Figure 8-1). If you click Button2, you get an alert box that displays the value of x.

Figure 8-1:
This input box asks for a value for the variable x.

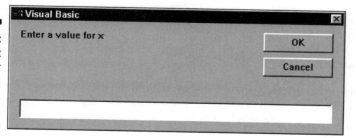

What number do you think will appear in the alert box? If you guess the same number that you enter into the input box, you're wrong. The answer is nothing! See Figure 8-2 for living proof. The scope for variable x consists only of the subroutine in which it is used. To VBScript, the two x variables are two entirely different variables.

Figure 8-2:
The value of
x is not what
you entered!

Broadening a variable's scope

If you want a variable's scope to be broader than a single procedure, declare it in a statement that is outside of any procedures. To declare a variable, use the Dim keyword (which you also use to declare an array). Here's an example:

```
Dim x
```

A variable that is declared outside of any subroutine or function is sometimes referred to as a *public* variable.

Listed in the following is the preceding example, but with one small but significant change. I use a Dim statement to declare the x variable outside of any subroutine. Doing so makes the variable valid in all procedures (subroutines and functions) in the document:

```
<SCRIPT LANGUAGE=VBScript>
Dim x
Sub Button1_OnClick()
    x = InputBox("Enter a value for x")
End Sub
Sub Button2_OnClick()
    Alert "x =" & x
End Sub
</SCRIPT>
<INPUT TYPE=button NAME=Button1 VALUE="Assign Value">
<INPUT TYPE=button NAME=Button2 VALUE="Show Value">
```

With this small change, clicking Button 2 displays the value you entered when you clicked Button 1.

To be able to use a variable or an array in any procedure, declare it outside of any subroutine or functions, but within the `<SCRIPT></SCRIPT>` tags.

Declaring multiple variables

If you need to declare more than one variable to be used in all procedures, you can use a series of Dim statements, like this:

```
Dim UserName
Dim CurrentMonth
Dim TotalCost
```

You also can declare multiple variables in a single statement, like this:

```
Dim UserName, CurrentMonth, TotalCost
```

Object Variables: A Special Type

VBScript supports a special type of variable called an *object variable*. An object variable is a variable that holds an object. (In Chapter 5, I describe the object model and discuss objects such as frames, documents, and forms.)

For example, assume that you have a form in your document, and the form contains a check box element. Here's HTML that accomplishes this:

```
<FORM NAME=Form1>
<INPUT TYPE=Checkbox>Send more information
</FORM>
```

You can write VBScript code to determine whether the check box is checked (that is, whether its Checked property is True). In the following code, the alert box displays True if the check box is checked and False otherwise:

```
Alert Document.Forms(0).Elements(0).Checked
```

The preceding code is a perfectly acceptable way to reference the check box object. But here's another way to do it, using an object variable:

```
Set MyCheckbox = Document.Forms(0).Elements(0)
```

The Set keyword is used to create an object variable. In this case, MyCheckbox is an object variable that holds the check box object. After you assign this object to an object variable, you can refer to that object using the object variable instead of the full object reference. Here's an example:

```
Alert MyCheckbox.Checked
```

Think of an object variable as a shortcut way of referring to an object. You can access all the object's properties and methods. Here's a statement that sets the check box's Checked property to True:

```
MyCheckbox.Checked = True
```

Using object variables is strictly optional. In some cases, you may find that your code executes faster if you use object variables (but usually, any speed difference is negligible). The real advantage of using object variables is that you can simplify your code. Instead of using a lengthy object reference, you can use a simple variable reference.

Here's VBScript code that writes text to a document in a frame. This code doesn't use an object variable:

```
Parent.Frames(0).Document.Open
Parent.Frames(0).Document.Write "<BODY BGCOLOR= ff00ff>"
Parent.Frames(0).Document.Close
```

Here's how that code looks after creating an object variable:

```
Set TheFrame = Parent.Frames(0).Document
TheFrame.Open
TheFrame.Write "<BODY BGCOLOR= ff00ff>"
TheFrame.Close
```

To assign an object to an object variable, use the Set keyword.

Forcing Variable Declaration

This section describes a technique that can potentially save you lots of frustration. The process requires a bit of additional effort, but it may be worth the trouble. I'm talking about forcing yourself to declare every variable you use in your code.

How to force yourself to declare all variables

If you include the following statement at the top of a `<SCRIPT>` block, VBScript forces you to declare every variable that you use in that block of script:

```
Option Explicit
```

If VBScript encounters a variable that has not been declared with a Dim statement, you get an error message like the one shown in Figure 8-3.

The Option Explicit statement only applies to the `<SCRIPT>` block in which it appears.

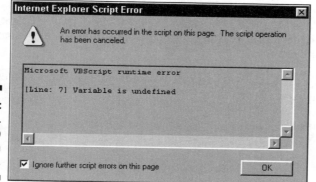

Figure 8-3:
Oops. . . .
You forgot to
declare a
variable.

Why force yourself to declare all variables?

Forcing yourself to declare every variable may seem a bit masochistic because it just means more work on your part (you need to type a few extra Dim statements to declare the variables). Actually, there's a very good reason to include the Option Explicit statement in your `<SCRIPT>` block: It can eliminate errors caused by typos.

Consider the following script:

```
<SCRIPT LANGUAGE=VBScript>
Sub ShowDiscount()
    DiscountPercent = .05
    Cost = 100
    Discount = Cost * DiscountPrecent
    Alert Discount
End Sub
</SCRIPT>
```

If you execute this code, you expect the alert box to display 5, which is 5 percent of 100. Actually, Discount has a value of 0 because a typo is in the assignment statement. Look closely, and you see that the second instance of DiscountPercent is spelled incorrectly.

Now take a look at the following modified version. I added an Option Explicit statement and declared the two variables:

```
<SCRIPT LANGUAGE=VBScript>
Option Explicit
Dim DiscountPercent, Cost
Sub ShowDiscount()
    DiscountPercent = .05
    Cost = 100
    Discount = Cost * DiscountPrecent
    Alert Discount
End Sub
</SCRIPT>
```

When you execute this subroutine, VBScript displays an error message about an undeclared variable — a sure sign that something's wrong. Think about which of these scenarios you would prefer:

- ✔ The subroutine executes okay, but provides the wrong answer when you may not even know it's wrong.
- ✔ VBScript warns you ahead of time that something's wrong.

Using the Option Explicit statement forces you to declare all variables and arrays that you use in the <SCRIPT> block.

Chapter 9

Controlling Program Flow and Decision-Making

In This Chapter

▶ An overview of the methods that let you control the flow of your VBA routines and make decisions

▶ How to use If-Then and Select Case structures

▶ How to perform looping in your procedures

*S*ome VBScript procedures start at the top and progress line by line to the bottom, never deviating from this top-to-bottom program flow. However, you often need to control the program flow of your routines by executing statements multiple times and testing conditions to determine what the routine does next. Ready or not, this kind of stuff comprises this chapter.

Go with the Flow, Dude

Programming newbies sometimes can't understand how a dumb computer can make intelligent decisions. The secret lies in a number of programming structures that are common to most programming languages. Table 9-1 provides a quick summary of these structures (all of which are explained later in this chapter).

Table 9-1   Programming Structures that Make Decisions

Structure	How It Works
If-Then	If condition is true, then do something.
If-Then-Else	If condition is true, then do something. Otherwise, do something else.
If-Then-ElseIf	If a condition is true, then do something. Otherwise, check to see whether another condition is true.

(continued)

Table 9-1 *(continued)*

Structure	How It Works
Select Case	Do any of several things, based on the value of something.
For-Next loop	Execute a series of statements a number of times.
Do-While loop	Do something while a condition is true.
Do-Until loop	Do something until a condition becomes true.
Do-Loop Until loop	Do something and then do it again until a condition becomes true.
Do-Loop While loop	Do something and then do it again while a condition is true.

If-Then Structure

Okay, I'm going out on a limb to say it: The most important control structure in VBScript is the If-Then structure. You'll probably use this commonly-used programming element on a daily basis. The good news: The If-Then structure is very easy to understand. You use If-Then structures all the time in real life. For example: If the water is boiling, then put in the pasta; If you pass Go, then collect $200.

As in human life, evaluating conditions and taking appropriate action is the key to success in writing programs. If this book works, you'll eventually share my philosophy that a successful VBScript procedure usually boils down to evaluating conditions and then acting upon them.

The basic syntax of the If-Then structure is

```
If condition Then instruction
```

The If-Then structure is used to conditionally execute a statement (or multiple statements). The condition part of the statement must represent a value that's either True or False. Most of the time, this condition is an expression that, when evaluated, returns True or False.

Examples of conditions

In this section, I present a few examples of expressions that return either True or False.

If the variable UserName contains nothing (an empty string), this expression returns True:

```
UserName = ""
```

If the variable Age has a value of 21 or greater, this expression returns True:

```
Age >= 21
```

If the background color of the current document is white, this expression returns True:

```
Document.Bgcolor = "#ffffff"
```

If the first element on Form1 of the current document is checked, this expression returns True:

```
Document.Form1.Elements(0).Checked
```

If the X variable contains 12 and the Y variable contains 24, this expression returns True. Note the use of the logical And operator (refer to Chapter 8 for more information about logical operators):

```
X = 12 And Y = 24
```

If the X variable contains a value less than 12 or the Y variable contains a value greater than or equal to12, this expression returns True. This example uses the logical Or operator:

```
X < 12 Or Y >= 24
```

The following expression uses the Not logical operator. This one requires some thinking. The expression always returns True, except when X equals 12 and Y equals 24. In other words, the Not operator makes True turn into False and makes False turn into True:

```
Not (X =12 And Y = 24)
```

An expression that's used as a condition in an If-Then statement must evaluate to either True or False.

If-Then examples

The following routine demonstrates the use of the If-Then structure. The code checks the current system time, by using the VBScript built-in Time function, and if the value returned by the Time function is less than .5 (that is, before noon), a message appears. If the Time function returns a value greater than or equal to .5, the routine ends and nothing happens:

```
Sub Window_OnLoad()
    If Time() <.5 Then Alert "Good Morning"
End Sub
```

If you want to display a different greeting in the afternoon (that is, if the Time function returns a value greater than or equal to .5), you can add another If-Then statement after the first one, like this:

```
Sub Window_OnLoad()
    If Time() < 0.5 Then Alert "Good Morning"
    If Time() >= 0.5 Then Alert "Good Afternoon"
End Sub
```

Note: I discuss the VBScript built-in Time function, along with several other useful functions, in Chapter 10.

If-Then with multiple instructions

If you need to execute more than one instruction if a condition is true, simply put each instruction on a separate line and use an End If statement to signify the end of the conditional instructions. Here's an example that executes three statements if a condition is true:

```
If UserName = "" Then
    NoName = True
    Msg = "You must enter your name."
    Alert Msg
End If
```

Supplying an Alternative: If-Then-Else

The If-Then statement has another form that lets you specify an action to take if the condition is true and another action to take if the condition is false.

```
If condition Then instruction Else other instruction
```

Again, the If-Then-Else structure should be a familiar concept. You hear statements like this all the time: *If it's a boy, then we'll name it Homer. Else, we'll name it Marge.*

Following is an example of the subroutine from the previous section, recoded to use the If-Then-Else structure:

```
Sub Window_OnLoad()
    If Time() < 0.5 Then Alert "Good Morning"_
            Else Alert "Good Afternoon"
End Sub
```

If-Then-Else with multiple instructions

In some cases, you need to provide multiple statements for the Then and Else parts. Doing so is quite straightforward, as you can see in the following example:

```
If UserName = "" Then
    NoName = True
    Msg = "You must enter your name."
    Alert Msg
Else
    Msg = "Hello " & UserName & ". Welcome!"
    Alert Msg
End If
```

Another option: If-Then-ElseIf

If the decisions your code needs to make are more complicated, you may want to use the If-Then-ElseIf structure. Here's the official syntax:

```
If condition1 Then
    instructions1
ElseIf condition2 Then
    instructions2
ElseIf condition3 Then
    instructions3
End If
```

This series of statements is interpreted as follows: If the first condition is true, follow the first set of instructions. If the first condition is false, check to see whether the second condition is true. If the second condition is true, follow the second set of instructions. If the second condition is not true, check to see whether the third condition is true and so on.

The real-life analogue to this structure is a statement like If you have a Corona, then I'll have one. If you don't have a Corona, then I'll have a Dos Equis. If you don't have a Dos Equis, then I'll have a Budweiser. If you don't have a Budweiser, then I'll have a Miller and so on.

You can use as many ElseIf statements as you need. Simply make sure that you use a final End If statement.

Here's an example that uses If-Then-ElseIf. It uses the VBScript Weekday function to return the day of the week (the result is a number between 1 and 7). The If-Then-ElseIf statements convert this value to a text string. The alert box displays the result, shown in Figure 9-1.

Figure 9-1:
A series of
If-Then-
ElseIf
statements
determines
the day of
the week.

```
X = Weekday(Now())
If x = 1 Then
    DayName = "Sunday"
ElseIf x = 2 Then
    DayName = "Monday"
ElseIf x = 3 Then
    DayName = "Tuesday"
ElseIf x = 4 Then
    DayName = "Wednesday"
ElseIf x = 5 Then
    DayName = "Thursday"
ElseIf x = 6 Then
    DayName = "Friday"
ElseIf x = 7 Then
    DayName = "Saturday"
End If
Alert "Today is " & DayName
```

Here's another example that displays a greeting when the document loads. The message is based on the time of day.

```
Sub Window_OnLoad()
    If Time() < 0.5 Then
        Alert "Good Morning"
    ElseIf Time() >= 0.5 And Time() < 0.75 Then
        Alert "Good Afternoon"
    ElseIf Time() >= 0.75 Then Alert "Good Evening"
    End If
End Sub
```

The Select Case Structure

The Select Case structure is useful for decision-making when three or more options are available (although it also works with two options and is a good alternative to the If-Then-Else structure).

The syntax for the Select Case structure is

```
Select Case expression
    Case value1
```

(continued)

(continued)

```
    Case value2
        instructions2
    Case value3
        instructions3
End Select
```

You can program as many cases as you like, and you can have any number of statements below each Case statement. All statements execute if the case is true. When VBScript executes a Select Case structure, the structure is exited as soon as a True case is found. In other words, after a match is found, VBScript doesn't waste time checking the other cases.

A Select Case example

Here's a practical example of using the Select Case structure. The following is another way of programming the If-Then-Else example presented in the previous section:

```
Select Case Weekday(Now())
    Case 1
        DayName = "Sunday"
    Case 2
        DayName = "Monday"
    Case 3
        DayName = "Tuesday"
    Case 4
        DayName = "Wednesday"
    Case 5
        DayName = "Thursday"
    Case 6
        DayName = "Friday"
    Case 7
        DayName = "Saturday"
End Select
Alert "Today is " & DayName
```

Because each case consists of only one line of instruction, you can take advantage of the VBScript multistatement-per-line character (the colon) and make this code more compact:

```
Select Case Weekday(Now())
    Case 1 : DayName = "Sunday"
    Case 2 : DayName = "Monday"
    Case 3 : DayName = "Tuesday"
    Case 4 : DayName = "Wednesday"
    Case 5 : DayName = "Thursday"
    Case 6 : DayName = "Friday"
    Case 7 : DayName = "Saturday"
End Select
```

A catch-all case

When you're writing code that uses Select Case, you can insert Case Else to handle all other conditions. In the following example, the variable WebBrowser holds a text string. The Select Case structure examines the contents of the WebBrowser variable and assigns text to the Msg variable:

```
Select Case WebBrowser
    Case "Navigator"
        Msg = "You're using a fine browser"
    Case "Explorer"
        Msg = "You're using the best browser"
    Case Else
        Msg = "You need to get a new browser"
End Select
```

Nested Select Case structures

As you may expect, you can nest Select Case structures as deeply as you want. In other words, you can use a Select Case structure inside of another Select Case structure. Simply make sure that you include a matching End Select statement for every Select Case statement.

Here's a simple example to demonstrate nested select case structures:

```
Select Case WebBrowser
    Case "Navigator"
        Msg = "You're using a fine browser"
    Case "Explorer"
        Select Case Version
            Case 2
                Msg="You need to upgrade!"
            Case 3
                Msg = "You're using the best browser"
        End Select
    Case Else
        Msg = "You need to get a new browser"
End Select
```

In this example, if the WebBrowser variable is Explorer, then another Select Case kicks in.

Note: The previous example also demonstrates how indenting can make your code easier to read. Here's the same example, but without any indentations. Pretty unintelligible, huh?

```
Select Case WebBrowser
Case "Navigator"
Msg = "You're using a fine browser"
Case "Explorer"
Select Case Version
Case 2
Msg="You need to upgrade!"
Case 3
Msg = "You're using the best browser"
End Select
Case Else
Msg = "You need to get a new browser"
End Select
```

Looping de Loops

One of the most useful programming concepts is looping. *Looping* is simply the process of repeating a block of statements a number of times. You may know the number of times to loop, or this number may be determined by the current values of variables in the program.

The most commonly used loop is the For-Next loop — but several other loops exist. I discuss them all in the following sections.

For-Next Loops

If you know how many times you need to loop, or if your code can determine how many times to loop, a For-Next loop is your best bet. The general structure of this loop is

```
For Counter = Start To Stop
    Instructions
Next
```

This structure may look more complex than it really is. Counter is a variable that keeps track of the number of loops. Start is the first number that's assigned to Counter, and Stop is the last number that's assigned to Counter.

A For-Next example

Following is a simple (and rather meaningless) example of a For-Next loop. This routine loops ten times and writes a random number to the document.

```
Document.Write "Here are some random numbers:"
Document.Write "<P>"
For x = 1 to 10
    Document.Write x & " " & Rnd()
    Document.Write "<BR>"
Next
```

Figure 9-2 shows the results of executing this script.

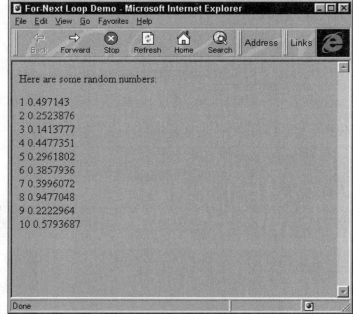

In this example, x (the loop counter variable) starts out as 1 and increases by 1 each time through the loop. When x is 10, the looping stops. The first Document.Write statement writes the value of x, a space, and then a random number to the document. The second Document.Write statement inserts a `<BR>` tag to skip to the next line.

When using For-Next loops, the loop counter is a normal variable. Therefore, you can change its value within the block of code that executes between the For and the Next statements. However, doing so is a bad practice you should avoid because changing the counter within the loop can have unpredictable results. In fact, take special precautions to ensure that the loop counter does not get changed by your code. Simply let the counter change by itself, with every iteration of the loop.

A For-Next example with a step value

A For-Next loop also can use a *step value* to specify how to increment the counter variable. Here's an example that uses a step value of 2. The counter variable, x, starts out as 1, and then is incremented by 2 each time through the loop. It takes on a value of 1, 3, 5, 7, and so on. Its final value is 19. So, the following code displays only the odd integers between 1 and 20:

```
For x = 1 to 20 Step 2
    Document.Write x
    Document.Write "<BR>"
Next
```

Looping backwards

The step value used in a For-Next loop can be a negative number. Using a negative number as the step value causes the counter value to be decremented rather than incremented. Here's a modified version of the previous example. This time, the code displays even integers, beginning with 20 and ending with 2:

```
For x = 20 to 1 Step -2
    Document.Write x
    Document.Write "<BR>"
Next
```

If you use a negative step value, the start value for the loop must be greater than the stop value. Otherwise, the code inside the loop doesn't execute at all.

For-Next and arrays

You can really appreciate For-Next loops when you use arrays (refer to Chapter 8 for details on arrays). If you need to do something with each element of an array, a For-Next loop is usually the way to go.

Here's a simple example that uses two For-Next loops with an array:

```
Sub Test_OnClick()
    Dim Nums(10)
    Randomize()
    For i = 1 To 10
        Nums(i) = Int((Rnd() * 100) + 1)
    Next
    For i = 1 To 10
        Msg = Msg & Nums(i) & " "
    Next
    Alert Msg
End Sub
```

In the first loop, each element of the Nums array is assigned a random integer between 1 and 100. In the second loop, a text string (stored in the Msg variable) is created. This string consists of the random values stored in the Nums array, with each value separated by a space. Finally, the alert box displays the message. Figure 9-3 shows an example.

Figure 9-3:
Two For-
Next loops
created this
message.

Listed in the following is a more sophisticated example, which uses a two-dimensional array (LinkArray) that consists of Web page descriptions and URLs. The For-Next loop creates hyperlink references and writes them to the document. The first time through the loop, the text written to the document is

```
<A HREF=http://www.coolmusic.com>A cool music site</A><BR>
```

The other elements in the array are handled the same way.

```
<SCRIPT LANGUAGE=VBScript>
Dim LinkArray(3,2)
LinkArray(1,1) = "A cool music site"
LinkArray(1,2) = "http://www.acoolmusicplace.com"
LinkArray(2,1) = "VBScript demos"
LinkArray(2,2) = "http://www.vbsdemosite.com"
LinkArray(3,1) = "Groucho Marx home page"
LinkArray(3,2) = "http://www.grouchomarxhome.com"
For i = 1 To 3
    Document.Write "<A HREF="
    Document.Write LinkArray(i,2)
    Document.Write ">"
    Document.Write LinkArray(i,1)
    Document.Write "</A><BR>"
Next
</SCRIPT>
```

Figure 9-4 shows the result of running this script.

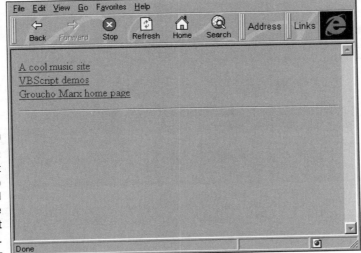

Figure 9-4:
A For-Next loop generated these hypertext links.

A nested For-Next example

VBScript also lets you *nest* loops. A nested loop is a loop inside of a loop. You can nest loops as deeply as you want.

The following example is an immediate script that uses a nested For-Next loop. It generates HTML code that creates a table.

```
<SCRIPT LANGUAGE=VBScript>
Rows = 8
Cols = 5
Document.Write "<TABLE BORDER=5 CELLPADDING=5>"
For r = 1 To Rows
    Document.Write "<TR>"
    For c = 1 to Cols
        Document.Write "<TD>"
        Document.Write "Row " & r & ", Col " & c
        Document.Write "</TD>"
    Next
Document.Write "</TR>"
Next
Document.Write "</TABLE>"
</SCRIPT>
```

Figure 9-5 shows how the document looks.

Row 1, Col 1	Row 1, Col 2	Row 1, Col 3	Row 1, Col 4	Row 1, Col 5
Row 2, Col 1	Row 2, Col 2	Row 2, Col 3	Row 2, Col 4	Row 2, Col 5
Row 3, Col 1	Row 3, Col 2	Row 3, Col 3	Row 3, Col 4	Row 3, Col 5
Row 4, Col 1	Row 4, Col 2	Row 4, Col 3	Row 4, Col 4	Row 4, Col 5
Row 5, Col 1	Row 5, Col 2	Row 5, Col 3	Row 5, Col 4	Row 5, Col 5
Row 6, Col 1	Row 6, Col 2	Row 6, Col 3	Row 6, Col 4	Row 6, Col 5
Row 7, Col 1	Row 7, Col 2	Row 7, Col 3	Row 7, Col 4	Row 7, Col 5
Row 8, Col 1	Row 8, Col 2	Row 8, Col 3	Row 8, Col 4	Row 8, Col 5

Figure 9-5:
VBScript code generated the HTML code for this table.

This example may seem rather complicated at first, but if you examine it closely, you can understand how it works.

The subroutine starts by assigning the number of rows and columns to two variables (Rows and Cols). A Document.Write statement generates the <TABLE> tag. Then the looping begins. Notice that two loops occur. The outer loop steps through the rows, and the inner loop steps through the columns. Document.Write statements generate appropriate HTML tags. Another Document.Write tag generates the text that appears in the cells. When the looping ends, the final Document.Write statement generates the closing </TABLE> tag.

Note: You can easily change the size of the table by entering new values for the Rows and Cols variables.

Do Until Loops

The Do Until loop is another type of looping structure available in VBScript. Unlike a For-Next loop, a Do Until loop doesn't loop a set number of times. Rather, it continues until a particular condition is true. Here's the Do Until syntax:

```
Do Until condition
    instructions
Loop
```

Here's a simple example that demonstrates how a Do Until loop works. The GetName subroutine displays an input box that asks for the user's name. The user's response is assigned to the Name variable. This assignment statement is inside of a Do Until loop. This means that the InputBox is repeatedly displayed until something is entered. If the user clicks OK or Cancel without making an entry, the input box reappears until the length of the Name is not equal to 0:

```
Sub GetName()
    Do Until Len(Name) <> 0
        Name = InputBox ("Enter your name")
    Loop
End Sub
```

Figure 9-6 shows this subroutine at work.

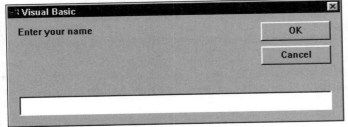

Figure 9-6: This input box appears repeatedly until the user enters a name.

Do While Loops

A Do While loop is very similar to the Do Until structure. The difference between the two is how the condition is stated. In a Do While loop, the loop executes *while* the condition is true. In a Do Until loop, the loop executes *until* the condition is true.

A Do While loop uses this syntax:

```
Do While condition
    instructions
Loop
```

Here's the GetName subroutine from the previous section, recoded to use a Do While loop instead of a Do Until loop. Notice that the Name variable is initialized to an empty string. If that statement isn't included, the loop does not execute because Name is equal to zero.

```
Sub GetName()
    Do While Len(Name) = 0
        Name = InputBox ("Enter your name")
    Loop
End Sub
```

Do-Loop Until Loops

A Do-Loop Until loop is a variation on the Do Until loop (the loop executes until a particular condition is true). The main difference is that the condition is tested *after* the statements in the loop execute. Therefore, the statements inside of a Do-Loop Until loop always execute at least once. Here's the syntax:

```
Do
    instructions
Loop Until condition
```

I recoded the GetName subroutine to use a Do-Loop Until loop. This is actually more efficient. Because the loop always executes at least once, you don't need to initialize the Name variable to an empty string (see the Loop Until preceding example):

```
Sub GetName()
    Do
        Name = InputBox ("Enter your name")
    Loop Until Len(Name) <> 0
End Sub
```

Do-Loop While Loops

A Do-Loop While loop is a variation on the Do While loop (the loop executes while a particular condition is true). The main difference is that the condition is tested *after* the statements in the loop execute. Therefore, the statements inside of a Do-Loop While loop always execute at least once. Here's the syntax:

```
Do
    instructions
Loop Until condition
```

The GetName subroutine, recoded to use a Do-Loop While loop, follows.

```
Sub GetName()
    Do
        Name = InputBox ("Enter your name")
    Loop While Len(Name) = 0
End Sub
```

Cheat Sheet For Looping

If you've read this chapter straight through, your head is probably reeling after reading about all the different types of loops. The type of loop that you use really depends on what you're doing. To help you decide the best loop for the job, I've prepared Table 9-2 to summarize the loops all in one handy spot.

Table 9-2	What's the Best Loop for the Job?			
	Uses an Index Counter	Always Loops At Least Once	Loops when a Condition Is True	Loops as long as a Condition Is False
For-Next	Yes			
Do Until				Yes
Do While			Yes	
Do-Loop Until		Yes		Yes
Do-Loop While		Yes	Yes	

Chapter 10

Getting Acquainted with Built-In Functions

- -

In This Chapter

▶ What you need to know to use the VBScript built-in functions

▶ Examples demonstrating common functions

▶ How to use the MsgBox and InputBox functions — special functions that display a dialog box

- -

*V*BScript, like most programming languages, includes a number of *built-in functions* that you can use in your scripts. If you've explored other chapters in this book, you've already seen some of these functions in the example scripts. For example, you may have seen the Time function, which returns the time of day, the Len function, which returns the length of a text string, and several others.

This chapter provides background details and introduces you to many more useful functions. This chapter shows how functions can make your VBScript code perform powerful feats, with little or no programming effort required.

The VBScript built-in functions are just part of the story. You also can use VBScript to create your *own* functions. Refer to Chapter 7 for the full story.

Using Functions in Your Code

When you use a built-in function in your code, you need to make sure that you:

- ✔ **Spell the function correctly.** You can use upper- or lowercase; it doesn't matter.

- ✔ **Put the arguments, if any, in a set of parentheses.** Separate each argument with a comma.

✓ **Specify the correct number of arguments and make sure that they contain the proper type of data.** If a function is expecting a value, providing a string as an argument may not work.

✓ **Use the argument as part of an expression or as its own expression.** This means that a function is always used in an assignment statement, and the function is always on the right side of the equal sign.

A function always returns a single item, and this item can be a number, a text string, or a logical value (True or False). Two special *user interface* (UI) functions — namely MsgBox and InputBox — have useful side effects: They display a dialog box.

If a function doesn't use any arguments, you can either omit the parentheses or include a set of empty parentheses. These two statements produce the same effect (they assign the current date and time to the ThisDay variable):

```
ThisDay = Now
ThisDay = Now()
```

Including the empty parentheses is a good idea, simply to make clear that you're dealing with a function rather than a variable.

Functions Galore

VBScript provides you with approximately 75 functions that you can use freely in your code. As is usually the case with mass quantities of things, some functions are more useful than others.

For a complete list of VBScript functions, along with a brief description of each one, refer to "VBScript Function Reference," located on the companion disk.

Function Examples

The best way, without a doubt, to become familiar with VBScript functions is to see them in action. This section presents VBScript code examples that use the more common functions. I organize these examples by function categories.

Conversion functions

Conversion functions do just what the category name implies: They convert something to something else.

The Chr function

The Chr function converts a character code (1 - 255) to a character. For example, Chr(65) returns the letter A, Chr(13) returns a (nonprinting) carriage return character, and Chr(34) returns a quotation mark character ("). Work with this stuff long enough, and you'll memorize lots of the more useful codes.

Here's VBScript code that writes a list of all characters to a document. Figure 10-1 shows the document that results. Notice that not all characters are printable.

```
For i = 1 To 255
    Document.Writeln Chr(i)
Next
```

Note: In the preceding example, I use the Writeln method rather than the Write method. Writeln inserts a blank space after writing the character. If I use the Write method, the characters appear as a single string of text with no spaces.

Figure 10-1:
All 255
characters.

The Chr function is most useful when you need to display a nonstandard character or a nonprinting character. For example, if you need to insert a line break into a message displayed in an alert box, use Chr(13), as follows:

```
Msg = "The background color code is" & Chr(13) &_
Document.Bgcolor
Alert Msg
```

Figure 10-2 shows the alert box. Notice that the message appears on two lines, thanks to the Chr function.

Figure 10-2:
Forcing a
line break in
an alert box
message.

The Asc function

The opposite of the Chr function, the Asc function returns the ASCII code for a particular character. For example, Asc(A) returns 65.

Following is VBScript that uses both the Chr and Asc functions. This simple coding and decoding script asks the user for a message, encrypts the message, and displays the encrypted message. Then the script converts the encrypted message back to the original and displays it.

```
Msg = InputBox ("Enter a message:")
Coded=""
For i = 1 To Len(Msg)
    Coded = Coded & Chr(Asc(Mid(Msg,i,1))+1)
Next
MsgBox Coded,13,"Here's the Coded Message"
Decode=""
For i = 1 To Len(Coded)
    Decoded=Decoded & Chr(Asc(Mid(Coded,i,1))-1)
Next
MsgBox Decoded,13,"Here's the Decoded Message"
```

Figure 10-3 shows the dialog boxes displayed by this code.

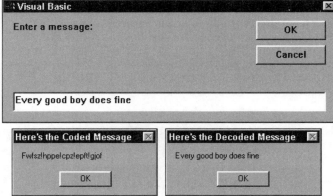

Figure 10-3:
The Chr
and Asc
functions
code and
then
decode the
message.

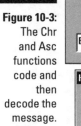

The script uses nested functions. The Mid function is nested in the Asc function, which is nested in the Chr function.

The encryption is done by simply adding 1 to the result of the Asc function and then passing this value as an argument to the Chr function. The decryption is done by subtracting 1 from the result of the Asc function and passing this value to the Chr function.

Note: This technique is not a very reliable form of encryption. But the point is to demonstrate the use of the Asc and Chr functions, not to provide a lesson in data security.

The Hex function

The Hex function converts a decimal value to its hexadecimal equivalent. Hex numbers use *Base 16* (decimal numbers, by comparison, use Base 10). This function is important because HTML color codes are often specified in hexadecimal. Refer to Chapter 6 for information about hex color codes.

Here is VBScript code that generates a random color code and applies the color to the document background. The code also uses three other functions: Randomize, Rnd, and Len (all discussed elsewhere in this chapter).

```
Randomize()
Color = Hex(Rnd()* 16777215)
Do Until Len(Color)=6
    Color = "0" & Color
Loop
Document.Bgcolor = Color
```

The Do-Until Loop structure ensures that the Hex value consists of six digits. The statement within the Do-Until Loop adds leading zeros to the Color variable until the length of the string is six characters.

Note: Oddly, VBScript doesn't provide a corresponding function to convert a Hex number to decimal. However, I developed such a function (Hex2Dec), and you can grab your very own copy in Chapter 15.

The Int and Fix functions

The Int and Fix functions are similar; they both remove the fractional part of a number (the numbers after the decimal point) and return the resulting integer value. The difference between the two functions is apparent when the number is negative.

✔ The Int function returns the first negative integer less than or equal to the number.

✔ The Fix function returns the first negative integer that's greater than or equal to the number.

Following is an example that generates a random number between 1 and 6, simulating the toss of a die. I use the Int function because the random number contains decimal places; Int simply removes the decimal places. Because negative numbers aren't involved, I can use Fix rather than Int and get exactly the same result.

```
DieToss = Int(6 * Rnd() + 1)
```

Date and time functions

Many Web page designers like to display the current date and time on a Web page — I'm not sure why, but including them is definitely a common thing to do. VBScript makes including the current date and time a piece of cake.

Current date and time functions

VBScript has functions that return the current date and/or time. Here's an example of three functions:

```
Document.Write Now()
Document.Write "<BR>"
Document.Write Date()
Document.Write "<BR>"
Dcument.Write Time()
```

Figure 10-4 shows how the browser displays this code.

Figure 10-4:
Displaying the current date and time.

08/24/96 11:33:28 AM
08/24/96
11:33:28 AM

Nesting date and time functions

Often, you'll want to work with a specific part of the date or time. Certain functions return only a part of a date (Year, Month, and Now), and other functions return only part of the time (Hour, Minute, and Second).

Here are examples that extract the parts of the current date:

```
ThisYear = Year(Now())
ThisMonth = Month(Now())
ThisDay = Day(Now())
```

Here are functions that extract the parts of the current time:

```
ThisHour = Hour(Now())
ThisMinute = Minute(Now())
ThisSecond = Second(Now())
```

You also can use these functions with any date or time, not only the current date or time. Here's an example that displays the year for a particular date:

```
Appointment = "July 4, 1997"
Alert Year(Appointment)
```

The alert box displays 1997.

Weekday function

The Weekday function returns an integer (from 1 to 7) that represents the day of the week for a particular date. Here's an example that displays the current day of the week in an alert box.

```
X = Weekday(Now())
If x = 1 Then
    DayName = "Sunday"
ElseIf x = 2 Then
    DayName = "Monday"
ElseIf x = 3 Then
    DayName = "Tuesday"
ElseIf x = 4 Then
    DayName = "Wednesday"
ElseIf x = 5 Then
    DayName = "Thursday"
ElseIf x = 6 Then
    DayName = "Friday"(continued)
```

(continued)

(continued)

```
ElseIf x = 7 Then
    DayName = "Saturday"
End If
Alert "Today is " & DayName
```

Math functions

Most functions in the Math category are trigonometric functions and don't really have a lot of practical applications for most Web pages. A few functions are more generally useful, however.

Trigonometric functions

If trig is your thing, you may be interested in these functions: Atn (arctangent), Cos (cosine), Sin (sine), and Tan (tangent). These functions work as expected, except that the argument must be expressed in radians, not degrees.

For example, Sin(90) returns 0.89399666 because the argument represents 90 radians, not 90 degrees (the sine of 90 degrees is 1).

The formula to convert degrees to radians is $\pi/180$. Here's a simple function that you can use to do the conversion:

```
Function Degrees(rad)
    Degrees = rad * (3.14159265358979 / 180)
End Function
```

After you insert this function, you can use it to do the conversion. Here's code that displays the sine of 45 degrees:

```
Angle = 45
Alert Sin(Degrees(Angle))
```

Random number functions

Unpredictability, or randomness, can play an important role in Web pages and make them more interesting to frequent visitors. The key player in programming randomness into your site is the Rnd function, which returns a random value between 0 and 1.

To get a random integer that falls between two values, use the following expression, where HighValue and LowValue are variables that hold the lowest and highest integers:

```
Int(Rnd() * ((HighValue + 1) - LowValue) + LowValue)
```

For example, if you want to generate a random integer between 10 and 50 (inclusive), use the following expression:

```
Int(Rnd()*((50 + 1) - 10) + 10)
```

Here's a simple example that displays a random "Lyle Lovett Quote of the Day" whenever the page is loaded or refreshed. If you use this technique, you'll probably want to include more than six quotes:

```
Dim Quote(6)
Randomize()
Quote(1) = "You got you some legs baby that just won't quit."
Quote(2) = "I married her just because she looks like you."
Quote(3) = "Penguins are so sensitive to my needs."
Quote(4) = "I don't like hippies and I don't like cornbread."
Quote(5) = "The world is full of creeps like me."
Quote(6) = "Put down that flyswatter and pour me some ice
            water."
RandomQuote = Int(6 * Rnd() + 1)
Document.Write "As Lyle Lovett says...<BR>"
Document.Write "<B>"
Document.Write Quote(RandomQuote)
Document.Write "</B>"
```

Figure 10-5 shows an example of how this code appears in the document.

Notice that I use the Randomize function in this example. This function initializes the random-number generator with starting value based on the system clock. If you don't use this statement, the same sequence of random numbers generates each time the page loads.

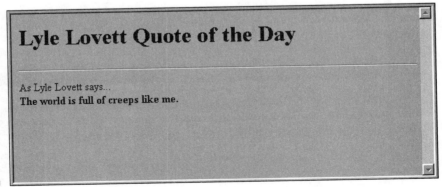

Figure 10-5:
This
document
displays a
random
quote.

String functions

VBScript has lots of useful functions that manipulate text strings. You owe it to yourself to get on the friendly side of these functions.

The Mid function

The Mid function is probably the most useful text function. This function lets you access any character or group of characters in a text string. The Mid function requires three arguments:

```
Mid(text,startpos,len)
```

Text is the text string that you're extracting characters from. Startpos is the position of the first character that you want to extract. Len is the number of characters to extract (Len is optional; if you omit this argument VBScript extracts one character).

Here's an example:

```
Text = "David Bromberg Band"
NewText = Mid(Text,6,8)
Alert NewText
```

When this code executes, the alert box displays Bromberg, which is the text that begins at position 6 and consists of eight characters.

The Mid function is useful in For-Next loops because it lets you work with each character in a text string. See the example in the section "The Len function," later in this chapter.

The Left and Right functions

You can use these two functions to extract part of a string from the left or the right. Here's an example of the Left function:

```
Text = "Microsoft Internet Explorer"
Alert Left(Text,9)
```

The alert box displays Microsoft, which are the leftmost nine characters of the text string. The Right function works the same way, but the text is taken from the right side of the string.

In the following example, the three color components of a six-digit hex color string are extracted and stored in three variables.

```
ColorValue = ""FFAACC"
RedPart = Left(ColorValue,2)
GreenPart = Mid(ColorValue, 3, 2)
BluePart = Right(ColorValue,2)
```

The Lcase and Ucase functions

The Lcase and Ucase functions convert text to uppercase and lowercase, respectively. Here's an example of the Ucase function:

```
FullName = "Michael Richard Jones"
Alert Ucase(FullName)
```

As you can see in Figure 10-6, the name converts to uppercase characters. The Lcase function works exactly the same way, except the text converts to lowercase characters.

Figure 10-6: Converting a string to uppercase.

Converting text to uppercase is useful when you need to compare two text strings that may not correspond exactly in terms of case. When the following code executes, the alert box displays No Match because the strings are not the same.

```
Text1 = "sample text"
Text2 = "Sample Text"
If Text1 = Text2 Then Alert "We've got a match" _
    Else Alert "No Match"
```

If you want to make the comparison based on the text content alone, regardless of the case, use the Ucase function to convert both strings to uppercase. Use the Lcase function to convert them to lowercase. Here's an example:

```
If Ucase(Text1)=Ucase(Text2) Then Alert "We've got a match" _
    Else Alert "No Match"
```

The Len function

The Len function returns the length of a string of text or a number. Here's an example:

```
Text = "Microsoft Internet Explorer"
Alert Len(Text)
```

In this case, the alert box displays 27, the number of characters in the text string.

The Len function comes in handy when you need to loop through each character in a text string using a For-Next loop. The following example counts the number of spaces in a string of text. The StringLength variable contains the number of characters in the Text variable and is used as the stop value in the For-Next loop.

```
Text = "What goes around comes around."
StringLength = Len(Text)
SpaceCount = 0
For i = 1 to StringLength
    If Mid(Text, i, 1) = " " Then SpaceCount = SpaceCount +1
Next
Alert "Number of spaces: " & SpaceCount
```

The Instr function

The Instr function returns the position of the first occurrence of one string within another. Here's the official syntax, which uses two arguments:

```
InStr(string1, string2)
```

String1 is the text that is being searched. String2 is the text you're looking for.

Here's an example:

```
Browser = "Microsoft Internet Explorer"
SearchFor = "Explorer"
Position = Instr(Browser, SearchFor)
Alert Position
```

When this code executes, the alert box displays 20 because *Explorer* was found beginning at the 20th character position in *Microsoft Internet Explorer*. If the string is not found, the Instr function returns 0.

Here's a more practical use of Instr. This example extracts the first name from a string that contains a person's full name.

```
FullName = "Liz Phair"
Position = Instr(FullName, " ")
FirstName = Left(FullName,Position - 1)
Alert "Hello " & FirstName
```

When this code executes, the alert box displays Liz. The Position variable holds the character position of the first and only space. Then I use the Left function to extract the characters. The second argument for the Left function is Position -1 so the space character itself is not included.

You can provide an additional argument to the Instr function to specify the position at which to start the search. This additional argument comes first in the list. For example, to look for a space character in a string starting at the fifth character, use this code:

```
Instr(5, Text, " ")
```

Variant functions

The Variant function category includes useful functions that let you test for certain types of data. Two of these functions, IsDate and IsNumeric, can come in quite handy when you write VBScript to validate data entered into forms.

Note: Refer to Chapter 13 for more information about validating data in forms.

The IsDate function

The IsDate function returns True if its argument can be interpreted as a date; otherwise, it returns False. Here's an example that displays a message depending on whether the user enters a valid date:

```
BirthDay = InputBox "Enter your date of birth."
If IsDate(BirthDay) Then Msg ="Thanks!" _
    Else Msg = "That's not a valid date!"
Alert Msg
```

VBScript is pretty flexible when it comes to interpreting dates. For example, VBScript interprets any of the following strings as a date:

dec 5, Dec 5 97, 12 5 97, 12/97, 12-5/97

Note: If the year is omitted, the current year is assumed. If the day is omitted, the first day of the month is assumed.

The IsNumeric function

The IsNumeric function returns True if its argument is a number; otherwise, it returns False. The following example demonstrates this function. The user is prompted to enter a value. If the response is not a number, an alert box appears.

```
Quantity = InputBox "How many?"
If Not IsNumeric(Quantity) Then Alert "Bad value!"
```

Notice that I use the Not operator to test the condition. The alert box only appears if the entry is *not* a number.

User Interface functions

Two VBScript functions go above and beyond the call of duty. Rather than simply return a value, these two User Interface (UI) functions also display a dialog box. In this section, I describe the MsgBox and InputBox functions.

MsgBox

The MsgBox function is similar to the Alert method of the Window object (see Chapter 6), but MsgBox is a lot more versatile. This function is a handy way to display information and to get simple input from users. The MsgBox function returns a code number that corresponds to whichever button is clicked.

Here's a simplified version of the MsgBox syntax:

```
MsgBox(prompt,buttons,title)
```

Prompt is the text displayed in the message box. Buttons is the code for the buttons that appear in the message box. Title is the text displayed in the message box title bar. The buttons and title arguments are optional.

You can use the MsgBox function two ways:

- ✔ **To display a message in a dialog box:** When the user clicks the OK button, the message goes away.

- ✔ **To get a response:** You can assign the value returned by the MsgBox function to a variable. The value corresponds to which button was clicked.

Creating a simple message box

This example shows how to use the MsgBox function to display a message. If you use the message box for this purpose, you don't have to include parentheses around the arguments. The following statement displays a message and does not return a result:

```
MsgBox "Click OK to load the next page."
```

Figure 10-7 shows how this message box appears on-screen.

Figure 10-7:
A simple
message
box.

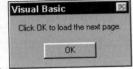

Getting a response from a message box

To get a response from a message box, you can assign the result of the MsgBox function to a variable. Here's an example:

```
Sub Button_OnClick()
    Ans = MsgBox("Do you want to go to my Links page?", 4)
    Select Case Ans
        Case 6 'Yes
'       ...[code if Ans is Yes]...
        Case 7 'No
'       ...[code if Ans is No]...
    End Select
End Sub
```

When this procedure executes, the Ans variable contains a value that corresponds to the button that is clicked — in this example, 6 for the Yes button, 7 for the No button. The Select Case statement determines the action to take, based on the value of Ans variable. The button values are described later in this chapter (see "Using the results of a MsgBox function").

Customizing message boxes

You can easily customize your message boxes because of the flexibility of the buttons argument. Table 10-2 lists the values that you can use for the button argument. You can specify whether an icon appears, which buttons to display, and which button is the default.

Table 10-2	Codes Used in the MsgBox Function
Codes	**Description**
0	Display OK button only
1	Display OK and Cancel buttons
2	Display Abort, Retry, and Ignore buttons
3	Display Yes, No, and Cancel buttons
4	Display Yes and No buttons
5	Display Retry and Cancel buttons
16	Display Critical Message icon
32	Display Warning Query icon
48	Display Warning Message icon
64	Display Information Message icon
128	Make the first button the default
256	Make the second button the default
512	Make the third button the default

To specify more than one of these codes for an argument, simply connect them with a + operator. The following statement displays a message box with Yes and No buttons (code = 4) and a question mark icon (code = 32). The second button (No) is the default button (code = 256):

```
Ans = MsgBox ("Continue?", 4 + 32 + 256, "Tell me...")
```

Figure 10-8 shows how this code looks.

Figure 10-8:
A message box with Yes and No buttons, plus a question mark icon.

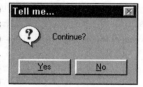

Using the results of a MsgBox function

If your message box has more than one button, you usually need to determine which button the user clicked. Table 10-3 shows the values for all the button clicks:

Table 10-3	Codes Returned by Button Clicks
Codes	**Description**
1	User clicked OK button
2	User clicked Cancel button
3	User clicked Abort button
4	User clicked Retry button
5	User clicked Ignore button
6	User clicked Yes button
7	User clicked No button

You can use an If-Then or a Select Case structure to specify what to do based on which button is clicked, as demonstrated in the following example. If the user clicks the Yes button, a new URL loads. Otherwise, nothing happens.

```
Sub Button_OnClick()
    Ans = MsgBox("Do you want to go to my Links page?", 4)
    If Ans = 6 then Window.Location.Href = "links.htm"
End Sub
```

The InputBox function

The InputBox function is useful for obtaining a single input from the user — a number or text. When you only need to get one value from a user, this function is often a better solution than using a text control in a form.

InputBox syntax

A simplified version of the InputBox function's syntax is

```
InputBox(prompt,title,default)
```

Prompt is text that is displayed in the input box. Title is the text that appears in the input box's title bar. Default is the default value. The title and default arguments are optional.

An InputBox example

Here's an example of how you can use the InputBox function:

```
VisitorName = InputBox("What is your name?",
"Welcome to my site!")
```

When this VBScript statement executes, the user sees the dialog box shown in Figure 10-9. Notice that this example uses only the first two arguments and does not supply a default value, which makes sense, unless you're the Web master at the Psychic Friends Network Web site. When the user enters his or her name and clicks OK, the value is assigned to the variable *VisitorName*.

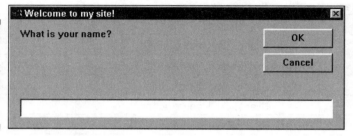

Figure 10-9: The InputBox function displays this dialog box.

The following example uses the third argument and provides a default value (1).

```
Msg = "How many copies would you like to order?"
TitleText = "Thanks for your order!"
Quantity = 1
Quantity = InputBox(Msg, TitleText, Quantity)
```

Figure 10-10 shows how this code looks to the user.

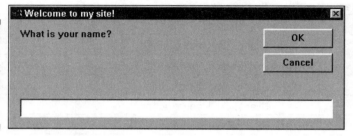

Figure 10-10: Using a default value for the InputBox function.

Finding out More about Functions

This chapter demonstrates the more common VBScript functions. "VBScript Function Reference," located on the disk, contains a complete list of the functions that are available to you. Almost every chapter in this book provides examples of using these functions.

Chapter 11

Correcting Errors and Exterminating Bugs

In This Chapter

▶ Types of errors you are likely to make

▶ How you can avoid making errors

▶ Bugs: What they are and how you can find them

▶ Program bugs you're likely to encounter

▶ Techniques to help you squash those bugs

*I*f the word bugs conjures up an image of a cartoon rabbit, this chapter can set you straight. I cover the broad topic of programming errors, including syntax errors as well as bugs. You discover how to recognize and correct errors and how to wipe the bugs off the face of your HTML document.

Make an Error? Me?

Everyone who writes computer programs makes errors. On the seriousness scale, errors can range from perfectly harmless to completely devastating. Actually, errors fall into two classes:

✔ **Syntax error:** Must be fixed before the code will run.

✔ **Program bug:** An error that may go unnoticed, but can rear its head at any time.

The fact is, all major software has bugs — a lot of bugs. It's been said that software that doesn't contain bugs is probably so trivial that it's not worth using.

Syntax Errors

A *syntax* error, sometimes known as a compilation error, is a language error. For example, you may

- ✔ Spell a VBScript keyword incorrectly.
- ✔ Omit the Next statement in a For-Next loop.
- ✔ Forget to insert an End Sub statement.
- ✔ Use an End Function statement when you should use an End Sub statement.
- ✔ Enter a set of mismatched parentheses.

This list is just for starters. You can have dozens of other types of syntax errors. You must correct every syntax error before the code will even execute.

A single syntax error is a showstopper. If you load an HTML document that contains one or more VBScript syntax errors, you know about it right away. Every line of your code is scanned for syntax errors. If one is found, you see an error message immediately. If the page loads and you don't see an error message, you know that your code is free of all syntax errors. Pat yourself on the back and pop open a bottle of bubbly.

The good news is that VBScript *always* lets you know when you've made a syntax error, and sometimes it even tells you exactly what you did wrong.

Anatomy of a syntax error message

Whenever VBScript encounters a syntax error, it pops up an error message, which is probably not an unfamiliar sight to you. Figure 11-1 shows how VBScript tells you about a syntax error. The exact error message, of course, varies, depending on your boo-boo.

Figure 11-1:
VBScript
can't
execute
your code
if it has a
syntax error.

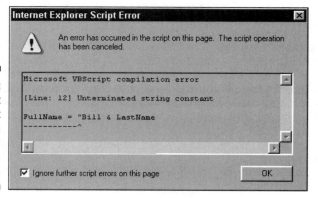

A pop-up syntax error message tells you the following information:

- ✔ **The scripting language that detected the error:** This language should be VBScript. If the error message mentions the JavaScript Compiler, that's a good sign that your `<SCRIPT>` tag is missing the `LANGUAGE = VBScript` attribute.

- ✔ **The line number and error description:** Line numbers start at the top of the document, including every line, even ordinary HTML statements. Blank lines also are counted. Unfortunately, you can't figure out a line number easily, unless your text editor displays line numbers.

- ✔ **The offending line of code:** The statement that caused the error is reproduced verbatim. Don't take this statement as gospel. Sometimes the error is *really* caused by a previous statement.

- ✔ **The location in the line where the problem occurred:** A caret (^) points to the character that appears to have caused the problem.

Avoiding syntax errors

As you may have surmised, a syntax error is really no big deal. You make the error, Internet Explorer tells you about it, you fix it, and then you move on. I don't know of any surefire way to avoid syntax errors. Some people are simply sloppy typists, which their code often reflects.

You can spend lots of time poring through each line of your code before you test it, but you'd be wasting your time. The best approach is to let the browser find your syntax errors. Fix the problem, save the file, and then reload. Keep doing this process until you've fixed all the syntax errors. I wish I could offer a more sophisticated method, but I can't.

Entomology 101: Program Bugs

A program *bug* is a common term for a problem with software. In other words, if software doesn't perform like it's supposed to, it is said to have a bug. Just because a document is free of syntax errors doesn't mean that it's free of *other* errors. You can have two types of program bugs:

- ✔ **Runtime errors:** These errors generate error messages, similar to the error messages you get for syntax errors.

- ✔ **Logical flaws in your code:** These types of bugs don't generate any error message. They manifest themselves by producing incorrect results.

Runtime errors

As the name implies, a runtime error occurs while the code is running. The most likely culprit is that the code is trying to do something with the wrong type of data. For example, your code may

✓ Attempt to divide by zero (which is illegal on this planet).

✓ Try to perform a mathematical operation on a text string (it doesn't work).

✓ Provide the wrong number of arguments for a function (a no-no).

✓ Try to write to a frame that is not displayed (can't do it, no matter how hard you try).

✓ Send the wrong type of data as an argument to a function (not a good thing).

The error messages that you see as a result of a runtime error are different than those generated by syntax errors. Figure 11-2 shows a typical runtime error message.

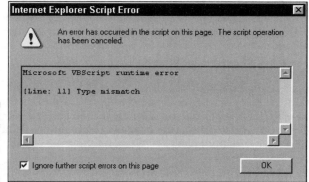

Figure 11-2: Houston, we have a problem.

Notice that the error dialog box identifies the problem as a runtime error, not as a syntax error. The dialog box also provides a line number and a description of the error. This description is not always very informative, and sometimes it's just plain wrong. Unlike a syntax error message, a runtime error message does not show you which statement caused the problem.

The error message may sometimes include a line that tells you the frame in which the error occurred. This line has nothing to do with Web page frames. In fact, I have no idea what this line means. Sometimes the line identifies the data that's invalid; at other times, it appears to be completely irrelevant. Go figure.

Correcting a runtime error is usually more difficult than correcting a syntax error. A runtime error, by its very nature, occurs while the code is running. If you're lucky, you can examine your code, figure out the source of the problem, and make changes in your code to avoid it. If you can't figure out the problem, you need to do some debugging.

Note: Some runtime errors may seem like they should be syntax errors. For example, if you spell a built-in function incorrectly, this error is not caught as a syntax error. Rather, you know about it when the code attempts to call the nonexistent function (you get a runtime error).

Logical flaws

Sometimes your code just doesn't work right. If you're lucky, you know that it doesn't work, and you can fix it before unleashing your Web page to the world. If you're not so lucky, the problem with your code occurs at an inopportune time, such as when a visitor to your Web site is about to do something important.

Logical flaws in your code can be extremely difficult to track down. The best way to identify such flaws is to test your code thoroughly under a variety of conditions. Then test your code more. And when you think you're finished testing your code, test it some more.

Identifying Bugs

The process of identifying and correcting bugs in your program is known as *debugging*. Debugging is a skill that you develop over time, so don't be discouraged if you find it to be a difficult process.

Before you can do any debugging, you must determine whether a bug actually exists. Two sure signs indicate that your code contains a bug:

- ✔ You see a runtime error message.
- ✔ The code simply doesn't work the way it should. Usually, but not always, this problem is readily apparent to you. Sometimes someone who is visiting your Web site informs you of this fact.

You need to remember that bugs have a way of appearing when you least expect them. For example, say you've written VBScript to validate user entries on a form. Just because your script works fine for your tests doesn't mean it works fine when it's unleashed on the world.

The best approach to debugging is thorough testing, under a variety of real-life conditions. Test your page by pretending that you're an obnoxious visitor who is trying to make your code crash. Enter numbers when strings are expected, enter negative numbers when positive numbers are expected, leave critical fields empty, and so on. In other words, go wild in your attempts to make the code crash and die. In the process, you can identify the weak spots so that you can fix them.

Avoiding Error Messages

It should go without saying, but I'll say it anyway: You should test your VBScript code thoroughly before posting your documents to your server. You want the scripts to work invisibly. In other words, visitors to your site won't even realize that all the cool stuff they're seeing is being brought to them through the wonders of VBScript. The worst thing that can happen is for a visitor to your site to be greeted with a VBScript runtime error message. That message may destroy their confidence in your site and may cause them to simply click the Back button to get outta there fast.

One way to completely avoid error messages is to use the following VBScript statement:

```
On Error Resume Next
```

This statement essentially causes VBScript to ignore any runtime errors and proceed as if nothing happened. Before you blindly insert this statement into every block of VBScript code, consider the trade-off. In some cases, ignoring an error is the best way to go. It causes no problems and, more importantly, prevents the display of the dreaded error message. The worst that can happen is that a noncritical piece of information doesn't appear.

But in other cases, ignoring an error can have serious consequences. If an error occurs when a user is submitting a form, for example, ignoring an error can result in the form not being submitted. In this case, the user would probably rather see the error than think that the form was submitted when it really wasn't.

Bottom line? Before choosing to ignore errors, consider all the possible consequences and then make your decision. No hard and fast rules apply here, so just use your better judgment.

WARNING!

> ## Where are the debugging tools?
>
> If you've used other programming languages, you may be familiar with debugging tools that let you:
>
> ✔ Step through code line by line.
>
> ✔ Display the value of any variable while the code is running.
>
> ✔ Stop execution at a specific line so that you can take a look at the values of certain variables.
>
> Sorry to be the bearer of bad news. Unlike most other programming languages, VBScript provides absolutely no assistance in the debugging process. In other words, you're on your own. Hopefully, this independence is a temporary situation, and some enterprising programmer will develop a full-scale VBScript debugging tool.

Stomping Those Bugs

In this section, I discuss how to fix an error after you've identified it — in other words, how to debug your code. The three most common methods of debugging VBScript code include

✔ Examining the code

✔ Inserting Alert statements at various locations in your code

✔ Writing variables to a frame

Examining your code

Perhaps the most straightforward debugging technique is to simply take a close look at your code and try to figure out the problem. If you're lucky, the error jumps right out, and you can quickly correct it.

Using Alert statements

TIP

A common problem is that one or more of your variables isn't taking on the values that you think it should. In such a case, monitoring the variable as your code runs is useful. One way to monitor the variable is to insert temporary Alert statements in your routine.

You also can use the MsgBox function rather than the Alert method. However, using Alert means one less keystroke, which can easily save you a minute or two over the course of your programming life.

For example, if you have a variable named Counter, you can insert the following statement in your code:

```
Alert Counter
```

When your routine executes, it displays the value of Counter when the Alert statement is encountered.

Displaying the value of two or more variables in the alert box is often helpful. The following statement shows the current value of LoopIndex and Counter (refer to Figure 11-3). Notice that I combine the two variables with the concatenation operator (&) and insert a space character in between them. Without this operator, the two values are strung together and appear as a single value (which isn't very helpful).

```
Alert LoopIndex & " " & Counter
```

Figure 11-3:
Using an
alert box to
display the
value of two
variables.

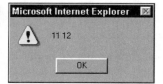

I use Alert functions frequently when I debug my code. I simply make sure that I remove them after I have identified and fixed the problem.

Monitoring a variable

If you place an Alert statement inside a For-Next loop to monitor the value of one or more variables, you'll find that responding to the alert boxes gets tedious. Therefore, you may want to take a more automated approach by writing a variable's value to a *floating frame*. This technique takes a bit of set-up work, but it may be worth it. A floating frame is a frame that you can insert into a document at any location.

You can write to a floating frame in three steps:

1. **Insert a temporary floating frame into your document.**
2. **Insert the DebugWrite subroutine (listed on the companion disk) into your document.**
3. **Insert a few strategically placed calls to the DebugWrite subroutine.**

The companion disk includes an example of this technique.

Bug Prevention Tips

In this section, I present general tips that may help you reduce the number of bugs in your code.

Develop your code in small bits

The best way to prevent bugs is to write code in small chunks and test it frequently. When I write VBScript, I find myself testing the code much more frequently than when I write in other languages, primarily due to the lack of VBScript debugging tools. Saving and testing hundreds of times for a single page is not uncommon for me.

Force variable declaration

Many bugs are the result of misspelled variable names. Examine the following code and try to spot a problem:

```
<SCRIPT LANGUAGE=VBScript>
InterestRate = .075
InterestRate = IntrestRate + .01
Alert InterestRate
</SCRIPT>
```

When you execute this code, you expect the alert box to display .076, right? In fact, the alert box displays .01. What's wrong with the code? Look at the second line closely. You find that the second instance of the variable name is spelled incorrectly. So, VBScript considers IntrestRate to be a new variable with a value of 0. Add .01 to 0 and you get .01, which is the value assigned to InterestRate.

Now look at this modified version of the code:

```
<SCRIPT LANGUAGE=VBScript>
Option Explicit
Dim InterestRate
InterestRate = .075
InterestRate = IntrestRate + .01
Alert InterestRate
</SCRIPT>
```

Notice the addition of the following statement:

```
Option Explicit
```

When you include this statement, you must declare every variable used in your code by using a Dim statement. Every undeclared variable results in an error message. Now, when you execute the code, you are alerted that an undeclared variable — the misspelled IntrestRate — is present.

Use consistent indentation

When you write VBScript, use indentation so that you can easily identify the structure of your code. Doing so makes matching For-Next loops, Select Case structures, and multiline If-Then statements much easier.

Remember a variable's scope

If your application uses multiple subroutines, don't forget that the scope of a variable normally consists of a single subroutine. If you want to use the same variable in multiple procedures, declare the variable outside of any procedure. For more details, refer to Chapter 8.

Test extreme cases

When you're testing your code, especially code that works with data obtained by a user, don't use the same data for each test run. Rather, vary your input and enter extreme values and even blatantly incorrect values (for example, if a field requires a date, enter a name). In other words, make no assumptions about the data that you're working with.

Let others test your code

One of the best ways to identify a problem is to let someone else try out your code. When writing code, the developer (you!) often gets so wrapped up in what he's doing that he overlooks simple problems. Sometimes, simply having someone else try out your page identifies these problems.

Test your code on the server

Although you'll be developing your VBScript code on a local machine, make sure that you test the final pages after you've loaded the page to your server. In rare instances, especially in applications that use ActiveX controls, you may encounter code that works fine on your local system, but has some problems when its loaded from a server. Therefore, it's always a good idea to test your work on the server that will ultimately be the document's final resting place.

Part IV
Doing Useful Stuff

The 5th Wave   By Rich Tennant

Re·al Pro′gram·mers

OH WOW!

MONDO-TECH

Real Programmers do their best work between 1 and 5 a.m.

In this part . . .

*I*n Part IV, the focus of this book shifts from discovering basic, yet essential, techniques to solving practical problems. Chapter 12 covers the HTML intrinsic controls, and Chapter 13 extends the discussion to include forms. Chapter 14 deals with frames, and Chapter 15 concludes the part with a dynamite collection of useful techniques that you can put to use immediately.

Chapter 12

Working with the HTML Intrinsic Controls

. . . .

In This Chapter

▶ What are HTML intrinsic controls? And what each control is good for

▶ An overview of each intrinsic control

▶ How to access intrinsic controls using VBScript

. . . .

*Y*ou may already be familiar with HTML intrinsic controls. These controls include user interface elements, such as buttons, check boxes, radio buttons, text boxes, and so on. Before the days of scripting languages, these controls were virtually useless unless you had a CGI *(Common Gateway Interface)* program installed on your server that could do something with them. Now that VBScript has arrived on the scene, you can make full use of these controls without using a CGI program.

HTML Intrinsic Controls: What's Available?

Standard HTML lets you insert several types of nontext items in a Web document. These items, known as *controls,* allow the user to interact with your page. These items also are sometimes known as *intrinsic controls,* which distinguishes them from other types of controls, such as ActiveX controls (see Part V).

Here's a list of the HTML intrinsic controls that you can use and manipulate with VBScript:

✔ **Button:** A clickable thingamajig.

✔ **Submit:** A special type of button control that sends the contents of a form to a Web server.

- **Reset:** A special type of button control that restores the original values for all the controls in a form.

- **Text:** A single-line control that holds words.

- **Textarea:** A multiline control that holds text, with or without a vertical scroll bar.

- **Password:** A text control that displays asterisks when text is entered.

- **Radio button:** A control that lets a user select from several options. Radio buttons always appear in groups of at least two. Selecting radio buttons automatically unselects the other radio buttons in the group.

- **Check box:** A control that is selected by the user to identify a choice. A check box is either on (checked) or off (not checked).

- **Select:** A control that presents a list of choices. It can resemble a list box or a drop-down list.

- **Hidden:** An invisible control that can hold text, but is not displayed on the page.

Note: Refer to "VBScript Function Reference," located on the disk, for a list of the properties, methods, and events for each intrinsic control.

Figure 12-1 shows an HTML document (available on the companion disk) that contains each previously described intrinsic control.

More object model stuff

The HTML intrinsic controls are deep in the object model (see Chapter 5). Each control is a member of the Elements array, which is contained in a Form object, which is contained in a Document object, which is contained in the Window object. Here's another way of looking at this object hierarchy.

```
Window
    Document
        Form
            Elements
```

You can use the intrinsic controls (which are Element objects) even if the document doesn't have a form defined with the `<FORM>` and `</FORM>` tags. If you omit these tags, an unnamed form is assumed.

The manner in which these controls relate to the object model is made clearer in Chapter 13 when I discuss forms. But if you haven't checked out that chapter, simply remember that these HTML intrinsic controls are actually objects that have properties, methods, and events (concepts covered in Chapter 6).

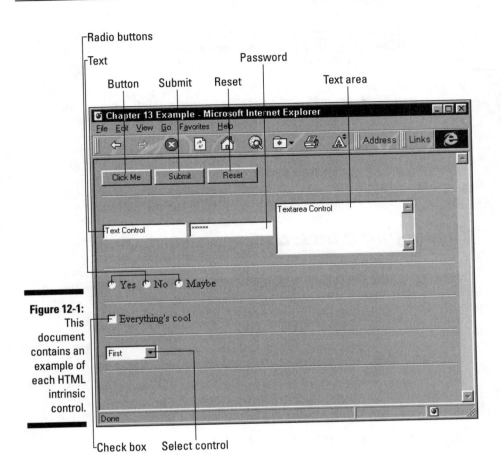

Figure 12-1:
This document contains an example of each HTML intrinsic control.

Button Controls

You probably know what a button control is. You click a button and (usually) something happens. If you've read other chapters in this book, you know that I use button controls a lot in the examples.

Here's an example of HTML code that inserts a button control into a Web document:

```
<INPUT TYPE=Button NAME=Button1 VALUE="Click Me">
```

The button's value property determines the text that is displayed on the button. When a button is clicked, it generates a click event that can call a subroutine. The subroutine's name consists of the button's name, an underscore character, and the word *onClick*. For example, clicking the button generated by the preceding HTML code executes a subroutine named Button1_OnClick. A subroutine that responds to an event is known as an *event handler* subroutine.

If you prefer to use a different subroutine to handle the click event that's generated when a button is clicked, you can specify the subroutine in the button's <INPUT> tag, like this:

```
<INPUT TYPE=Button NAME=MyButton VALUE="Click Me"
       ONCLICK=MySub>
```

In this case, clicking the button executes the subroutine named MySub.

Displaying a message

The following code is an event handler subroutine that displays a message when a button named MsgButton is clicked. This subroutine displays the current URL loaded in the window:

```
Sub MsgButton_OnClick()
    Msg = "You are currently reading the document located at"
    Msg = Msg & Chr(13) & Window.Location
    Msgbox Msg
End Sub
```

Changing a button caption

The caption displayed on a button is its *Value* property. You can change the button's Value by using VBScript.

This section contains a clever example of a button (named TimeButton) with the caption *Click For the Time of Day*. Clicking the button executes the subroutine TimeButton_OnClick, which changes the button's caption to the current time of day. Here's the clever part: The TimeButton_OnClick subroutine uses the setTimeout method, which executes another subroutine after a certain amount of time has passed. In this case, VBScript waits 2000 milliseconds (two seconds) and executes the RestoreButton subroutine, which restores the button's Value property.

Following is the code listing:

```
<SCRIPT LANGUAGE=VBScript>
Sub TimeButton_OnClick()
    TimeButton.Value=Time()
    X = setTimeout ("RestoreButton",2000,"VBScript")
End Sub
Sub RestoreButton()
    TimeButton.Value = " Click for the Time of Day "
End Sub
</SCRIPT>
<INPUT TYPE=Button NAME=TimeButton _
Value="Click For the Time of Day">
```

Opening a new URL

The following simple event handler subroutine opens a new URL in the window. Clicking the button named SearchButton calls the SearchButton_OnClick subroutine. In this example, clicking the button connects to the AltaVista search site:

```
Sub SearchButton_OnClick()
    Navigate "http://www.altavista.digital.com"
End Sub
```

You also can use the following statement to connect to the AltaVista search site:

```
Window.Location = "http://www.altavista.digital.com"
```

Simulating the Back and Forward buttons

Simulating the behavior of your browser's Back and Forward buttons is easy. Here's HTML code that generates two buttons named GoBack and GoForward:

```
<INPUT TYPE=Button Name=GoBack Value=Back>
<INPUT TYPE=Button Name=GoForward Value=Forward>
```

The following code contains two event handler subroutines for these buttons. The GoBack_OnClick subroutine loads the previous URL in the History object. The GoForward_OnClick procedure loads the next URL in the History object.

```
Sub GoBack_OnClick()
    Window.History.Back
End Sub
```

```
Sub GoForward_OnClick()
    Window.History.Forward
End Sub
```

Submit and Reset Controls

The Submit and Reset controls are buttons that perform a special action. For example, clicking a Submit button sends the information contained in the controls in a form to a Web server. Clicking a Reset button clears the form and restores it to its original state.

Here's HTML code that generates these two buttons. Notice that the <INPUT> tags don't specify a Value property (that is, a caption) for the button. The Value properties display automatically for Submit and Reset buttons.

```
<INPUT TYPE=Submit>
<INPUT TYPE=Reset>
```

Refer to Chapter 14 for examples that use the Submit and Reset controls.

Text Controls

Text controls are handy and quite versatile because they serve two distinct purposes:

- **Text controls can be used as an input field:** The user can enter text or a value into a text control.
- **Text controls can be used as an output field:** Your VBScript code can write text or a value into a text control. For example, your code can perform a calculation and display the result in a text control.

Here's HTML code that generates a text control:

```
<INPUT TYPE=Text NAME=Text1 SIZE=50>
```

The `SIZE=` attribute is optional. You can include the attribute to control the width of the text control (measured in the approximate number of characters it holds). You also can use a `VALUE=` parameter to insert the specified text when the page loads.

Text is the default value of the `TYPE` attribute for the `<INPUT>` tag. So if you omit the `TYPE=` attribute, the browser displays a text control.

Using a text control for input

The companion disk contains an example that demonstrates how to use a text control for input.

Most of the time, you can use text controls to get some type of input from the user. Here's HTML that generates a text control and a button control. The text control is designed to get the user's name.

```
Name:
<INPUT TYPE=Text NAME=UserName SIZE=30>
<P>
<INPUT TYPE=Button Name=Button1 Value="Greet Me">
```

A note about the <FORM> </FORM> tags

Intrinsic controls are often used in an HTML form, which is designated by using a <FORM> and a </FORM> tag. In fact, older browsers don't even display these controls unless they are placed inside a form.

To keep things simple, the examples in this chapter do not use the `<FORM>` and `</FORM>` tags. If you use these tags to define a form, pay attention to the placement of your VBScript code that accesses the controls.

You can insert your VBScript inside or outside of the <FORM></FORM> tags. If your VBScript code is inside the <FORM></FORM> tags, you don't have to do anything special.

If the VBScript code is outside the <FORM> </FORM> tags, you'll want to give the form a name by using the NAME parameter. Here's an example:

```
<FORM NAME=OrderForm>
```

Qualify your references to the form's controls by preceding the control names with the form name, separated by a dot. For example, if you have a text control named NameBox located on a form named OrderForm, you can refer to it in your code like this:

```
UserName = OrderForm.NameBox.Value
```

If the form doesn't have a name, you can still refer to controls in the form, but you need to refer to the Forms array of the Document object. Here's an example of how to refer to a text control in the first (unnamed) form in a document:

```
UserName =Document.Forms(0).NameBox.Value
```

Listed in the following is the event handler subroutine for the button. This subroutine checks the Value property of the text control. If the Value equals "", nothing has been entered into the text control, and the TheName variable holds the generic name User. If the text control is not empty, the text is assigned to the TheName variable. Finally, the message box displays a simple greeting.

```
Sub Button1_OnClick()
    If UserName.Value = "" Then
        TheName = "User"
    Else
        TheName = UserName.Value
    End If
    MsgBox "Hello " & TheName
End Sub
```

Figure 12-2 shows this example in action.

Using a text control for output

You also can write text to an input control by using VBScript. Using programming terminology, your VBScript code sets, or changes, the Value property of the text control object.

The companion disk contains an example that demonstrates how to use a text control for output.

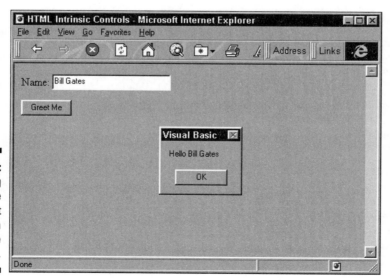

Figure 12-2:
Displaying
the value
from a text
control in a
message
box.

The following HTML code generates a text control, named Results, and a button, named Button1:

```
<INPUT TYPE=Text NAME=Results SIZE=40>
<P>
<INPUT TYPE=Button Name=Button1 Value="Click Me">
```

Here's a listing of the event handler for the button control. Clicking the button increments the Counter variable and displays text in the text control.

```
Dim Counter
Sub Button1_OnClick()
  Counter = Counter + 1
  Results.Value = "You clicked the button " & Counter & "times."
End Sub
```

Notice that the Counter variable is defined outside of the procedure. Doing so makes the Counter variable a global variable — which means that the Counter variable retains its value even when the Button1_OnClick subroutine ends. See Chapter 8 for more information about global variables.

Figure 12-3 shows how these controls appear in the browser.

Figure 12-3:
Using a text
control to
write text to
a Web page.

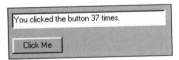

Understanding the OnFocus and OnBlur events

When the user activates a control, that control has the *focus*. When the user deactivates the control, that control has the *blur* (strange terminology, I know). You can monitor this change of focus and perform an action when it occurs.

Note: The term *blur* comes from the world of JavaScript. Other varieties of Visual Basic use the term *LostFocus* to describe what happens when a user deactivates a control.

Here's HTML code that adds text controls to a document:

```
1. <INPUT TYPE=text NAME=Text1 ONFOCUS=ShowStatus(1)><BR>
2. <INPUT TYPE=text NAME=Text2 ONFOCUS=ShowStatus(2)><BR>
3. <INPUT TYPE=text NAME=Text3 ONFOCUS=ShowStatus(3)><BR>
4. <INPUT TYPE=text NAME=Text4 ONFOCUS=ShowStatus(4)><BR>
Status: <INPUT TYPE=text NAME=Status SIZE=50
             ONFOCUS=ShowStatus(0)>
```

The <INPUT> tags for the text controls specify a subroutine (ShowStatus) to execute when the focus changes to the control. Notice that I specify a different argument for each control.

Here's a listing of the ShowStatus event handler subroutine that executes when one of the text boxes gets the focus:

```
Sub ShowStatus(x)
    If x <>0 Then
        Status.Value="You are now in TextBox " & x
    Else
        Status.Value=""
    End if
End sub
```

This subroutine checks the value of the argument passed to it, which is x in this case. If x does not equal 0, the routine changes the value of the text control named Status. If x equals 0, the Status text control has been activated, and the status text is set to "".

Refer to Figure 12-4 to see how this example looks.

Textarea Control

The textarea control works just like a text control, with a few exceptions:

- ✔ The textarea control can hold more than one line of text (the text wraps around automatically, just like a word processor document).

- ✔ The textarea control is generated by <TEXTAREA> and </TEXTAREA> tags (not an <INPUT> tag).

- ✔ The textarea control displays a vertical scrollbar along its right edge.

- ✔ The textarea control can contain nonprinting characters. For example, if the user presses Enter while working with a textarea control, this action generates two ASCII characters: 13 (carriage return) and 10 (line feed).

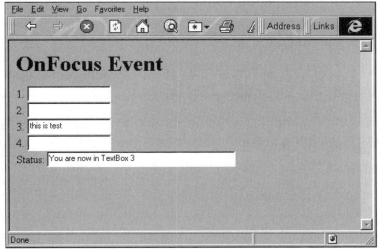

Figure 12-4:
The Status
text control
is updated
whenever
the focus
changes.

The properties, methods, and events for a textarea control are identical to those for the text control. Here's an example that generates a textarea control:

```
<TEXTAREA NAME=Textarea1 ROWS=10 COLS=50></TEXTAREA>
```

The ROWS= and COLS= attributes specify the height and width of the control. If you want text to appear in the textarea control when the page loads, insert the text between the <TEXTAREA> and </TEXTAREA> tags.

The companion disk contains an example that *parses* the contents of a textarea control. Parsing is the process of breaking each line of the text into separate items. The code loops through each character entered, searching for the line breaks.

Password Control

The password control is identical to a text control, with one exception: Text entered by the user, or by your VBScript code, appears in the text box as a series of asterisks. You may be familiar with passwords on computer systems. In almost every case, typing your password spits out asterisks to prevent people who are looking over your shoulder from seeing what you typed.

Note: Unlike the text control, the password control doesn't respond to any events.

Here's an example of HTML code to generate a password control:

```
<INPUT TYPE=Password NAME=Password1 SIZE=5>
```

Figure 12-5 shows how the password control looks in a browser.

If you're considering using a password control and VBScript to restrict access to a Web page, think again. To determine whether the user entered the correct password, your VBScript must compare the text entered by the user with the correct password. To perform this comparison, the correct password must be in your VBScript code. Any halfway savvy user can use the View⇨Source command, browse though your code, and figure out what the correct password is. Therefore, a password control is most useful when the information entered is sent to the server, where another program determines whether the password is correct.

Radio Button Controls

If you're as old as I am, you may remember the radios that used to be installed in cars back in the '50s and '60s. In the days before electronic tuners, you pressed a button to change the station. Pressing a button caused another

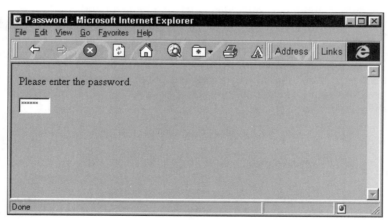

Figure 12-5:
An example of a password control. Typing in this field produces an asterisk for each character entered.

button to pop out. Now you know where the term *radio button* originated. These controls always appear in groups of at least two. Only one item in a group of radio buttons can be selected at any time, which makes them an ideal way to force a user to make a single choice.

You can think of a set of radio buttons as an item on a multiple choice test. Only one item can be selected. Selecting a new choice automatically cancels the previous choice. Here's HTML code that generates a set of radio buttons.

```
<INPUT TYPE=Radio NAME=Age VALUE=1>18 or younger<BR>
<INPUT TYPE=Radio NAME=Age VALUE=2>19 - 29<BR>
<INPUT TYPE=Radio NAME=Age VALUE=3>30 - 49<BR>
<INPUT TYPE=Radio NAME=Age VALUE=4>50 or older<BR>
<INPUT TYPE=Radio NAME=Age VALUE=5>None of your business<BR>
```

Figure 12-6 shows how these controls appear in the browser.

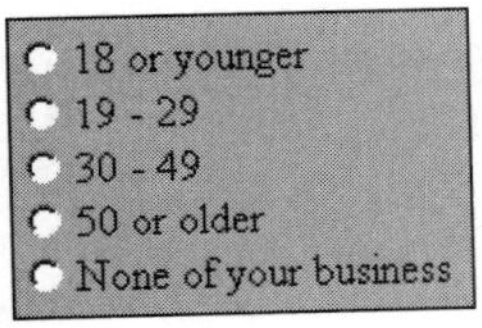

Figure 12-6:
Five radio
buttons.

C 18 or younger
C 19 - 29
C 30 - 49
C 50 or older
C None of your business

To make one of the choices the default, add a CHECKED attribute to one of the <INPUT> tags. For example:

```
<INPUT TYPE=Radio NAME=Age VALUE=5 CHECKED>None of your
              business
```

If you don't include the CHECKED parameter, no choice is selected when the page loads.

Notice that each <INPUT> tag has the same name: Age. Using a common name is how different sets of radio buttons are grouped together. If the same page (or the same form) had another set of radio buttons, you would use a different name for the second set.

Here's HTML that creates two sets of radio buttons. Notice that each set of buttons has a different name.

```
1. Do you use a computer at home?
<INPUT TYPE=Radio NAME=Q1 VALUE=1>Yes
<INPUT TYPE=Radio NAME=Q1 VALUE=2>No
<P>
2. Do you use a computer at work?
<INPUT TYPE=Radio NAME=Q2 VALUE=1>Yes
<INPUT TYPE=Radio NAME=Q2 VALUE=2>No
```

The VALUE attribute is optional. You can use this parameter if you want to associate a particular value to a radio button.

Executing a subroutine when a radio button is clicked

If you want to execute a subroutine when the user clicks a radio button, specify the subroutine in the <INPUT> tag using the ONCLICK parameter. Associating a subroutine with a radio button doesn't work like a normal button. In other words, if you have a radio button named Age, clicking the button does not automatically execute a subroutine named Age_OnClick.

Here's an example of specifying a subroutine, named AgeClick, to execute when a radio button is clicked. Notice that each radio button passes a different argument to the AgeClick subroutine:

```
<INPUT TYPE=Radio NAME=Age ONCLICK="AgeClick(1)">18 or
          younger
<INPUT TYPE=Radio NAME=Age ONCLICK="AgeClick(2)">19-29
<INPUT TYPE=Radio NAME=Age ONCLICK="AgeClick(3)">30-49
<INPUT TYPE=Radio NAME=Age ONCLICK="AgeClick(4)">50 or older
<INPUT TYPE=Radio NAME=Age ONCLICK="AgeClick(5)">None of your
          business
```

Here's an example of the AgeClick subroutine. This routine assigns the value that is passed to it to the AgeRange variable. For example, if the user clicks the second radio button, AgeRange has a value of two.

```
Sub AgeClick(x)
    AgeRange = x
End Sub
```

Determining which radio button is selected

In the previous section, I demonstrate how to execute a subroutine whenever a radio button is clicked. That's one way to determine which choice the user made. Another way is to examine the Checked property of the radio buttons.

Because each set of radio buttons has the same name, use an index number to examine a particular button. The first button has an index number of 0, the second is numbered 1, and so on. Here is HTML code to generate three radio buttons. The third button is the default button, and it's assigned a value of 0.

```
<INPUT TYPE=Radio NAME=Sex VALUE=1>Male<BR>
<INPUT TYPE=Radio NAME=Sex VALUE=2>Female<BR>
<INPUT TYPE=Radio NAME=Sex VALUE=0 CHECKED>Unknown<BR>
```

Here's a subroutine that determines which radio button is clicked. In this case, the document also has a button named Button1. Clicking the button displays a message box that shows which radio button is selected.

```
Sub Button1_OnClick()
    For i = 0 To Sex.Count -1
        If Sex(i).Checked Then UserSex=Sex(i).Value
    Next
    Msgbox UserSex
End Sub
```

This subroutine uses the Count property to determine how many elements are named Age. In this case, Age.Count equals 3, but because the elements are numbered beginning with 0, the For-Next loop needs to start with 0 and end with 1 less than the value returned by Age.Count. Within the loop, the Checked property of each element is examined. If the Checked property is True, the AgeRange variable is assigned that element's value. The Message box displays either 0 (Unknown), 1 (Male), or 2 (Female).

To have the result return text (such as *Male, Female,* or *Unknown*), use text for the VALUE attribute, like this:

```
<INPUT TYPE=Radio NAME=Sex VALUE=Male>Male<BR>
<INPUT TYPE=Radio NAME=Sex VALUE=Female>Female<BR>
<INPUT TYPE=Radio NAME=Sex VALUE=Unknown CHECKED>Unknown<BR>
```

Figure 12-7 shows this example in use.

Figure 12-7:
Determining
which radio
button is
selected.

Check Box Control

If a radio button control is like a multiple choice test item, then a check box control is like a true/false test item. A check box control is either checked, or it's not, which makes it an ideal choice for user input that is *binary* in nature: yes/no, on/off, true/false, and so on.

Here's HTML code that inserts two check box controls into a document.

```
<INPUT TYPE=Checkbox NAME=Email>Reply by Email <BR>
<INPUT TYPE=Checkbox NAME=Fax>Reply by Fax
```

Figure 12-8 shows how the check boxes appear in the document.

Figure 12-8:
Two
checkbox
controls.

Remember that, unlike radio buttons, check boxes are always independent of each other. In the preceding example, the user can click one box, both boxes, or no boxes.

If you include a CHECKED attribute in the <INPUT> tag, the check box is checked when the page loads. You can use the defaultChecked property to determine whether the check box has a CHECKED attribute.

To execute a subroutine when the user clicks a check box, you can create a subroutine with a name that corresponds to the check box's name, an underscore, and the word *OnClick*. Here's an example that executes when the check box named Email is clicked:

```
Sub Email_OnClick()
    If Email.Checked Then EmailResponse = True _
        Else EmailResponse = False
End Sub
```

This subroutine examines the Checked property of the check box and assigns either True or False to a variable named EmailResponse.

Select Control

A select control displays what is commonly known as a list box or a drop-down list box. This control is a good choice when the user needs to select from a list of items. Depending on how you set up the list box, the user can select one item or multiple items.

Use the <SELECT> and </SELECT> tags to generate a select control. Place the options that will be displayed by the control between these tags, with each preceded by an <OPTION> tag. If you want one of the options to be selected as the default selection, include a SELECTED attribute in the <OPTION> tag.

Here's an example of HTML that generates a select control. The June item is selected by default:

```
<SELECT NAME=Select1 SIZE=6>
    <Option>January
    <Option>February
    <Option>March
    <Option>April
    <Option>May
    <Option SELECTED>June
    <Option>July
    <Option>August
    <Option>September
    <Option>October
    <Option>November
    <Option>December
</SELECT>
```

Figure 12-9 shows how this list box appears in the browser.

Figure 12-9:
A select
control.

The select control has two important attributes that determine how it looks and behaves:

- 🖋 SIZE: The number of items to display at one time. If SIZE equals one, the select control looks like a drop-down list rather than a list box. If SIZE is greater than or equal to the number of options, the control does not display a scrollbar.
- 🖋 MULTIPLE: If this parameter is included, the user can select multiple items from the list.

 Sometimes, you may find that the list box is too narrow for your liking. In some cases, the text of the items may not even be fully displayed. To solve this problem, add several nonbreaking spaces to the end of the longest item in the list. To insert a nonbreaking space, use the following HTML code: Here's an example:

```
<Option>January   
```

Figure 12-10 shows two select controls. The wider control on the right shows the effect of adding nonbreaking spaces to one of the options.

Which item is selected?

When working with a select control, the big question is how to determine which item is selected. The easy answer is to use the selectedIndex property to get the index number of the selected item. Getting the text of the option is a bit more tricky.

 The following is HTML code that generates a select control and a button:

```
<SELECT NAME=Select1 SIZE=6>
    <Option >Apples
    <Option>Peaches
    <Option>Watermelon
    <Option>Pears
```

```
        <Option>Plums
        <Option>Oranges
        <Option>Tangerines
        <Option>Strawberries
</SELECT>
<P>
<INPUT TYPE=Button Name=Button1 Value="Click Me">
```

Clicking the button named Button1 executes the following subroutine, which displays the selected item's index number and text. Figure 12-11 shows an example of the message box that appears when the button is clicked.

```
Sub Button1_OnClick()
    ItemNum = Select1.selectedIndex
    ItemText = Select1.Options(ItemNum).Text
    Msg = "You selected Item #" & ItemNum +1 & ": " &
            ItemText
    Msgbox Msg
End Sub
```

The selected Index property determines the index number of the selected item and is rather straightforward. Determining the text associated with the selected item is the Text property of the specific Option. Here's another more complicated way to get the text of the selected item without using the intermediate variable ItemNum:

```
ItemText=Select1.Options(Select1.selectedIndex).Text
```

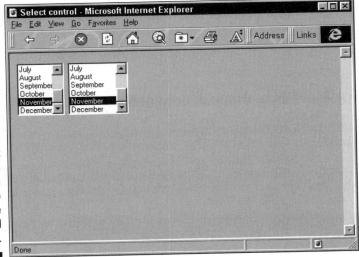

Figure 12-10: The control on the right uses nonbreaking spaces to make the control wider.

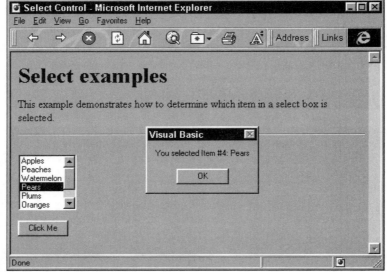

Figure 12-11:
Displaying
the selected
item index
number
and text.

Determining multiple selections

If you use the MULTIPLE attribute in the <SELECT> tag, the user can select multiple items from the select control by pressing Ctrl as he clicks the items. The following HTML code creates a select control that allows multiple selections (see Figure 12-12).

```
<SELECT NAME=Select1 SIZE=4 MULTIPLE>
    <Option >First Quarter Report
    <Option>Second Quarter Report
    <Option>Third Quarter Report
    <Option>Fourth Quarter Report
</SELECT>
```

As you may expect, you can use VBScript to determine all the items that are selected. The following subroutine demonstrates this.

```
Sub Button1_OnClick()
    For i = 0 to Select1.Options.Count -1
        If Select1.Options(i).Selected = 1 Then
            msg = msg & " " & Select1.Options(i).Text
        End if
    Next
    Msgbox msg
End Sub
```

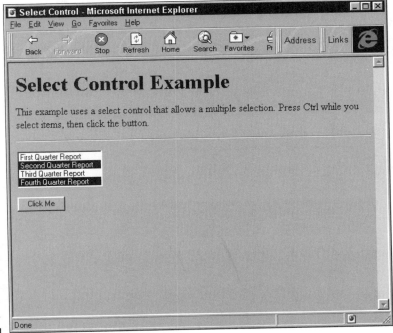

Figure 12-12:
This select
control lets
the user
select more
than one
option.

The Button2_OnClick subroutine uses a For-Next loop to loop through the array of options. The number of options in the list is determined by

```
Select1.Options.Count
```

Because the option numbering begins with 0, the loop stops at one less than the value returned by Select1.Options.Count.

If an item is selected, its Selected property returns 1; otherwise, it returns 0. The If statement checks to see if each option is selected. If so, it adds the option's Text property to the msg variable. Finally, the MsgBox displays the msg variable, which consists of the text of each selected item.

Hidden Control

The hidden control is useful only if you submit a form. This control is sort of like a variable. You can assign a value to it, but the hidden control doesn't display on the page. When the form is submitted, the value in any hidden controls also are sent.

Refer to Chapter 13 for an example that uses the hidden control.

Chapter 13

Working with Forms

In This Chapter

▶ Using VBScript to work with HTML forms

▶ Referring to controls on a form

▶ Examples that demonstrate client-side form validation techniques

▶ Preventing submission of a form that contains invalid data

▶ Using VBScript to generate forms and controls

▶ Using VBScript to display a compact list of links

An HTML form is a blessing and a curse. The blessing is that a form is the only commonly accepted way to get information from a visitor to your Web site. The curse is that a form never seems able to do quite enough, and working with one can be frustrating.

In this chapter, I attempt to reduce the amount of cursing that often accompanies using forms. VBScript can make a huge difference for you when working with forms because you can do clever things that are otherwise impossible.

Read Me First!

The examples in this chapter deal with conventional HTML forms. The examples contain the intrinsic HTML controls that you can display in almost any browser. (Chapter 12 provides details and examples of the HTML intrinsic controls used in HTML forms.) You can produce more attractive forms and have more control over their appearance if you use ActiveX controls in your forms.

In general, though, a good rule of thumb is that if you can get by with using an intrinsic form element, rather than an ActiveX control, go for it! Using ActiveX controls adds more overhead to your page and may require the user to download the control, which takes time. I discuss ActiveX controls in Part V.

HTML Forms: A Refresher Course

Web page designers use forms primarily to get information from Web site visitors. I've seen forms for product order forms, visitor questionnaires, online quizzes, and guest book signings. The visitor enters information onto the form by using standard HTML controls, such as text controls, check boxes, radio buttons, and so on. (Refer to Chapter 12 for details on these controls.) The information is sent back to the server where it is processed — often by a CGI program designed specifically for that purpose. Usually, the server sends back another HTML document to confirm the receipt of the information.

For example, a Web page may include an order form like the one shown in Figure 13-1. The visitor fills out the information in the form and then submits the form by clicking a button. This submission sends the contents of the controls (that is, their values) to the server, where they are interpreted and processed. When the server receives this information, it sends another HTML document, which thanks the user for the information.

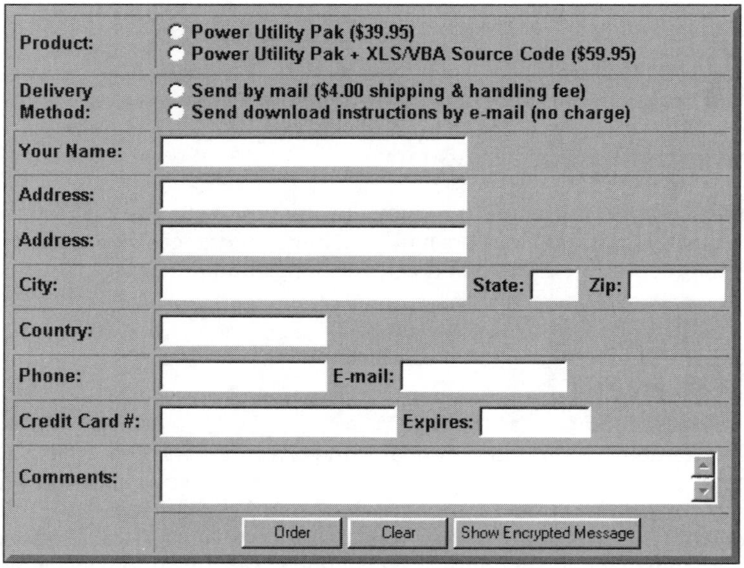

Product:	○ Power Utility Pak ($39.95) ○ Power Utility Pak + XLS/VBA Source Code ($59.95)
Delivery Method:	○ Send by mail ($4.00 shipping & handling fee) ○ Send download instructions by e-mail (no charge)
Your Name:	
Address:	
Address:	
City:	State: [ ] Zip: [ ]
Country:	
Phone:	E-mail:
Credit Card #:	Expires:
Comments:	

[Order] [Clear] [Show Encrypted Message]

Figure 13-1:
An example
of an order
form.

Defining a form

You can create your form on an HTML page by using the `<FORM>` and `</FORM>` tags. You can provide a name for the form by using the `NAME` attribute for the `<FORM>` tag. Here's an example of a complete, albeit short, form definition:

```
<FORM NAME=Form1 ACTION="../cgi-bin/process">
Name:
<INPUT TYPE=Text NAME=Text1>
<P>
Password:
<INPUT TYPE=Password NAME=Text1>
<P>
<INPUT TYPE=Submit>
</FORM>
```

Figure 13-2 shows how this form appears in the browser.

Notice these points about the code for the form in Figure 13-2:

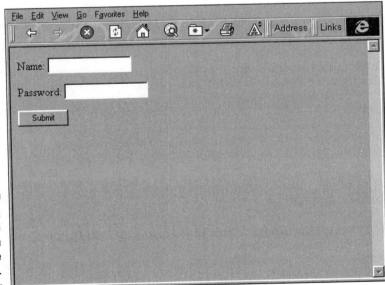

Figure 13-2:
A simple form with three controls.

- ✔ The form begins with a `<FORM>` tag and ends with a `</FORM>` tag.
- ✔ The form's name is Form1.
- ✔ When the form is submitted, a CGI program named process handles it.
- ✔ The form contains normal text and other HTML tags.
- ✔ The form contains three controls: a text control, a password control, and a submit control.

A Web page can have any number of forms defined. Forms can even be placed inside other forms, which is almost never a good idea. If your Web page needs more than one form, make sure that the `<FORM>` and `</FORM>` tags don't overlap with other `<FORM>` and `</FORM>` tags.

Adding form controls

The controls in a form are intrinsic HTML controls that are placed on a page using any of the following HTML tags:

- ✔ `<INPUT>`
- ✔ `<SELECT></SELECT>`
- ✔ `<TEXTAREA></TEXTAREA>`

In addition to HTML intrinsic controls, form controls also can be ActiveX controls. However, information supplied in an ActiveX control is not submitted automatically. You can use a VBScript procedure to assign the ActiveX control value to a hidden HTML intrinsic control, which adds some complexity to the process.

Refer to Chapter 12 for information about the HTML intrinsic controls. And check out Part V for details on ActiveX controls.

Validating a form

One critical component of working with forms is verifying that the form's data is valid. The process of determining whether the data is okay is known as *validating* the form. For example, the form may require the user to enter a phone number. You need a way to verify that a phone number is entered. For example, you can check to make sure that the field is not blank (simple validation), or you can write code to check the characters entered to ensure that they are all numbers, hyphens, or parentheses (more thorough validation). Of course, validation only goes so far. I don't know of a way to determine that the phone number provided is actually a working number!

Before the days of scripting languages (such as VBScript), the server always validated forms. In practical terms, *server-side* validation means additional time — sometimes *a lot* of additional time — waiting for the server to validate and confirm the data. Depending on the time of day, the type of connection, and the speed of the server, the user may find this wait to be intolerable and simply move on to another site, which can mean a lost sale or a turned-off potential customer. As you see later in this chapter, VBScript provides a solution: *client-side* form validation.

VBScript and HTML Forms: A Winning Combination

How does VBScript fit into this form's processing picture? VBScript fits in several ways:

- **Generating forms and controls:** You can use VBScript to generate HTML code that produces forms and controls within forms. This code can save you lots of time and can make your forms more dynamic.

- **Client-side data validation:** Rather than send the form data back to the server for validation, VBScript can do the job in a flash by informing the user immediately if a problem exists.

- **Miscellaneous uses:** Use your imagination. But if your brain cells aren't firing properly, I provide a clever example later in this chapter that demonstrates how to use VBScript to create a very compact list of hyperlinks.

I discuss these topics and provide examples later in this chapter. But before you can do anything useful with VBScript and forms, you need to know how to refer to the controls contained in a form, which I cover in the next section.

Referring to Controls

To do something with a control in a form, you need to know how to refer to the control. You can refer to a control in two ways:

- By its relative position in the form
- By its name

Referring to a control by its position in the form

In the scripting object model (see Chapter 5), each Form object contains a collection of controls, known as the *Elements* collection. You can refer to a control by its position within the Elements collection. For example, say you have a Web document that has a form named Form1, and the first control in this form is a text control named Text1. To assign the contents of this text control to a variable named UserText, you can use the following VBScript assignment statement:

```
UserText = Form1.Elements(0).Value
```

The first item in the Elements collection has an index number of 0, not 1.

If you want to know how many elements are in a form, you can access the Count property of the Elements collections:

```
NumControls = Form1.Elements.Count
```

You can access the last control in the form using this statement:

```
UserText = Form1.Elements(Form1.Elements.Count-1)
```

You need to subtract 1 from the total number of controls because the numbering of the Elements collection begins with 0.

Referring to a control by name

You may want to refer to a control by its name. Besides being a more user-friendly approach, referring to a control by its name can help prevent errors. For example, you may write VBScript code to refer to the fourth element in a form. If you later modify the form and insert a new control before the fourth element, the fourth element becomes the fifth element, and you have to change your VBScript code.

To refer to a control by its name, precede the control's name with the form's name and a dot. For example, you may want to assign the contents of a text control to a variable named UserText. If the text control is named Text1 and it's contained in a form named Form1, you can use the following statement:

```
UserText = Form1.Text1.Value
```

You also can access a control by name within the Elements collection. Here's an example:

```
UserText = Form1.Elements("Text1").Value
```

An example

At this point, you may be confused. Why would anyone ever want to refer to a control by its position rather than by its name? Well, occasionally using *index numbers* has its advantages. Here's an example that demonstrates when you may want to avoid using names:

```
<FORM NAME=Form1>
Month 1: <INPUT TYPE=Text NAME=Jan><BR>
Month 2: <INPUT TYPE=Text NAME=Feb><BR>
Month 3: <INPUT TYPE=Text NAME=Mar><BR>
Month 4: <INPUT TYPE=Text NAME=Apr><BR>
Month 5: <INPUT TYPE=Text NAME=May><BR>
Month 6: <INPUT TYPE=Text NAME=Jun><BR>
<INPUT TYPE=Button Name=Button1 Value=Send>
</FORM>
```

The preceding HTML code generates a form with six text controls and a button (see Figure 13-3). The user is expected to make an entry in each field. A subroutine performs simple validation when the user clicks the Send button. The VBScript code needs to check each field to make sure that none of them is empty.

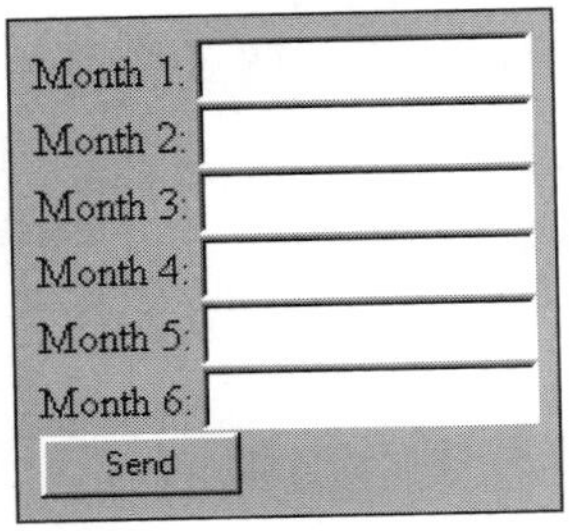

Figure 13-3:
This form
has six text
controls.

Month 1: [   ]
Month 2: [   ]
Month 3: [   ]
Month 4: [   ]
Month 5: [   ]
Month 6: [   ]
[Send]

Following is the Button1_OnClick subroutine, which uses a For-Next loop to examine each text control. If any of these controls is empty, the subroutine assigns False to the DataOK variable. The result? If any of the fields is empty, the user receives an appropriate message. Otherwise, the message box displays *Thanks!*:

```
Sub Button1_OnClick()
    DataOK = True
    For i = 0 to 5
        If Form1.Elements(i).Value = "" Then DataOK=False
    Next
    If Not DataOk Then
        Msgbox "Please complete all fields"
    Else
        Msgbox "Thanks!"
    End If
End Sub
```

Referring to controls by using an index number offers a big advantage: You don't need to write code to check each item separately. Here's how the routine is written using the control names:

```
Sub Button1_OnClick()
    DataOK = True
    If Form1.Jan.Value = "" Then DataOK=False
    If Form1.Feb.Value = "" Then DataOK=False
    If Form1.Mar.Value = "" Then DataOK=False
    If Form1.Apr.Value = "" Then DataOK=False
    If Form1.May.Value = "" Then DataOK=False
    If Form1.Jun.Value = "" Then DataOK=False
    If Not DataOk Then
        Msgbox "Please complete all fields"
    Else
        Msgbox "Thanks!"
    End If
End Sub
```

Using object variables

In Chapter 8, I touch on the topic of *object variables*. An object variable is a variable that holds an object, such as a check box or a select control. You can't simply assign an object to a variable. You use the Set keyword to create an object variable. Following is a VBScript statement that creates an object variable named UserText:

```
Set UserText = Form1.Text1
```

After you define the object variable, you can use it in place of the complete reference to the object. For example, to display the text contained in Form1.Text, you can use the following code:

```
Msgbox UserText.Value
```

Using an object variable can simplify your coding. Several examples in this chapter use object variables.

Generating Forms and Controls with VBScript

In this section, I discuss how you can use VBScript to generate the controls within a form. The trick involves using the Document.Write method to send HTML code to the current document or to a document in another frame.

Generating alphabet radio buttons

Figure 13-4 shows a Web page that displays 26 radio buttons, one for each letter of the English alphabet. Writing the HTML code to produce these controls is not difficult, but doing so is tedious. In my book of rules, when a task is tedious, you need to let the computer do the work.

Following is the VBScript code that produces the 26 radio buttons. Standard HTML code defines the form, and a simple VBScript For-Next loop generates the additional HTML code to produce the 26 controls:

```
<FORM NAME=Form1>
<SCRIPT LANGUAGE=VBScript>
For i = 65 to 90
    Document.Write "<INPUT TYPE=Radio>" & Chr(i)
    Document.Write "<BR>"
Next
</SCRIPT>
</FORM>
```

The loop starts at 65, ASCII code for the letter A, and ends with 90, ASCII code for the letter Z. Refer to "The Chr function" in Chapter 10 for more about ASCII code.

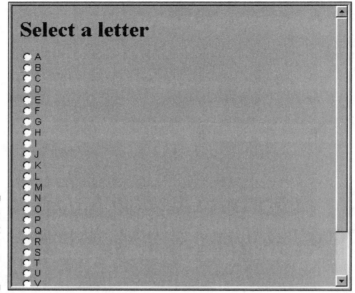

Figure 13-4:
VBScript
generated
these radio
buttons.

Generating a list of numbers

Figure 13-5 shows a Web page that contains a select control with 1,500 options — integers from 1 to 1,500. Nobody wants to write the HTML code to generate this control. But, as you can see in the following listing, using VBScript to generate the <OPTION> tags makes generating this control a piece of cake.

Figure 13-5:
This select
control
has 1,500
options —
thanks to
VBScript.

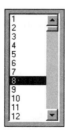

```
<FORM NAME=Form1>
<SELECT NAME=Number SIZE=12>
<SCRIPT LANGUAGE=VBScript>
For i = 1 to 1500
```

```
    Document.Write "<OPTION> " & i
Next
</SCRIPT>
</SELECT>
</FORM>
```

Generating a list of dates for the current month

Figure 13-6 shows an HTML document that has a select control. The options in this control consist of each day of the current month. So, the number of options varies, depending upon the month.

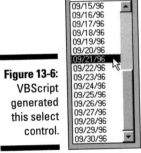

Figure 13-6:
VBScript
generated
this select
control.

The following listing shows the VBScript code that generates the select control.

```
<FORM NAME=Form1>
<SELECT NAME=Dates SIZE=1>
<OPTION SELECTED> Select a Date
<SCRIPT LANGUAGE=VBScript>
ThisMonth = Month(Now())
ThisYear = Year(Now())
TheDay= DateSerial(ThisYear,ThisMonth,1)
Do While Month(TheDay) = ThisMonth
    Document.Write "<OPTION> " & TheDay
    TheDay=TheDay + 1
Loop
</SCRIPT>
</SELECT>
</FORM>
```

The preceding example uses standard HTML code to generate the form and *begin* creating the select control. VBScript kicks in when you need to put in the <OPTION> tags. It uses a Do While Loop construct (refer to Chapter 9) to generate each date in the current month. The loop starts with the first day of the current month and ends when the month of the date is no longer equal to the current month.

This technique has two advantages:

- ✔ The select control always displays the dates for the current month, so you don't need to edit the document each month.

- ✔ Eliminating the need to enter all the <OPTION> tags manually saves you time.

Client-Side Data Validation

For many people, the key selling point of VBScript is its ability to perform client-side validation of HTML forms. Traditionally, form validation was performed entirely on the server side. When a user completed a form, the form was submitted back to the server. At the server site, a CGI program determined whether the entries were valid. If not, the server sent the form back to be modified. This process not only used extra bandwidth, but also slowed things down considerably.

With a scripting language like VBScript, form validation can be performed before the form is actually submitted to the server. In other words, the data headed for the server is validated using code contained in the HTML document. The results are a faster response time, less bandwidth usage, and less work for the server, which may already be overloaded.

What gets validated?

The types of validation needed depend entirely on the form's use. Here are a few examples that may strike a familiar chord:

- ✔ **If a text field must be completed, make sure that the field is not empty.** You can verify that a text field is not empty by checking to see whether the control's Value property equals "" (an empty string) or whether its length is 0.

- ✔ **If the user is required to make a selection from a set of radio buttons, make sure that a button is actually selected.** Sometimes you may be able to bypass this check by setting a default button (such as *no response*) that is selected when the form loads.

- **If the user is required to enter a date, make sure that the entry is actually a date.** You can use the VBScript IsDate function to verify that the entry is a date.

- **If the user is required to enter a value, make sure that the entry is actually a value.** You can use the VBScript IsNumeric function for this validation. You also may need to ensure that the value is not negative, or that it's within a certain numerical range.

- **If the user is required to enter a credit card number, make sure that the card number is valid.** You can use my CreditCard function to validate the card number (see Chapter 15).

- **If the user is required to enter a specific type of information, such as a full name, you can do checks to improve the chances that the data is valid.** For example, if a full name is required, you can check for the existence of at least one space character.

The preceding examples demonstrate the more common types of data validation. The exact method that you use depends, of course, on your data.

The OnSubmit event

After the user completes the form, he can submit it to the server using one of two methods:

- Clicking the Submit button for the form.
- Pressing Enter.

Either action generates an onSubmit event for the form. Validating a form's contents consists of doing checks when the onSubmit event occurs. Depending on the outcome of these checks, your code does one of two things:

- Cancels the submit event by setting the Submit event to False
- Allows the submit event to occur by setting the Submit event to True

---

A word about the examples

The examples in this chapter that use the `<FORM>` tag omit one key component for this tag: the `ACTION` attribute. This attribute points to a URL (often a CGI program) that handles the values submitted. Therefore (with one exception), these examples do not actually submit any data. If you adapt these examples for you own use, you need to supply the URL for the `ACTION` attribute.

The easiest way to validate a form's contents is to use a function to handle the onSubmit event and place your validation code inside the function.

Here's a simple example that validates a form called MyForm, which contains a single text control named Text1. The function checks to see whether Text1 is empty. If so, the function cancels the onSubmit event. If Text1 is not empty, the form is submitted.

```
<SCRIPT LANGUAGE=VBScript>
Function MyForm_OnSubmit()
    If MyForm.Text1.Value = "" Then
        MsgBox "You must enter some text!"
        MyForm_OnSubmit = False
        Exit Function
    End If
    MyForm_OnSubmit = True
    Msgbox "Thanks for the info"
End Function
```

Notice that the name of the subroutine is the form's name, followed by an underscore and *OnSubmit*. This function executes when the user clicks the Submit button or presses Enter.

Note: You can write code that executes the Submit method for a form. For example, the following statement, when executed, submits a form named OrderForm (and also triggers the onSubmit event):

```
OrderForm.Submit
```

Validating a form: Example one

Take a look at Figure 13-7, which shows a simple form in a Web page. The user is expected to enter two values: name and birth date.

Here's the HTML code that produces the form:

```
<FORM NAME=Form1>
Name:<BR>
<INPUT Type=text, NAME=UserName><BR>
Birthday:<BR>
<INPUT Type=text, NAME=Birthday><BR>
<P>
<INPUT Type=Submit><BR>
</FORM>
```

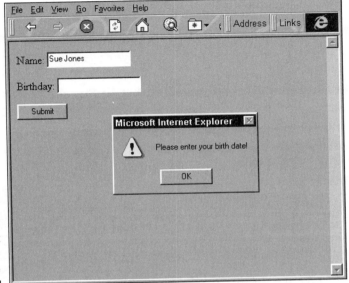

Figure 13-7:
A simple
form that
must be
validated.

Following is the event handler subroutine that executes when the user clicks the Submit button or presses Enter. This subroutine ensures that valid data is entered into the two input fields.

```
<SCRIPT LANGUAGE=VBScript>
Function Form1_OnSubmit()
    If Form1.UserName.Value = "" then
        Alert "Please enter your name!"
        Form1_OnSubmit=False
        Exit Function
    End If
    If Form1.BirthDay.Value = "" then
        Alert "Please enter your birth date!"
        Form1_OnSubmit=False
        Exit Function
    End If
    If Not IsDate(Form1.BirthDay.Value) Then
        Alert "You entered an invalid birthday!"
        Form1_OnSubmit=False
        Exit Function
    End If
    Form1_OnSubmit=True
    Alert "Thanks for the information!"
End Function
</SCRIPT>
```

The subroutine does three validation steps:

1. **The subroutine checks to make sure that the Name field is not blank.**

   If the field is blank, the subroutine displays a message and cancels the onSubmit event.

2. **The subroutine checks to make sure that the Birthday field is not blank.**

   If the field is blank, the subroutine displays a message and cancels the onSubmit event.

3. **The subroutine uses the IsDate function to ensure that the Birthday field contains a valid date.**

   If the field doesn't contain a valid date, the subroutine displays a message and cancels the onSubmit event.

If the form passes all three tests, the form is submitted, and the user gets a thank-you message.

Validating a form: Example two

Figure 13-8 shows a simple, but quite attractive, form designed to create and send an e-mail message. The information in this form needs to be validated before it is sent.

Note: If you load the example from this book's disk, be aware that it's a real, live working example. In other words, the information in the form will actually be sent to a Web server, converted to an e-mail message, and sent to the author of this book. You must be online to send the e-mail. If you want to adapt this form for your own use, you can modify the reference to the CGI program that receives and processes the information. Contact your Internet service provider for details. Your provider probably has a similar program available.

The names of the elements in this form, named Form1, are listed in Table 13-1.

Table 13-1	Elements in Form1
Name	*Control Type*
Subject	A text control
ReturnMail	A text control
Message	A textarea control
Reply	A checkbox control
Clear	A reset button
Send	A submit button

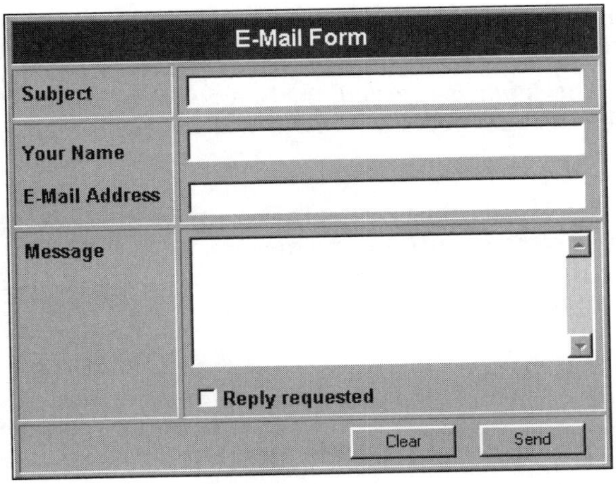

Figure 13-8:
This form
needs to be
validated
before the
information
is sent.

When the user clicks the Send button or presses Enter, an OnSubmit event is generated. The OnSubmit event executes the following validation function:

```
Function Form1_OnSubmit()
'    Check for an empty message
    If Form1.Message.Value="" then
        Alert "You don't want to send a blank message, do
            you?"
        Form1_OnSubmit = False
        Exit Function
    End If
'    Make sure email address is provided if reply is requested
    If Form1.Reply.Checked = "True" Then
        If Form1.ReturnMail.Value="" Then
            Msg = "If you want a reply to this message "
            Msg = Msg & "you must provide your e-mail address."
            Alert Msg
            Form1_OnSubmit = False
            Exit Function
        End If
    End If
    Form1_OnSubmit = True
End Function
```

Using this function, only the critical fields get validated. In fact, the function makes only two checks:

> ✔ **It makes sure the Message field is not empty.** There's no point in sending an empty message.
>
> ✔ **If the Reply check box is checked, the function verifies that the ReturnMail text box is not empty.** (An e-mail address is required for a reply.)

If either of these checks fails, the user gets a descriptive message (see Figure 13-9), the onSubmit event is canceled, and the form is not submitted. If the form passes both tests, the information is sent to the server where it is converted into e-mail and sent to the author of this book — me!

Figure 13-9:
An example of a message displayed if form data is not valid.

Using Form Controls For a Link List

The companion disk contains an example that demonstrates yet another way to use VBScript with forms. In this example, the form holds controls that let the user select a hyperlink in a particular category.

Figure 13-10 shows a document that contains radio buttons, a select control, and a button control. The radio buttons display three categories of links.

Figure 13-10:
Providing a list of links in a select control.

When the user selects a category, the select control displays a list of links in the selected category. The user selects a link and then clicks the button to load the URL for that link. This method of listing links is useful because it provides a very compact way to present a large number of links.

If you spend any time working with the select control, you probably know that you cannot change the options in the control after the page is loaded. So how, you may ask, does clicking a radio button change the options in the select control? The answer is VBScript. In this example, VBScript writes the HTML code to a floating frame that holds the select control. The HTML code creates the select control on the fly. The result is a select control that appears to do the impossible. Chalk another one up for the magic of VBScript.

If you're interested in using this technique, I urge you to view the source document on the companion disk.

Chapter 14

Working with Frames

In This Chapter

▶ How frames fit into the object model

▶ Referring to objects in a different frame

▶ Clever ideas involving borderless frames

▶ Using the SetTimeOut method as a timer

More and more Web sites these days make use of frames. Using frames allows the Web page designer to display more than one document at a time — each document in a different frame. Like them or not, frames have become a pervasive part of the World Wide Web. I don't get into the various philosophies about using frames in Web pages, because people usually love 'em or hate 'em, but I do tell you all you need know about accessing frames with VBScript. For more information about how frames and Web pages fit together, refer to my discussion of the object model in Chapter 5.

Frames: Not Just For Pictures Anymore

In Chapter 5, I point out that a Frame object is contained in the Window object. I also mention that a Frame object is a member of the Frames collection, and that frames are numbered beginning with 0: Frames(0) is the first frame, Frames(1) is the second frame, and so on.

A Frame Object is much like a Window object because a frame can hold only one Document object. But a Document object in a Frame can contain other frames that hold other Document objects. If your head is spinning, don't despair. Work with this stuff long enough, and it can make perfect sense.

In terms of objects, here's an example of a typical hierarchy. The Window object contains two Frame objects, and each Frame object holds a Document object:

```
The Window object
  Document object
    Frame object #1
      Document object
    Frame object #2
      Document object
```

A Frame Example

To get the ball rolling, I start out with an example. The following HTML code creates two vertical frames, each of which occupies 50 percent of the browser window:

```
<HTML>
<HEAD>
<TITLE>Frame Maker</TITLE>
</HEAD>
<BODY>
<FRAMESET COLS="50%,50%">
  <FRAME SRC="left.htm" NAME="LeftFrame">
  <FRAME SRC="right.htm" NAME="RightFrame">
</FRAMESET>
</BODY>
</HTML>
```

Figure 14-1 shows how the browser looks when the document that creates the frames loads.

In this example, the left frame is named LeftFrame and contains a document named left.htm, which contains a button. The document is listed in the following. Notice that no subroutine handles the button's OnClick event. I show you how to handle the event in the next section.

```
<HTML>
<HEAD>
<TITLE>Left Frame</TITLE>
</HEAD>
<BODY>
<H1>Left Frame</H1>
<INPUT Type=Button Name=Test Value="Click Me">
</BODY>
</HTML>
```

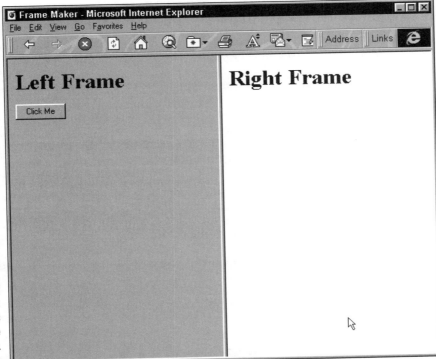

Figure 14-1:
Two frames,
each of
which
occupies
half of the
window.

The right frame is named RightFrame and contains the right.htm document, which has a background color of FFFFFF (white).

Here's the complete listing of right.htm:

```
<HTML>
<HEAD>
<TITLE>Right Frame</TITLE>
</HEAD>
<BODY BGCOLOR=White>
<H1>Right Frame</H1>
</BODY>
</HTML>
```

Referring to a different frame

Now, the question is whether VBScript code in a frame can refer to another frame. The answer must be yes — otherwise, I wouldn't have posed the question.

To demonstrate communication within the frame, add the following subroutine to the left.htm document:

```
Sub Test_OnClick()
    Alert Parent.Frames(1).Document.Bgcolor
End Sub
```

This subroutine is an event handler for the button. Clicking the button displays an alert box that shows the background color of the document in the right frame. Figure 14-2 proves that the subroutine works (the alert box displays #ffffff, which is the hex code for the color white).

Although the Alert statement works, you may be wondering *why* it works. Take another look at what is displayed by the Alert statement:

```
Parent.Frames(1).Document.Bgcolor
```

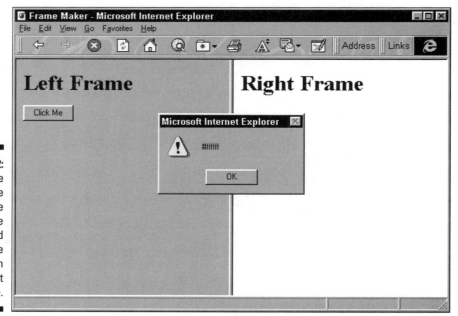

Figure 14-2:
Clicking the
button in the
left frame
displays the
background
color of the
document in
the right
frame.

Here's what's going on, from left to right:

- ✔ Parent returns the Window object, because the Window object is the parent of the document in the left frame.

- ✔ Frames(1) returns the second member of the frames collection in the Windows object. Remember, frames are numbered beginning with 0, so the left frame is frame 0 and the right frame is frame 1.

- ✔ Document returns the document contained in the right frame.

- ✔ Bgcolor returns the background color of the document in the right frame.

Other ways to refer to a frame

Using the frame's index number, beginning with 0, is only one way to refer to a frame. You also can use the frame's name in place of the index number:

```
Alert Parent.Frames("RightFrame").Document.Bgcolor
```

Or you can use the following statement:

```
Alert Parent.Frames.RightFrame.Document.Bgcolor
```

Either statement performs exactly like the original statement.

```
Alert Parent.Frames(1).Document.Bgcolor
```

Still confused?

This book's disk includes an example that may clear things up for you. As you can see in Figure 14-3, the example uses two frames. Clicking any button in the left frame displays an alert box that displays a particular item. For example, click the button for Parent.Location.Href, and the alert box displays the Href property of the Location object for the frame's parent. In other words, the alert box displays the URL for the document that created the frames.

If you're confused about referring to other objects, I urge you to try out the preceding example and click buttons. I guarantee that this experience reduces, or maybe even eliminates, confusion.

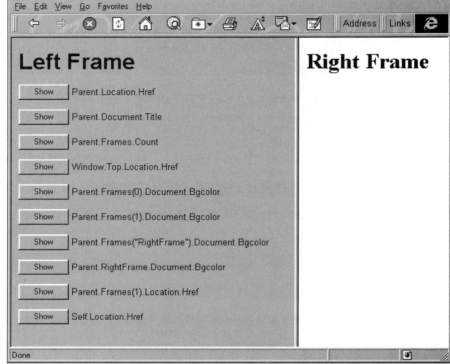

Figure 14-3:
This example demonstrates various aspects of the object model.

Another Frame Example

In this section, I present another example to demonstrate how to refer to objects involving frames.

The following listing is an HTML document named loader.htm, which generates three frames, as shown in Figure 14-4. Using three frames is a relatively common arrangement you can see frequently while cruising the Web. The top frame typically holds a logo or banner. The left frame often holds hyperlinks, which load a particular page into the frame on the right.

```
<HTML>
<HEAD>
</HEAD>
<BODY>
<FRAMESET ROWS="15percent,85percent">
  <FRAME SRC="top.htm" NAME="TopFrame">
  <FRAMESET COLS="15percent,85percent">
  <FRAME SRC="left.htm" NAME="LeftFrame">
  <FRAME SRC="doc0.htm" NAME="RightFrame">
</FRAMESET>
</FRAMESET>
</BODY>
</HTML>
```

Notice that each frame has its own HTML source document and a name
(TopFrame, LeftFrame, and RightFrame).

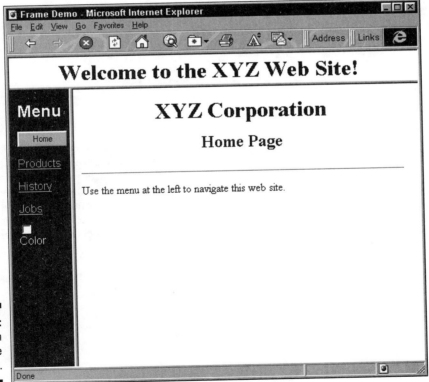

Figure 14-4:
A common
three-frame
setup.

Refer back to Figure 14-4 and notice that the document in the left frame displays a button, three hyperlinks, and a check box. These objects are set up as follows:

- ✔ Clicking the button loads the home page (the original document, or doc0.htm) into the right frame.
- ✔ Clicking the first hyperlink loads doc1.htm into the right frame.
- ✔ Clicking the second hyperlink loads doc2.htm into the right frame.
- ✔ Clicking the third hyperlink loads doc3.htm into the right frame.
- ✔ The check box determines whether colors are used in the top frame.

I discuss each of these elements in the following sections.

Using a button to load a URL into a different frame

You may be interested in the event handler for the button object. Clicking the button loads the home page (doc0.htm) into the right frame. Here's the code:

```
<SCRIPT LANGUAGE=VBScript>
Sub HomeButton_OnClick()
    Parent.Frames(2).Location.Href="doc0.htm"
End Sub
</SCRIPT>
```

Remember, the VBScript code for the button is contained in the left.htm document, which is loaded into the left frame. The parent object for the left.htm Document object is the Window object, so using Parent returns a reference to the Window object. The Window object contains a Frames collection, and the third member of the Frames collection (with an index number of 2) is the frame named RightFrame. The Location property of the Frame object returns the Location object, and the statement is setting this object's Href property — which determines the document to load.

Here are two more ways to load a new document into the frame. These methods use the frame's name rather than its index number:

```
Parent.Frames("RightFrame").Location.Href="doc0.htm"
Parent.RightFrame.Location.Href="doc0.htm"
```

Loading a URL into a different frame by using a hyperlink

The hyperlinks in the left frame don't use any VBScript — the documents are loaded into the frame using pure HTML. Here's the HTML code that generates the hyperlinks:

```
<A HREF=doc1.htm TARGET="RightFrame">Products</A><P>
<A HREF=doc2.htm TARGET="RightFrame">History</A><P>
<A HREF=doc3.htm TARGET="RightFrame">Jobs</A><P>
```

Notice that I use the name of the frame as the target for the hyperlink.

Changing the colors in a different frame

The final item in the left frame, the check box, demonstrates how to change properties of an object in another frame. In this case, the check box determines the background color and foreground color of the Document object in the Frame object named TopFrame. Here's the HTML that generates the check box:

```
<FORM NAME=Form1>
  <INPUT Type=Checkbox Name="BannerColor">Color
</FORM>
```

Here's the event handler subroutine for the check box, which is contained in left.htm. This subroutine executes when the check box is clicked:

```
Sub BannerColor_OnClick()
    Select Case Document.Form1.BannerColor.Checked
        Case "True"
            Parent.TopFrame.Document.Bgcolor="FF0000"
            Parent.TopFrame.Document.Fgcolor="FFFF00"
        Case "False"
            Parent.TopFrame.Document.Bgcolor="FFFFFF"
            Parent.TopFrame.Document.Fgcolor="000000"
    End Select
End Sub
```

The preceding routine uses a Select Case structure to take action, based on whether the check box is checked. The referencing is similar to that used for the button click previously described. If the check box is checked, the colors of the document in the top frame are changed to red (FF0000) and yellow (FFFF00). If the check box is not checked, the colors are set to black (FFFFFF) and white (000000).

The following statements refer to the document in the top frame and produce the same effect:

```
Parent.Frames("TopFrame").Document.BgColor="FF0000"
Parent.Frames(0).Document.BgColor="FF0000"
```

More Ways to Load Documents

In this section, I demonstrate more ways to load a document when frames are involved.

Figure 14-5 shows an example, which is available on this book's disk. This example demonstrates several useful techniques that involve loading documents.

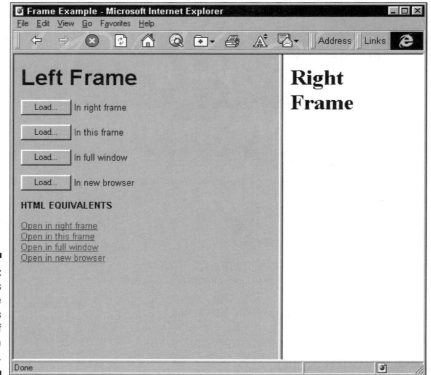

Figure 14-5:
This
example
demonstrates
ways of
loading a
document.

In the sections that follow, refer to Figure 14-5 for reference. The left frame, frame 0, is named LeftFrame. The right frame, frame 1, is named RightFrame. The examples in the following sections are VBScript statements that are contained in the document in the left frame.

Loading a document in another frame

Following are three different ways to load a document named newdoc.htm into the right frame. These statements have the exact same effect:

```
Parent.Frames("RightFrame").Location.Href="newdoc.htm"
```

```
Parent.Frames(1).Location.Href="newdoc.htm"
```

```
Parent.RightFrame.Location.Href="newdoc.htm"
```

The preceding VBScript statements are equivalent to the following HTML code:

```
<A HREF="newdoc.htm" TARGET="RightFrame">Open newdoc.htm</A>
```

Loading a new document in the current frame

Following are five different ways to load a document named newdoc.htm into the current frame (LeftFrame). These statements have the exact same effect:

```
Parent.Frames("LeftFrame").Location.Href="newdoc.htm"
```

```
Parent.Frames(0).Location.Href="newdoc.htm"
```

```
Parent.LeftFrame.Location.Href="newdoc.htm"
```

```
Self.Location.Href="newdoc.htm"
```

```
Window.Location.Href="newdoc.htm"
```

The preceding VBScript statements are equivalent to the following HTML code:

```
<A HREF="newdoc.htm" TARGET="_self">Open newdoc.htm</A>
```

Loading a document in the browser's full window

Following are three ways to load a document named newdoc.htm into the browser's window, which replaces the current document. These statements have the exact same effect:

```
Parent.Location.Href="newdoc.htm"
```

```
Parent.Navigate "newdoc.htm"
```

```
Top.Location.Href="newdoc.htm"
```

You also can get the same effect if you use either of the following lines of HTML code:

```
<A HREF="newdoc.htm" TARGET="_top">Open newdoc.htm</A>
```

```
<A HREF="newdoc.htm" TARGET="_parent">Open newdoc.htm</A>
```

Note: Using "_parent" as the TARGET attribute for the <A> tag opens the document in the parent of the current frame. In this case, using "_parent" as the TARGET attribute has the same effect as using "_top" as the TARGET attribute because the frame's parent is the Window object. If the frame is contained in another frame, "_parent" returns the containing frame, not the Window object.

Loading a document in a new browser window

The following statement opens the newdoc.htm document in a new browser window. It uses the Open method of the Window object:

```
Window.Open "newdoc.htm", "Window Name"
```

You also can open the document by using the following HTML code:

```
<A HREF="newdoc.htm" TARGET="_blank">Open newdoc.htm</A>
```

Floating Frames

One of the perennial problems Web page designers face is creating interactive pages — pages that respond to user actions. As you can find out in this section, VBScript and *floating frames* provide an excellent solution to this problem.

Before VBScript and floating frames existed, if you wanted to display new information in response to a user's action, you had only two possibilities:

- **Display another document:** This document can be existing, or it can be generated on the fly by a CGI program. In either case, an irritating delay almost always occurs before the document is visible to the user.

- **Display the information in a text control or textarea control:** These two controls are the only intrinsic HTML elements that can be changed while they are on-screen. Disadvantages? You have no control over the appearance of the text — it's just plain old text in a white box, and the user can easily edit or erase the information in a text or textarea control.

Microsoft Internet Explorer 3.0 provides floating frames as a solution. Floating frames are useful because they can appear anywhere in a document. A normal frame must occupy at least one side of the window. A floating frame, on the other hand, can float anywhere in the document. And a floating frame can be borderless. If the floating frame's background color is the same as the main document's background color, the frame blends in perfectly and appears to be part of the document.

The fact that a frame can appear anywhere, and without a border, provides you with great new possibilities. For example, a Web page can appear as if it is being changed dynamically in response to a user's actions. To do so, you generate HTML code with your VBScript and then send the code to the floating frame using the Document.Write method.

Updating a page dynamically with a floating frame

To demonstrate the potential of using a floating frame, a simple example that calculates the total price of an order of widgets is shown in Figure 14-6. The document consists of a simple form, including a text control and a button. The floating frame is located directly below the controls and has no frame, so it blends in with the document.

The user enters a quantity into the text box and clicks the button. The total price is written to the document in the floating frame. To the user, it appears as if the document itself is being updated, which is impossible.

The HTML document

Here's the entire HTML document:

```
<HTML>
<HEAD>
<TITLE>Chapter 15 Example</TITLE>
<SCRIPT LANGUAGE=VBScript>
Sub Calc_OnClick()
    On Error Resume Next
    Price=19.95
    Q = Document.Form1.Quantity.Value
    TotalCost= Q * Price
    msg = "<BODY BGCOLOR=" & Document.BgColor & "><B>"
    msg = msg & "The total price for " & Q & " widgets is $"
    msg = msg & TotalCost & "."
    Parent.Frames(0).Document.Write msg
    Parent.Frames(0).Document.Close
End Sub
</SCRIPT>
</HEAD>
<BODY>
<H1>Widget Price Calculator</H1>
<HR>
The current price of a widget is $19.95. Specify how many
you would like to order, then click the Calc button.
<FORM Name=Form1>
<B>Quantity:</B>
<INPUT TYPE=Text NAME=Quantity Value=0 SIZE=5>
<INPUT TYPE=Button NAME=Calc Value=" Calc! ">
</FORM>
<IFRAME SRC="priceinfo.htm" WIDTH=600 HEIGHT=100 FRAMEBORDER=0>
</IFRAME>
</BODY>
</HTML>
```

Note: Using this document requires an additional empty document, named priceinfo.htm — which is used as the source document for the floating frame.

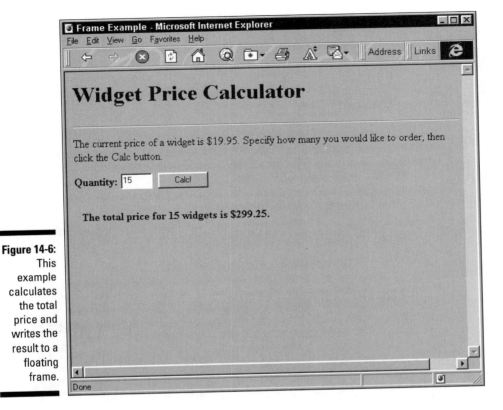

Figure 14-6:
This example calculates the total price and writes the result to a floating frame.

How it works

I use Parent.Frames(0) to refer to the floating frame (which doesn't have a name). The Document.Write statements simply send HTML code to the frame. Notice that I use Document.Close to close the document after writing to it. If you omit this statement, subsequent text is appended to the document.

Note: To keep it simple, I don't do any type of error checking in the preceding example. Rather, I use the On Error Resume Next statement to handle errors by ignoring them. So, for example, if you enter a non-numeric entry into the text box, you don't get an error message, but the results shown in the floating frame are meaningless.

A more sophisticated borderless frame example

Figure 14-7 shows a more sophisticated example of writing HTML to a borderless frame. In this example, clicking an option button writes a description of that option to the frame.

The document and the VBScript code are quite straightforward. You can examine the source document (which is included on the companion disk) on your own to see how it works. Here are a few things to note:

- ✔ The document uses a two-dimensional array (see Chapter 8) to hold the option button text and the descriptions.

- ✔ VBScript code generates HTML code that creates the option buttons (see Chapter 13 for details on this technique).

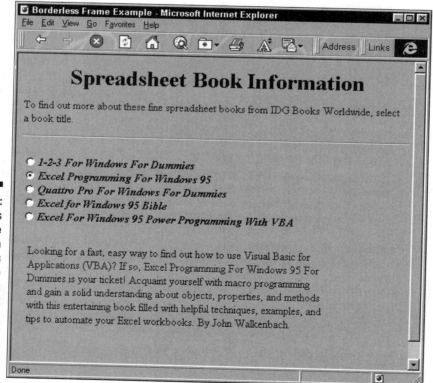

Figure 14-7: This example uses a borderless frame to update the document when the user clicks an option button.

✔ The application is very easy to modify. For example, adding new options requires no additional programming. Simply extend the array and enter new text and descriptions.

✔ Because all information is stored in the computer's memory, clicking an option button results in a virtually instantaneous display of information. A new document isn't loaded.

Fun With Floating Frames

As with most things related to the World Wide Web, frames also have a lighter side. In this section, I present three less serious examples that demonstrate a few things you can do with floating frames.

Simple animation effects

Web site developers like the idea of movement on their pages, which accounts for the widespread use of scrolling marquees and animated GIF files. As you'll see, you can use VBScript to add life to a dead page. The example in this section demonstrates how to change the colors of floating frames in a continuous loop. If you set things up right, this type of animation can be a pretty slick effect.

The example of changing colors is shown in Figure 14-8. Because IDG Books hasn't yet figured out a way to display movement in its book pages, you need to load the document into your browser to see it in action.

The page contains two small floating frames, one on either side of the heading. Each frame contains a different document, and each document displays only one word, either *VBScript* or *Enhanced*. The VBScript code in the main document reverses the foreground and background colors of the documents in the frames, twice per second. The visual effect is that of a colored box moving back and forth across the page.

The example uses the SetTimeOut method. This method executes a subroutine after a specified time period has elapsed. SetTimeOut takes three arguments:

✔ *Procedure:* The procedure to execute when the specified delay has elapsed.

✔ *Delay:* The time to wait before the procedure executes. This time is expressed in milliseconds, where 1,000 milliseconds equal one second.

✔ *Language:* The language the procedure is written in, which is VBScript.

If you're interested in this type of effect, consult the source document for the example file.

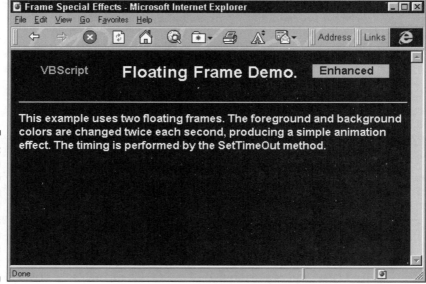

Figure 14-8:
This page
uses two
floating
frames, and
the colors
change in a
continuous
loop.

A VBScript message flasher

Internet Explorer supports the `<MARQUEE>` tag, which displays a moving message on the Web page. In this example, I present an alternative: a message flasher. This example displays a series of messages in a floating frame. You can display as many messages as you like for a specific amount of time. You also can control the color of each message.

Figure 14-9 shows an example of the message flasher. When you look at the figure, just use your imagination and pretend that you see multiple messages flashing. The following HTML code generates the floating frame:

```
<IFRAME SRC=empty.htm WIDTH=380 HEIGHT=30 FRAMEBORDER=No></
          IFRAME>
```

Message flasher code

When the document is opened, the following Window_On load subroutine executes. This routine defines the messages and the color for each message using a two-dimensional array named Msg. Notice that three global variables are available in all procedures: Msg, the array; MsgNum, which keeps track of which message is being displayed; and MsgDelay, which determines how long to display the messages.

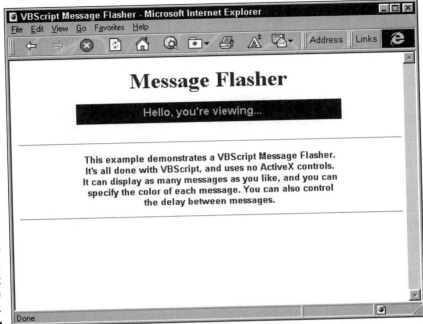

Figure 14-9:
VBScript
message
flasher.

```
<SCRIPT LANGUAGE="VBScript">
Dim Msg(4,1)
Dim MsgNum
Dim MsgDelay
Sub Window_OnLoad()
    Msg(0,0)="Hello, you're viewing..."
    Msg(0,1)="#00ff00"
    Msg(1,0)="...a VBScript Message Flasher!"
    Msg(1,1)="#ff0000"
    Msg(2,0)="It uses a floating frame."
    Msg(2,1)="#ff00ff"
    Msg(3,0)="Pretty cool, huh?"
    Msg(3,1)="#ffff00"
    Msg(4,0)="The message will now repeat."
    Msg(4,1)="#00ffff"
    MsgDelay=2000 '2 seconds
    MsgNum=0
    Call ChangeMessage()
End Sub
</SCRIPT>
```

The Msg array stores the message text in its first dimension and the hex color code in its second dimension.

The MsgDelay variable holds the number of milliseconds to display each message. Before the subroutine ends, the following ChangeMessage subroutine is called:

```
Sub ChangeMessage()
    Set MsgFrame=Document.Frames(0).Document
    MsgFrame.Write "<BODY BGCOLOR=Black TOPMARGIN=5>"
    MsgFrame.Write "<B><CENTER>"
    MsgFrame.Write "<FONT FACE=ARIAL SIZE=3 COLOR="
    MsgFrame.Write Msg(MsgNum,1) & ">"
    MsgFrame.Write Msg(MsgNum,0)
    MsgFrame.Close
    ID=SetTimeOut("ChangeMessage",MsgDelay,"VBscript")
    MsgNum=MsgNum+1
    If MsgNum = Ubound(Msg,1)+1 Then MsgNum=0
End Sub
```

The ChangeMessage subroutine starts by declaring an object variable to represent the floating frame. A series of statements uses the Write method to generate HTML code and sends the code to the floating frame. For example, when MsgNum is 0, the following HTML code is written to the frame:

```
<BODY BGCOLOR=Black TOPMARGIN=5>
<B><CENTER>
<FONT FACE=ARIAL SIZE=3 COLOR=#00ff00>
"Hello, you're viewing..."
```

After the HTML code is sent to the document in the frame, the ChangeMessage subroutine uses the SetTimeOut method to schedule another call to the ChangeMessage subroutine. The delay between calls is determined by the value of MsgDelay, which is set in the Window_OnLoad subroutine. Finally, the MsgNum variable is incremented. If MsgNum is greater than the number of messages, then it's set to 0 — which makes the messages repeat forever, or until the user opens a new document.

Customizing the message flasher

The message flasher example is easy to customize. You can easily change the messages and add new messages. If you add new messages, simply make sure that the Msg array is dimensioned to correspond to the number of messages.

Frame animation — big time!

The example in this section is similar to the previous example, but much more impressive.

Figure 14-10 shows a browser window that uses nine (count 'em) frames. The only purpose for eight of these frames is to provide a colorful border for the center frame. But, being unsatisfied with simply a colorful border, I add slick animation effects using VBScript. When this document is loaded, the colors change rapidly in a marqueelike fashion.

If you don't try any other examples in the book, don't miss this one. You'll be amazed at its attention-grabbing effect.

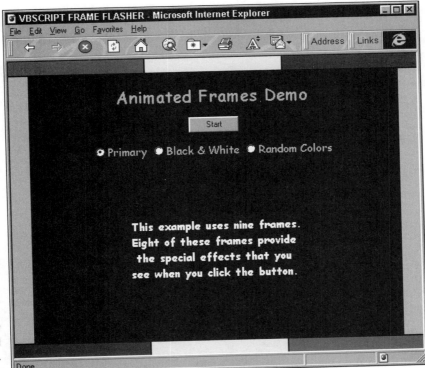

Figure 14-10:
This document uses nine highly animated frames.

Chapter 15

Useful Code Snippets
That You Can Steal

・・・・・・・・・・・・・・・・・・・・・・・・・・・・・・・・・・・・・

In This Chapter

▶ Descriptions of several useful VBScript procedures that you may find useful

▶ How to view and use the code

・・・・・・・・・・・・・・・・・・・・・・・・・・・・・・・・・・・・・

*I*t's been said that there's no such thing as a new idea. I'm not sure that the statement is true, but I do know that Web page designers often need to accomplish the same sorts of things someone else has already done. With that in mind, I developed several useful VBScript routines that you can adapt for your own use with little or no modification.

I describe these routines in this chapter, but I don't present the code (this book has a limited number of pages!). As always, you can view them and take what you want from this book's disk.

Number Formatting Functions

VBScript is a great programming language, but work with it long enough and you can find glaring omissions. For example, you may have noticed that VBScript doesn't provide a way to format numbers. The examples in this section present three custom formatting functions.

Formatting dollars and cents

My FormatDollars function displays a value in currency format: A dollar sign, and rounded to the nearest penny. Figure 15-1 shows a number displayed without using the FormatDollars function and an example of how the numbers appear after they're processed by the FormatDollars function.

After adding the FormatDollars function to your document, you can display a formatted value by using a VBScript statement like the following:

```
MsgBox "The net price is " & FormatDollars(NetPrice)
```

Figure 15-1:
Before and after using the Format Dollars Funciton.

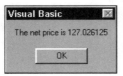
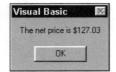

Formatting percentages

My FormatPct function displays a value formatted as a percentage. This function takes two arguments:

✔ The number to be formatted

✔ The number of decimal places to display

Figure 15-2 shows examples of numbers before and after they're processed by the FormatPercent function.

Using these functions in your HTML documents

If you find the functions in this chapter useful, feel free to use them in your own HTML pages. Here's how to do it:

1. Fire up Internet Explorer and open the file on the sample disk that contains the Chapter 15 examples.

2. Click the link for the document that contains the function you're interested in.

3. Choose the View➪Source command to display the entire HTML document in a separate window using Notepad.

4. Fire up your favorite editor and open the HTML document in which you want to use the function.

5. Activate the Notepad window that you opened in step 3.

6. Copy the function, which includes all the text beginning with `Function` and ending with `End Function`, and paste it to your document. The best place to paste it is within the `<HEAD>` and `</HEAD>` tags.

7. Modify your HTML code to use the function. You may want to study the original document to get some tips.

Number	Output of the FormatPercent Function
.1972 (2)	19.72%
1 (0)	100%
.99723223 (1)	99.7%
-.9976 (2)	-99.76%
1.01 (4)	101.0000%
.87723232 (5)	87.72323%
.23 (5)	23.00000%
Non-Number	INVALID

Figure 15-2: Displaying a value as a percentage with the Format Percent function.

Spelling out numeric values

The DollarText function takes one argument, a number, and returns a text string that spells out the numbers in English, using dollars and cents. Here's an example of how to use DollarText:

```
Msgbox DollarText(134.7842)
```

Figure 15-3 shows an example of the DollarText function. The value is rounded to the nearest penny.

Figure 15-3: The DollarText function.

One Hundred Thirty-Four Dollars and Seventy-Eight Cents

Note: Steve Mark developed this function. The DollarText function is truly a fine piece of coding and is not easy to write — I tried to write such a function and gave up. Steve wrote the function for use in the Excel Visual Basic for Applications language. I made a few modifications, and it runs like a charm in VBScript. Thanks to Steve for allowing me to share it with the world.

Displaying a Friendly Date and Time

VBScript makes displaying the current date and time in a document very easy. In fact, a single statement that uses the Now function does the job:

```
Document.Write "Today is " & Now()
```

Figure 15-4 shows the result of executing the statement. Although the Now function is quite functional, the output format looks like something that came from a computer and is not exactly friendly. Besides, who really needs to have the time displayed to the second?

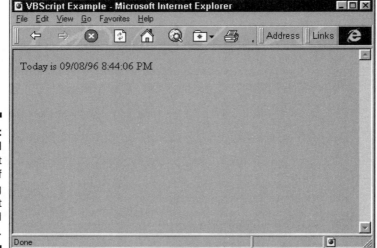

Figure 15-4:
The normal VBScript method of displaying the current date and time.

Because Web page designers seem to have a real need for this sort of thing, and because I've seen very bad coding attempts, I developed several functions that let you display formatted dates and times nicely.

The DayName function returns the day of the week in English for any date. Following are a few examples of using the DayName function:

```
MsgBox DayName(Now())
```

```
MsgBox DayName(Dateserial(1997,12,25))
```

```
MsgBox DayName("Dec 25 1997")
```

The MonthName function returns the name of the month for any date. If you execute the following statement on Christmas Day, the message box displays *December:*

```
Msgbox MonthName(Now())
```

The function works for any valid date.

The FriendlyDate function accepts a date as an argument and returns a nicely formatted string, which includes the day of the week. Figure 15-5 shows an example of the FriendlyDate function in use. The following statement displays the date for the last day of 1999, which makes for a very wild four-day weekend.

```
Msgbox FriendlyDate("Dec 31 1999")
```

Figure 15-5:
The
FriendlyDate
function.

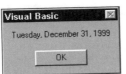

The FriendlyTime function works like the FriendlyDate function, but it displays a nicely formatted time, as shown in Figure 15-6. Here's the statement that displays the message box:

```
Msgbox "The current time is " & FriendlyTime(Now())
```

Figure 15-6:
An example
of using the
FriendlyTime
function.

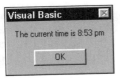

The FriendlyNow function ties everything together and provides an easy way to generate a date and time. Figure 15-7 shows the difference between using a plain Now function and using the FriendlyNow subroutine. Here's the code used to generate the text:

```
Document.Write Now()
Document.Write "<P>"
Document.Write FriendlyNow()
```

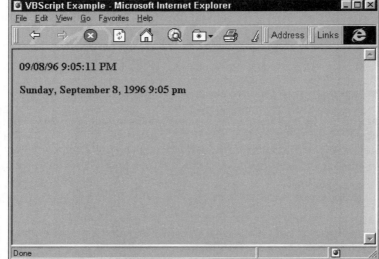

Figure 15-7:
Using the
Now
function and
using the
FriendlyNow
function.
Which do
you prefer?

Converting Hex to Decimal

VBScript provides a built-in function, Hex, that converts a decimal value to its hexadecimal equivalent. If you need to convert in the other direction, Hex to decimal, you're out of luck. You can develop your own conversion function, or you can snag a copy of my Hex2Dec function.

Detecting a VBScript-Compatible Browser

The following code illustrates how to perform a VBScript-compatibility browser check automatically. If the document is loaded into a browser that can interpret VBScript, a new document, vbs/index.htm, is opened automatically, and VBScript does the detection. If the browser cannot interpret VBScript, then the VBScript code is ignored and nothing happens:

```
<HTML>
<HEAD>
<TITLE>XYZ Corporation</TITLE>
<SCRIPT LANGUAGE=VBScript>
<!--
Window.Location.Href = "vbs/index.htm"
-->
</SCRIPT>
</HEAD>
```

```
<BODY>
<H1>XYZ Corporation</H1>
<P>
Welcome to our Web site. You are not using a
VBSript-compatible browser.
</BODY>
</HTML>
```

Audio Greeting Based on the Time of Day

As you know, Web pages ain't just for text anymore. Multimedia plays an increasingly large role. It's very common to visit a Web site and see a greeting that depends on the time of day — for example, Good Morning, if you access the site before noon. The greeting is easy to program with VBScript. The example on the companion disk demonstrates how to set up an audio greeting, based on the time of day.

Note: For added interest, these WAV files are in Japanese.

To try out the example, make sure that you have the *Play sounds* option turned on in Internet Explorer. To check the setting for the option, use the View➪Options command and then click the General tab.

Validating a Credit Card Number

If you use a form in which the user enters a credit card number, you may want to grab a copy of my CardType function. This function uses one argument, a credit card number, and returns a text string that identifies the type of credit card. If the number is not a valid credit card number, the function returns INVALID. Figure 15-8 shows the demo page located on this book's disk. Try the demo using your own credit card numbers.

If you decide to use this function, be aware that information sent over the Internet is often routed through several different sites. Consequently, it is possible (although quite unlikely) that a credit card number can be intercepted on its journey to your server. One solution is to encrypt the credit card number before it is sent.

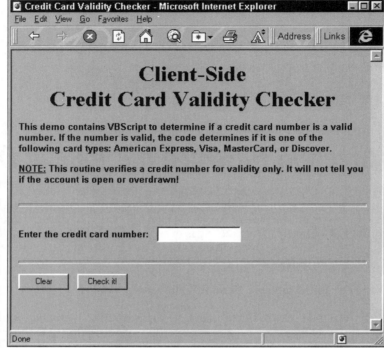

Figure 15-8:
This page
uses the
CardType
function to
determine
whether a
credit card
number is
valid.

A Scrolling Status Bar Message

The Window object's Status property corresponds to the text in the browser's status bar. You can use VBScript to change the text in the status bar. Here's a simple example:

```
Window.Status = "Welcome to my site!"
```

When this statement executes, the browser's status bar displays the text. You can take advantage of the Status property and use VBScript to display a scrolling message in the status bar. Figure 15-9 shows a message in the status bar. If you want to see this in action, open the example document on this book's disk.

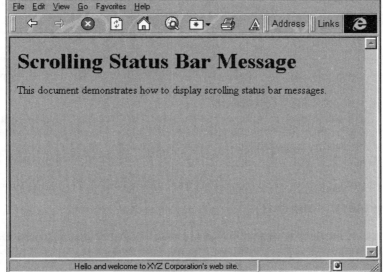

Figure 15-9:
This Web
page uses
VBScript to
display a
series of
scrolling
status bar
messages.

Special FX

Web page designers are always looking for a new visual effect that makes their
pages stand out in the crowd. So I developed a few VBScript routines that can
give your Web page a different look.

Background fade-in

If you've accessed index.htm on the companion disk, you may have noticed an
unusual effect when the page is loaded: The background color seems to fade in.
This fade-in is one of my favorite VBScript special effects and is very simple to
set up. Simply insert the following code, which is an immediate script — not a
subroutine — at the top of your document:

```
<SCRIPT LANGUAGE=VBScript>
For i = 16 To 255 Step 2
    x=Hex(i)
    Document.Bgcolor = x & x & "00"
Next
</SCRIPT>
```

The code fades the background color to yellow (FFFF00), starting with white (000000). This fade-in is done within a For-Next loop. You can modify this code to display different colors.

My *WavyText function* is a weird one. This function makes generating wavy text easy. Figure 15-10 shows an example of a document that uses the WavyText function.

I developed a custom function called *FadeText*. This function lets you display text on a Web page with a fade-out effect. The function is quite flexible, and you can produce a wide variety of interesting effects.

Sorting an Array

Sorting an array is a common task among programmers. *Sorting* simply means putting the values in the array in either ascending or descending order. Many algorithms for sorting an array exist.

Figure 15-10:
The WavyText function generates this text effect.

Figure 15-11 shows an example on this book's disk. Click the Generate button to create an array of 100 random integers and then click the Sort button to sort the array in descending order.

Choosing Lottery Numbers

Sorting has many uses — including drawing random numbers. Figure 15-12 shows an example that makes selecting random lottery numbers easy. You can specify how many numbers are in the pool and how many random numbers you want to generate.

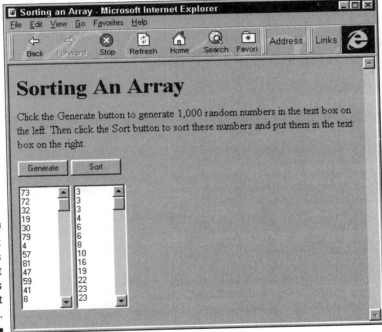

Figure 15-11: This document demonstrates how to sort an array.

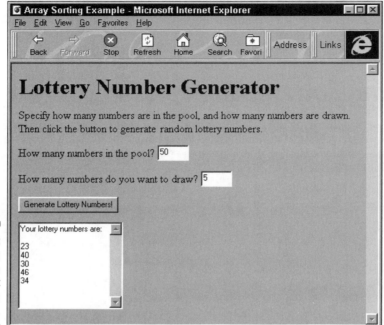

Figure 15-12:
Using
sorting to
select
random
lottery picks.

Part V
Incorporating ActiveX Controls

The 5th Wave

By Rich Tennant

Re·al Pro·gram·mers

Real Programmers don't sleep - their systems just temporarily go down.

In this part . . .

Part V is devoted to ActiveX controls. These controls can enhance your Web pages with power and flexibility that you may have thought impossible. Chapter 16 serves as an introduction and overview, and Chapter 17 provides the details you need to start using ActiveX controls immediately. In Chapter 18, I discuss the HTML Layout control, which is guaranteed to make your mouth water.

Chapter 16

ActiveX Controls: What, Where, and Why

. . . .

In This Chapter

▶ Discovering ActiveX controls

▶ Why you want to use ActiveX controls

▶ Where to get ActiveX controls

▶ Why ActiveX controls are safe

▶ The pros and cons of using ActiveX controls

. . . .

*I*f your goal is to produce an exciting and dynamic Web site (and that *should* be your goal), you definitely need to know about ActiveX controls. As I explain in this chapter, ActiveX controls enable your Web pages to perform amazing feats that are otherwise difficult or impossible. Using ActiveX controls overcomes many limitations you may have encountered using plain HTML, or even HTML and VBScript. But before you start incorporating ActiveX controls into your code, you may need background information, which is the purpose of this chapter.

Okay, So What Is an ActiveX Control?

An ActiveX control is a *component* (also known as an *object*) that can be incorporated into an HTML document to provide normally nonexistent functionality. For example, a Web document may use an ActiveX control that displays an interactive chart. Normally, interactive charting is not within the powers of HTML, but by including the ActiveX control, the Web page developer has essentially extended the limits of normal Web activities.

Two quick examples

Before you get hopelessly lost, I want to throw out two quick examples to put this into perspective. For hands-on experience, and an opportunity to view the source code behind the documents, you may want to try out these examples, which are on the companion disk.

An ActiveX Label control

As you may know, after a Web page is loaded into a browser, the page is pretty much frozen in time. In other words, you can't change any text on the page. You can try every trick you know, using VBScript or any other tools you can find, but you won't figure out a way to change the text inside of a document's `<H1></H1>` tag after the page is loaded.

Wouldn't it be nice if there was a way to add a text element to your page that could be changed after the page was loaded? Without much effort, I'm sure you can think of a half dozen potential uses for such a text element.

Well, folks, this element exists: the ActiveX Label control. You can insert this control into your Web page using a relatively simple sequence of tags. When the page displays, you can use VBScript to do any of the following:

- ✔ Change the text displayed by the control
- ✔ Change the font, size, color, or attributes of the text
- ✔ Make the text invisible

Figure 16-1 shows a document that uses an ActiveX Label control as the document heading. I add a few buttons to demonstrate what you can do to this label. Clicking the buttons, which are standard HTML intrinsic controls, executes VBScript procedures that change the properties of the ActiveX Label control. For example, clicking the Font button cycles through three different fonts. Clicking the Size button increases the size of the text by one point. Clicking the Color button toggles the text color between black and red.

An ActiveX ScrollBar control

In Chapters 12 and 13, I discuss the HTML intrinsic controls: buttons, check boxes, radio buttons, and so on. Although these controls are quite useful, they are not that flexible. For example, you have no control over the fonts or colors the controls use. Changing the items in a Select control after the page has been loaded is impossible, and the selection of intrinsic controls leaves a bit to be desired (a scrollbar control to let a user select a value by clicking or dragging the scroll bar is desirable).

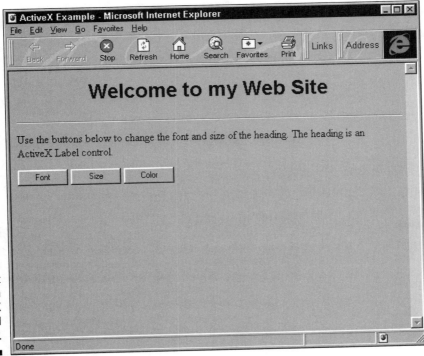

Figure 16-1:
This document uses an ActiveX Label control.

Microsoft, if you haven't already figured this out, developed an ActiveX ScrollBar control that you can use in your Web documents. Figure 16-2 shows a document that uses three ScrollBar controls. In this example, these controls are used to adjust the red, green, and blue components of the document's background color. Again, all these enhancements are done using VBScript.

The ActiveX ScrollBar control looks a lot like an HTML intrinsic control, but, as you can discover in the next section, the control is quite different.

Where Do You Get ActiveX Controls?

If you're ready to acquire ActiveX controls, be aware that they fall into three general categories:

- ✔ Controls that are available to anyone, free of charge
- ✔ Commercial controls that must be licensed and for which there are fees
- ✔ Shareware controls that can be used for a small fee

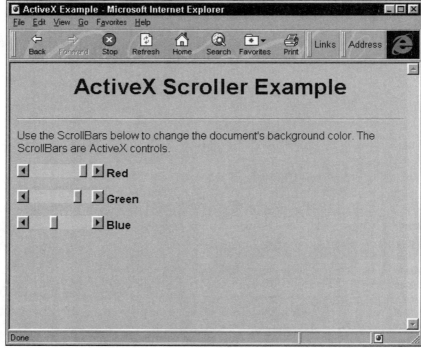

The best place to find out more about ActiveX controls is — where else — on the Web. This book's disk contains links to sites that are good places to start your quest for ActiveX controls.

Types of controls

As I write these pages, more than 2,000 ActiveX controls are available (yes, somebody actually keeps track of these controls), but not all these controls are written for use on Web pages. Here's a list of the types of ActiveX controls that are currently available for use in Web pages.

- ✔ **User interface controls:** These controls consist of scroll bars, buttons, spinners, pop-up menus, and more versatile alternatives to standard HTML intrinsic form elements.

- ✔ **Video controls:** These controls allow viewing of video clips on a Web page.

- ✔ **Animation controls:** Many ActiveX controls enable the display of animations.

- ✔ **Charts and maps:** ActiveX controls that display charts and maps are available. Several controls display charts and maps interactively.

✔ **Calendar controls:** These controls display a calendar on which the user can perform actions by clicking dates.

✔ **Document viewers:** These controls allow the display of specially formatted documents.

✔ **Real-time data acquisition:** A good example of this control is a stock ticker control, which displays stock prices in a moving marquee.

The preceding list of controls is by no means exhaustive. The potential of ActiveX controls is virtually unlimited. New controls are written daily. Browse around on the Web, and you can find ActiveX controls that don't fit into any of these categories.

ActiveX controls from Microsoft

If you're just discovering ActiveX controls, you may want to focus on the controls available from Microsoft. The controls that exist that may keep you busy for awhile.

Microsoft Forms 2.0 controls

Perhaps the best starter set of ActiveX controls is the Microsoft Forms 2.0 controls. These controls are included with the HTML Layout control (which I discuss in detail in Chapter 18). The HTML Layout control is included in the complete installation of Microsoft Internet Explorer 3.0.

If you don't have a copy of the HTML Layout control, the most efficient approach to getting one is to download a copy of Microsoft's ActiveX Control Pad, which you definitely need and which is available free of charge. The ActiveX Control Pad includes the HTML Layout control and all the Forms 2.0 controls.

To download these files, use the links provided on the companion disk.

Note: If you've installed Microsoft Office 97 on your computer, you already have these controls because they are also included with Office 97. You can use these controls in your Web pages as well as in Office 97 documents. For example, when you create a custom dialog box using Excel 97, you use the Forms 2.0 controls.

All the Forms 2.0 controls are contained in a single file, named fm20.dll, which is stored in your windows/system folder. Table 16-1 briefly describes the Forms 2.0 controls.

Table 16-1 The Microsoft Forms 2.0 ActiveX Controls

Control	What it does
ActiveX Hot Spot control 1.0	Overlaid over other objects to detect mouse movements or mouse actions. Useful only within an HTML Layout.
ActiveX Image control 1.0	Inserts an image that's stored in a file.
CheckBox	A check box; an alternative to the HTML intrinsic check box control.
ComboBox	A combo box; an alternative to the HTML intrinsic select control.
CommandButton	A command button; an alternative to the HTML intrinsic button.
Image	Embeds an image; the image is not stored in a file.
Label	A label.
ListBox	A list box; an alternative to the HTML intrinsic select control.
OptionButton	An option button; an alternative to the HTML intrinsic radio control.
ScrollBar	A scroll bar.
SpinButton	A spin button.
TabStrip	A tab strip; as used in multitabbed dialog boxes.
TextBox	A text box; an alternative to the HTML intrinsic text or textarea controls.
ToggleButton	A toggle button control.

Other Microsoft ActiveX controls

The Microsoft Web site has a special location that contains a number of additional ActiveX controls that the company has developed. These controls can be downloaded and used freely. Table 16-2 lists and describes the controls that are available at this site as I write this book. More may exist when you visit the page.

The companion disk contains a link to Microsoft's ActiveX Gallery page, which contains ActiveX controls that you can download.

Each control is contained in a separate *.ocx file. For example, the Microsoft Chart ActiveX object is stored in iechart.ocx.

Table 16-2   ActiveX Controls Available from Microsoft

Control	Description
Animated Button	A button that can display different images when clicked.
Chart	Displays data in a variety of chart formats.
Gradient	Creates gradient color fills in Web pages.
Label	Displays text labels at any angle and with unusual effects.
Marquee	Displays scrolling text in a window.
Menu	A button that can display a menu.
New Item	Displays an image until a specified date.
Pop-up Menu	Displays a pop-up menu.
Pop-up Window	Displays an image in a pop-up window.
Pre-loader	Pre-loads images and other components into the local cache.
Stock Ticker	Displays real-time market data.
Timer	Generates an event at a specified time interval.
View Tracker	Lets you determine what the user is currently viewing on your page.
PowerPoint Animation Player	Creates Microsoft PowerPoint presentations and animations.

Other sources for ActiveX controls

New ActiveX controls appear almost daily. And some Web sites are completely devoted to ActiveX controls.

The companion disk contains a list of links that you can access to find out more about ActiveX controls.

The Technology behind the Magic

As I mention in this chapter, an ActiveX control is an element that's inserted into a Web document. More technically, the Web document contains a reference to an *object* that is installed and registered on a computer. Installing an ActiveX object consists of downloading it to a local hard drive and registering it in the Windows registry so that other applications know it exists. The Windows registry is essentially a master database that contains information about the programs installed on a computer.

When an ActiveX-compatible browser encounters a Web document that contains an ActiveX control, the browser goes through the following steps:

1. **The browser checks the local system registry to verify that a particular control is already installed on the computer.**

2. **If the control is already installed, the browser displays the Web document and displays the control on the page.**

   Not all ActiveX controls create a viewable image, but most do. For example, a Timer control is invisible — it does its thing behind the scenes.

3. **If the control is *not* already installed on the computer, the browser tries to locate that control, downloads it, and installs it automatically on the computer.**

   Depending on the security level set in the browser, the browser may or may not ask if it's okay to install the control.

4. **If the control cannot be installed automatically, or if the user refuses the request to install it, the Web document cannot use the control, and the Web page may or may not be completely unusable.**

   Whether or not a control can be installed automatically depends upon the information supplied in the <OBJECT> tag for the ActiveX control.

Downloading a control

If you access a URL containing an ActiveX control that is already installed on your computer, everything works just fine. You may not even realize that the Web site is using an ActiveX control.

If the control is not installed on your computer, the control must be downloaded, installed, and registered before it can be used. Fortunately, this process can happen automatically, but while it occurs there is a delay. The length of the delay depends on the size of the control.

After the control is downloaded and installed on your computer, you don't need to download it again. If you access the same page later, the browser knows that the control is on your computer and doesn't download it again. After a control is downloaded and installed, it works for all Web sites that use that particular control.

If a particular control is not on your computer, how does the browser know where to find it? Good question. The answer is that the codebase for the control is specified in the <OBJECT> tag for the control. The *codebase* is a URL that specifies a location from which the control is downloaded.

Security for controls

Using ActiveX controls can be dangerous. The vast majority of ActiveX controls is perfectly safe, but writing destructive ActiveX controls is possible. For example, you can access a Web site that uses an unknown control. You may think the control looks interesting, so you choose to download it to try it out. Before you know it, your hard drive is completely unusable. Although this scenario is highly unlikely, it is possible. As I write this book, I received word of an ActiveX control that, when installed, caused the computer to shut down. The developer of this control is not malicious; rather, he just wanted to prove that you can create a destructive ActiveX control.

Because of the potential danger involved with using ActiveX controls, security features are included with Internet Explorer, including the ability for you to specify various security levels.

Figure 16-3 shows the Security tab of Internet Explorer's Options dialog box. Choose the View➪Options command to get to this dialog box. In the following sections, I describe the relevant parts of this dialog box — the controls located in the Active content section.

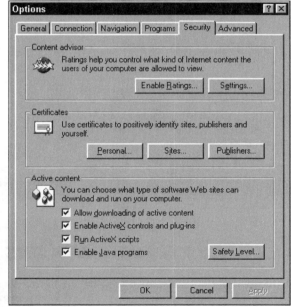

Figure 16-3:
The Security tab of Internet Explorer's Options dialog box.

✔ **Allow downloading of active content.** If this setting is not enabled, Internet Explorer does not download any nonstandard content, such as video, audio, and other multimedia.

✔ **Enable ActiveX controls and plug-ins.** This setting determines whether the browser uses ActiveX controls. If you want to completely disable ActiveX controls, clear the check mark from this check box. If you do so, you cannot try out the ActiveX examples I developed.

✔ **Run ActiveX scripts.** This setting determines whether Internet Explorer executes VBScript or JavaScript code. If no VBScript example works for you, make sure that this setting is turned on.

✔ **Enable Java programs.** This setting determines whether Internet Explorer executes Java programs encountered on the Web site.

✔ **Safety Level button.** This button brings up another dialog box, shown in Figure 16-4. This dialog box lets you determine how Internet Explorer deals with potential security problems. For most users, the High setting works just fine. But if you develop Web pages that use ActiveX controls, you may want to use the Medium setting.

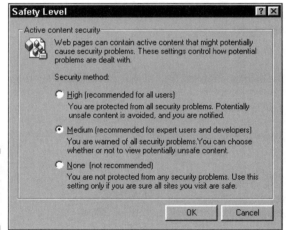

Figure 16-4:
The Safety
Level dialog
box.

Using ActiveX Controls: Pros and Cons

Sure, ActiveX controls are great, but they aren't a panacea. In this section, I present a list of the pros and cons related to using ActiveX controls in your Web pages.

The Pros

Using ActiveX controls has more pros than cons. I may be a bit biased — or maybe the pros really *do* outnumber the cons.

- ✔ **You can perform the impossible.** As I mention earlier in the chapter, ActiveX controls let your Web pages perform feats that are otherwise impossible. The beauty of ActiveX controls is that they perform after the Web document is loaded. In other words, they can make a stagnant Web page an active Web page. ActiveX controls, combined with a good knowledge of VBScript, can make your Web site stand out in the crowd.

- ✔ **An established standard.** ActiveX controls have been around for a few years, but haven't been available for use in Web pages until the release of Microsoft Internet Explorer 3.0. Visual Basic programmers have used ActiveX controls, formerly known as OLE controls, VBX controls, or OCX controls, for a while. ActiveX controls are sometimes compared to Java applets and Netscape plug-ins. ActiveX controls can do anything an applet or plug-in can do, but an advantage is that ActiveX controls can also be used in applications unrelated to the Web.

- ✔ **Endorsed by Microsoft.** Like it or not, Microsoft is a heavy hitter in the software world. Microsoft originated the concept of ActiveX controls and has made a major investment in them. To many, the investment is a good sign that this technology isn't just another flash in the pan.

- ✔ **Thousands of developers.** ActiveX controls are reusable software components created by a variety of software vendors. As such, you can probably locate a control that does exactly what you want. If you can't locate one, you can always hire someone to write an ActiveX control for you, or do it yourself if you have the knowledge.

- ✔ **Easy to control.** You can add ActiveX controls to your Web pages by using the HTML `<OBJECT>` tag. The `<OBJECT>` tag includes a set of parameters that specify which data the control uses and determine the appearance and behavior of the control. You can use VBScript code to manipulate the control.

The cons

In the interest of fairness, here's a shorter list of items that describe the darker side of ActiveX controls.

- ✔ **Not supported by all browsers.** As I write this book, Internet Explorer is the only browser that supports ActiveX controls, but at least one Netscape Navigator plug-in that adds this feature to Netscape Navigator still exists. I expect to see native support for ActiveX controls in a future version of Netscape Navigator. For more information on the topic, refer to the sidebar "Using ActiveX controls with Netscape Navigator," later in this chapter.

- ✔ **Downloading delays.** If you have a dial-up connection to the Internet, you may be aware that certain sites seem to take *forever* to load. Graphic-intensive Web pages have always been a problem, and ActiveX controls add even more delay. The good news is that a particular control needs to be downloaded only once and is available on your computer and quickly called into action when it's needed again.

- ✔ **Potential danger.** I discuss the potential danger of using ActiveX controls earlier in this chapter. If you're careful about accepting the download of controls, however, using ActiveX controls isn't a problem.

Chapter 17

Using ActiveX Controls:
The Gory Details

. . . .

In This Chapter

▶ Using the `<OBJECT>` tag to insert an ActiveX control in your HTML document

▶ Referring to ActiveX controls using VBScript

▶ Finding out about properties, methods, and events for ActiveX controls

▶ Introducing the Microsoft ActiveX Control Pad, a handy tool for working
  with ActiveX controls

▶ Demonstrating ActiveX controls with informative examples

. . . .

*T*his chapter is designed to give you a taste of ActiveX controls. As I indicate,
a huge variety of controls is available, and many of them are much more
impressive than what appears in the simple examples in the chapter.

In this chapter, you can find out how to activate your HTML documents. I tell
you everything you need to know to start using ActiveX controls in your Web
pages. This chapter includes lots of examples that demonstrate controls, and
you should be able to adapt these examples to your own needs.

This chapter focuses exclusively on the ActiveX controls that were developed
by Microsoft. Other ActiveX controls operate similarly, but each control has its
own unique set of properties, methods, and events.

If you haven't done so, I highly recommend that you read Chapter 16 before
proceeding with this chapter. Chapter 16 provides the necessary background
information to help you fully understand this chapter.

The <OBJECT> Tag: It Gets Ugly

To insert an ActiveX object in your HTML document, use the <OBJECT> tag. Be forewarned: The information between the <OBJECT> and the </OBJECT> tags can be daunting, but as I describe later in this chapter, the ActiveX Control Pad generates the <OBJECT> tag for you automatically.

An example <OBJECT> tag

Following is a complete HTML document that includes an ActiveX Label object. The ActiveX object is defined between the <OBJECT> and the </OBJECT> tags.

```
<HTML>
<BODY>
<OBJECT ID="Label1" WIDTH=400 HEIGHT=32
   CLASSID="CLSID:978C9E23-D4B0-11CE-BF2D-00AA003F40D0
  CODEBASE="http://activex.microsoft.com/controls/
mspert10.cab">
   <PARAM NAME="ForeColor" VALUE="0">
   <PARAM NAME="BackColor" VALUE="12632256">
   <PARAM NAME="VariousPropertyBits" VALUE="268435483">
   <PARAM NAME="Caption" VALUE="Welcome to my Web Site">
   <PARAM NAME="Size" VALUE="4630;503">
   <PARAM NAME="FontName" VALUE="Arial">
   <PARAM NAME="FontEffects" VALUE="1073741825">
   <PARAM NAME="FontHeight" VALUE="200">
   <PARAM NAME="FontCharSet" VALUE="0">
   <PARAM NAME="FontPitchAndFamily" VALUE="2">
   <PARAM NAME="ParagraphAlign" VALUE="3">
   <PARAM NAME="FontWeight" VALUE="700">
</OBJECT>
<HR>
This document uses an ActiveX control.
</BODY>
</HTML>
```

The <OBJECT> tag attributes

Notice that the <OBJECT> tag extends across three lines. Using multiple lines is optional (I wrote the tag in multiple lines to make it easier to read). The <OBJECT> tag attributes vary with the object. For this particular example, the <OBJECT> tag contains the following attributes:

- ✓ **ID:** The name for the control. You can give the control any name you like. Making the name descriptive of the control that it represents is a good idea.

- ✓ **WIDTH:** The width of the control.

- ✓ **HEIGHT:** The height of the control.

- ✓ **CLASSID:** The ClassID of the control. This attribute is the most important because its number uniquely identifies the control.

- ✓ **CODEBASE:** The URL that contains a copy of the control so that it can be downloaded, if it's not already installed on the computer. CODEBASE is optional, but good to include.

The <PARAM> *tags*

Before the closing </OBJECT> tag, a number of <PARAM> tags appear. These <PARAM> tags specify the initial settings for certain properties of the object. The ActiveX Label control has many additional properties. If a property is not specified in a <PARAM> tag, the default setting is used. In the preceding example, 12 property settings are specified.

Using the <PARAM> tags is one way to initialize a control's properties. You also can set these properties using VBScript. For example, you can create a Window OnLoad subroutine and set the properties in it.

More about the CODEBASE attribute

Using the CODEBASE attribute in your <OBJECT> tag is optional, but you should get in the habit of always using it. If a user loads a document that uses an ActiveX control and the control is not already installed, the control is downloaded automatically from the URL specified in the CODEBASE attribute. If the CODEBASE attribute is missing, the user cannot use the control.

For Microsoft Forms 2.0 ActiveX controls, you can use the following URL, which points to the Microsoft Web site:

```
http://activex.microsoft.com/
   controls/mspert10.cab
```

This URL is supposedly the permanent location for the CAB file, which automatically installs the latest version of the HTML Layout control and all the Forms 2.0 controls. Anyone who installs the complete version of Internet Explorer 3.0 already has these controls.

Because the Microsoft site tends to have quite a bit of traffic, you may want to provide a copy of the mspert10.cab file at your own site and use your own URL in the CODEBASE attribute. Legally, providing a copy at your site is okay because the license agreement permits redistribution of the HTML Layout control CAB file.

Introducing the ActiveX Control Pad

The Label control example in the previous section demonstrates that the `<OBJECT>` tag can be slightly overwhelming. Hardly anyone writes these `<OBJECT>` tags manually. Instead, they use a handy tool that does it automatically: Microsoft's ActiveX Control Pad.

The ActiveX Control pad is available to you free of charge, courtesy of the folks in Redmond.

This book's disk contains a link that points to the download site for the ActiveX Control Pad.

Complete coverage of the ActiveX Control Pad is beyond the scope of this book. The product itself includes an online help file that describes how to use it. In the sections that follow, I briefly describe the four key components of the ActiveX Control Pad:

- ✔ An HTML text editor
- ✔ An ActiveX control editor
- ✔ The Script Wizard
- ✔ An HTML Layout Editor

Note: The following discussion is based on Version 1.0 of the ActiveX Control Pad. Hopefully, this product continues to evolve. A later version may be available as you read this book.

HTML text editor

When you start up the Control Pad, you work in an HTML text editor (refer to Figure 17-1). As an HTML editor, Control Pad is certainly nothing to write home about. Don't even *think* about adopting this as your main HTML editor. In fact, Control Pad makes Windows Notepad look advanced — Control Pad doesn't even have a Search command!

Control Pad does have one nice feature. The left margin displays icons that correspond to the `<OBJECT>` and `<SCRIPT>` tags in your document. Click an icon, and you're transported to the ActiveX control editor or the Script Wizard.

Figure 17-1:
The ActiveX
Control Pad
is centered
around an
HTML text
editor.

ActiveX control editor

When you select the Edit⇨Insert ActiveX Control command, the Control Pad displays a list of all ActiveX controls installed on your computer. Select a control, and a new window opens up that lets you adjust the control interactively. As you can see in Figure 17-2, you can use the Properties dialog box to view or set properties for the control.

Figure 17-2:
The
Properties
dialog lets
you adjust
the control
interactively.

After you set the control's properties to your liking, click the Close button and the Control Pad inserts the `<OBJECT>` tag into your document. Figure 17-3 shows how the `<OBJECT>` tag looks.

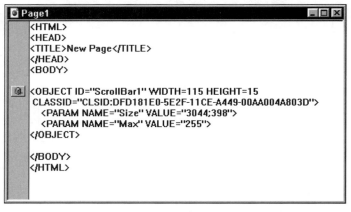

Figure 17-3:
The Control Pad generates the `<OBJECT>` tag based on your choices in the Properties dialog box.

Script Wizard

The Script Wizard is an interesting component of the Control Pad that lets you create VBScript or JavaScript code by using point and click action. The Script Wizard is really designed for those users who don't program, and it's useful only for very simple scripts. The Script Wizard is not at all efficient, and you will usually want to write the scripts manually. You can choose from List View, which shows actions assigned to events, or Code View, which shows the actual VBScript code.

However, the real advantage of the Script Wizard, even for programming pros, is that it shows you a list of properties and events for each ActiveX object.

HTML Layout editor

The HTML Layout editor component of the Control Pad lets you add an ActiveX Layout control and then edit it in a WYSIWYG manner. You can add other objects to the Layout and determine precisely the location, size, transparency, and layering of controls. When you save an HTML Layout, the Control Pad creates a file with an .alx extension that is separate from the HTML file for the page.

Chapter 18 is devoted to the HTML Layout control.

Hands-On: Using the ActiveX Control Pad

Using the Control Pad isn't difficult, but you may need time to become familiar with it. In the sections that follow, I provide an introduction to the ActiveX Control Pad to give you a feel for what you can do with the Control Pad. In the example in this section, I

- ✔ Create a new HTML document.
- ✔ Add an ActiveX SpinButton control to the document.
- ✔ Add an ActiveX Label control.
- ✔ Use the Script Wizard to connect these controls: Clicking the SpinButton changes the value in the Label.

Creating a new document

Figure 17-4 shows the ActiveX Control Pad after I issue the File⇔New HTML command. Control Pad inserts standard HTML tags into the new document.

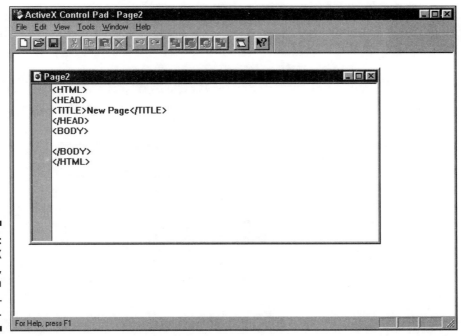

Figure 17-4:
The ActiveX Control Pad, with an empty HTML document.

Inserting an ActiveX Label control

To insert an ActiveX control into the document, move the cursor to the location where the control goes. For this example, move the cursor between the <BODY> and </BODY> tags. Choose the Edit⇨Insert ActiveX Control command, and you get a dialog box like the one shown in Figure 17-5. This dialog box lists all the controls installed on your computer. Select the control named Microsoft Forms 2.0 Label and click the OK button.

Note: The controls that are listed in the Insert ActiveX Control dialog box vary. Certain controls displayed in this list may not be suitable for HTML documents.

Figure 17-5:
The Insert
ActiveX
Control
dialog box
lists all
controls
installed on
your
computer.

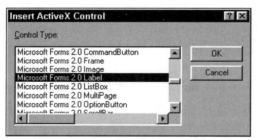

As shown in Figure 17-6, the ActiveX Control Pad displays the ActiveX control in a graphical window named Edit ActiveX Control and also displays a Properties box that lists each of the control's properties and current settings.

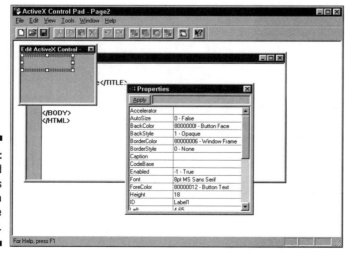

Figure 17-6:
Inserted
controls
appear in a
separate
window.

Changing Label control properties

You can use the Properties box to change properties of the Label control. You also can change some properties, such as the object's size, directly with the mouse. To change a property using the Properties box, select the property and then make the change in the edit box at the top of the Properties box. Some properties present a list of possible settings in a drop-down box.

For this example:

1. **Make the label smaller, because it just displays a number, and set the Width property to 36 and the Height property to 12.**

2. **Enter 1 for the label Caption.**

3. **Center the text in the label by changing the TextAlign property to 2-Center.**

   TextAlign is an example of a property that you can set using the drop-down list in the Properties box.

4. **Change the font for the label to Arial 10-point and Bold.**

   To do so, double-click the Font line in the Properties box and select the font, size, and style from the dialog box that pops up.

When you're satisfied with the property settings, close the control's window by clicking the Close button, which is the small X button on the right side of the title bar. The Control Pad then inserts the <OBJECT> tag and code for the control into your HTML document. Figure 17-7 shows the <OBJECT> tag for the ActiveX Label control.

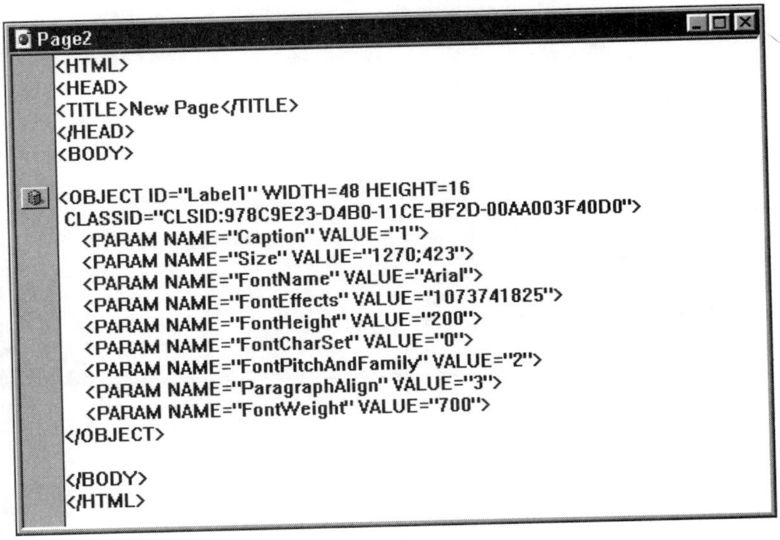

Figure 17-7:
The code for a Label control is generated by the ActiveX Control Pad.

```
Page2
<HTML>
<HEAD>
<TITLE>New Page</TITLE>
</HEAD>
<BODY>

<OBJECT ID="Label1" WIDTH=48 HEIGHT=16
CLASSID="CLSID:978C9E23-D4B0-11CE-BF2D-00AA003F40D0">
    <PARAM NAME="Caption" VALUE="1">
    <PARAM NAME="Size" VALUE="1270;423">
    <PARAM NAME="FontName" VALUE="Arial">
    <PARAM NAME="FontEffects" VALUE="1073741825">
    <PARAM NAME="FontHeight" VALUE="200">
    <PARAM NAME="FontCharSet" VALUE="0">
    <PARAM NAME="FontPitchAndFamily" VALUE="2">
    <PARAM NAME="ParagraphAlign" VALUE="3">
    <PARAM NAME="FontWeight" VALUE="700">
</OBJECT>

</BODY>
</HTML>
```

Inserting an ActiveX SpinButton control

The next step is to insert the SpinButton control. Because the SpinButton will be located directly to the right of the label, move the cursor between the `</OBJECT>` tag for the label command and the `</BODY>` tag. Choose the Edit⇨Insert ActiveX Control command and select Microsoft Forms 2.0 SpinButton from the list of controls.

Set the properties using the Properties box. For this example:

1. **Set the Min property to 1, which means that the spinner's lowest value is 1.**

2. **Set the Max property to 12, which means the spinner's highest value is 12.**

Close the control's Window by clicking the Close button. The document now contains the code for this new control. Figure 17-8 shows the document, which contains `<OBJECT>` tags for two ActiveX controls.

If you need to change control properties after the control is inserted, click the icon to the left of the `<OBJECT>` tag for the control. Clicking this icon displays the control and lets you change properties using the Properties box.

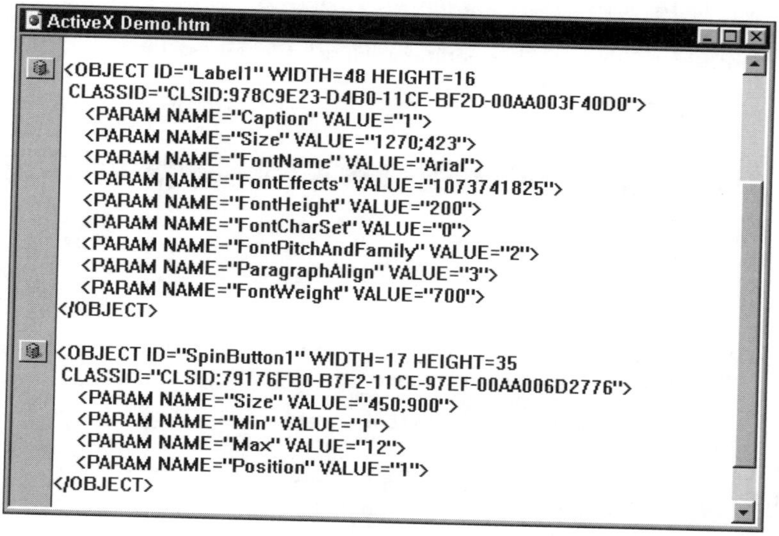

Figure 17-8:
The HTML document, after adding the SpinButton control.

```
ActiveX Demo.htm                                          _ □ ×

<OBJECT ID="Label1" WIDTH=48 HEIGHT=16
 CLASSID="CLSID:978C9E23-D4B0-11CE-BF2D-00AA003F40D0">
    <PARAM NAME="Caption" VALUE="1">
    <PARAM NAME="Size" VALUE="1270;423">
    <PARAM NAME="FontName" VALUE="Arial">
    <PARAM NAME="FontEffects" VALUE="1073741825">
    <PARAM NAME="FontHeight" VALUE="200">
    <PARAM NAME="FontCharSet" VALUE="0">
    <PARAM NAME="FontPitchAndFamily" VALUE="2">
    <PARAM NAME="ParagraphAlign" VALUE="3">
    <PARAM NAME="FontWeight" VALUE="700">
</OBJECT>

<OBJECT ID="SpinButton1" WIDTH=17 HEIGHT=35
 CLASSID="CLSID:79176FB0-B7F2-11CE-97EF-00AA006D2776">
    <PARAM NAME="Size" VALUE="450;900">
    <PARAM NAME="Min" VALUE="1">
    <PARAM NAME="Max" VALUE="12">
    <PARAM NAME="Position" VALUE="1">
</OBJECT>
```

Adding HTML

So far, this document contains only two ActiveX controls. You can add text above or below the controls. For example, you can add the following code directly below the `<BODY>` tag:

```
<H1>ActiveX Control Demo</H1>
Click the spinner to change the value displayed in the label.
```

Viewing the document

Save the document and see how it looks in the browser. Figure 17-9 shows the document displayed in Internet Explorer.

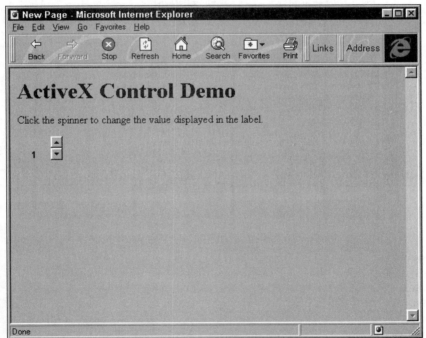

Figure 17-9:
This document contains two ActiveX controls.

Using the Script Wizard

So far, the two controls appear in the document but aren't connected together. You can click the SpinButton control all you want, but nothing happens. This document needs a VBScript event handler subroutine to handle the SpinButton clicks. Here are two ways to get the event handler code into the document:

- ✔ **Write a VBScript subroutine manually.** To do so, you need to know what event is generated when the SpinButton is clicked.
- ✔ **Use the Script Wizard to write the event handler code.**

Because this section demonstrates the ActiveX Control Pad's features, I use the Script Wizard to write the event handler code.

To activate the Script Wizard, choose the Tools⇨Script Wizard command, which displays a new window (shown in Figure 17-10).

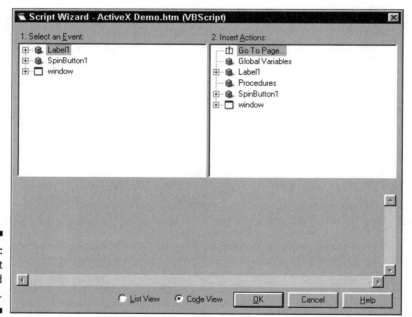

Figure 17-10:
The Script
Wizard
window.

The window has three parts:

- ✔ **The upper-left part contains a list of all objects in the document.** You can expand this list, by clicking the + symbols, to show all available events for each object.

- ✔ **The upper-right part also contains a list of objects, plus a few other items.** The list expands to show properties and methods.

- ✔ **The bottom part of the window varies, depending upon which option is set (either List View or Code View).**

For this example, make sure that the Code View option is selected. Because no code exists, the panel is empty.

1. **In the left window, click the + symbol to the left of the SpinButton1 object to display a list of events for that object.**

   The event of interest is the Change event. For this example, when the SpinButton changes, the Label's Caption property displays the SpinButton's value.

2. **Click the Change event.**

   The bottom window displays the beginning of an event handler subroutine named SpinButton1_Change.

3. **In the right window, click the + symbol next to the Label item.**

   The list expands to show actions for that control.

4. **Double-click the Caption item for the Label1 control.**

   Examine the window at the bottom. It contains a reference to Label1.Caption.

5. **Type an equal sign (=) in the lower window.**

6. **In the right window, scroll down and click the + symbol for the SpinButton1 control.**

   It expands to show actions.

7. **Double-click Value.**

   A reference to SpinButton1.Value appears to the right of the equal sign in the lower window. At this point, the window looks like Figure 17-11.

8. **Click OK to close the ScriptWizard.**

   You return to the document.

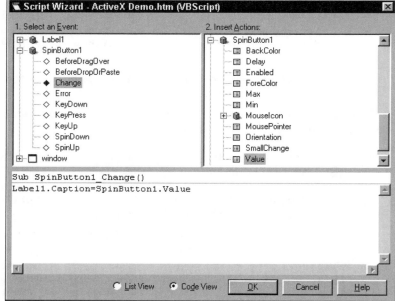

Figure 17-11:
The Script
Wizard
window,
after
creating the
SpinButton1_
Change
subroutine.

The document now contains the following subroutine, courtesy of the Script Wizard:

```
<SCRIPT LANGUAGE="VBScript">
<!--
Sub SpinButton1_Change()
    Label1.Caption = SpinButton1.Value
End Sub
-->
</SCRIPT>
```

Note: The VBScript code generated by the Script Wizard is not very well formatted. It doesn't use any indenting. Also, each subroutine the code generates appears within its own set of `<SCRIPT>` and `</SCRIPT>` tags.

Testing the script

Save the document and try it out in your browser. If all goes well, clicking the SpinButton causes the Label's caption to display the SpinButton's value.

More about the Script Wizard

If you follow the preceding exercise, you may have a better understanding for how the Script Wizard works. You also may think that generating a one-line subroutine requires a lot of work.

I am the first to agree that the Script Wizard is not the most efficient way to produce VBScript. To me, the value of the Script Wizard is that it tells you the properties and methods available for a particular object.

Here are a few additional points about the Script Wizard:

- ✔ **It has two modes: Code View and List View.** List View displays descriptions of the event-handlers, and Code View displays the actual code. Because you know about VBScript, you may want to always use Code View.

- ✔ **You can manually edit code in the Code View display, which is usually the most efficient way to edit it.**

- ✔ **Use the online help to find out more about the properties, methods, and events.** The Help computer covers all of the Microsoft Forms 2.0 controls.

- ✔ **In Code View, the Script Wizard adds the End Sub statement for you.** Don't add the statement yourself, otherwise it appears twice in your document — and generates an error.

This brief overview doesn't really do justice to the Script Wizard. Click the Help button for more information about using the Script Wizard.

Discovering Properties and Methods

Each ActiveX control has its own unique set of properties, methods, and events. Here are four ways to find out which properties and methods are available.

- ✔ **Locate the documentation for the ActiveX object.** The Microsoft Forms 2.0 ActiveX controls are documented in the online Help file for the ActiveX Control Pad. Figure 17-12 shows an example of this Help file.

- ✔ **Use the Microsoft ActiveX Control Pad.** As I note in the previous section, you can use the Properties box to review or change properties. You also can use the Script Wizard to find out about the events and methods for an object.

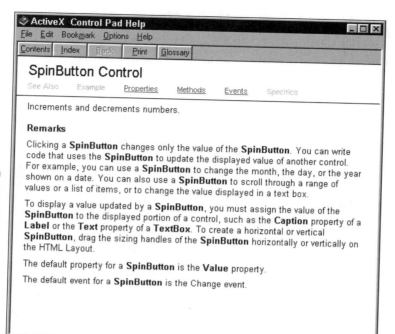

Figure 17-12:
The ActiveX
Control
Pad's Help
file
describes
the
Microsoft
Forms 2.0
controls.

🖝 **Obtain a copy of VBCompanion by Apex Software.** This product lets you view the properties and methods for every control installed on your computer. Go to Apex's Web site for information:

```
http://www.apexsc.com/
```

🖝 **Look at code someone else has written.** If you can find a Web page that uses the control you're interested in, you can often get valuable tips by examining the document containing the control.

ActiveX Examples

In this section, I present examples that use ActiveX controls from Microsoft. These examples give you an idea of what you can do with ActiveX controls. The examples are available on this book's disk, so you may want to try them out and view the complete source listings.

The ActiveX Marquee control

You may be familiar with Internet Explorer's <MARQUEE> tag. This tag lets you display scrolling text in a Web page. Microsoft also has an ActiveX control that does marquees. This control lets you specify an HTML document or a graphic image to scroll in a window.

Figure 17-13 shows an example of the ActiveX Marquee control on a Web page. I add two buttons to start and stop the vertical scrolling. The document that scrolls in the marquee is actually converted to a graphic, so a delay may occur if the document is large. Converting a document to a graphic image gives you precise control over scrolling, down to an individual pixel.

The ActiveX PopUp Menu control

You can present a choice to a visitor to your Web page in many ways. The ActiveX PopUp Menu control offers another way. This control displays a list of items in a menu that pops up at the current mouse pointer position. Figure 17-14 shows an example of this control in use. Clicking the button executes a subroutine that executes the PopUp method of this control, causing the PopUp menu to appear.

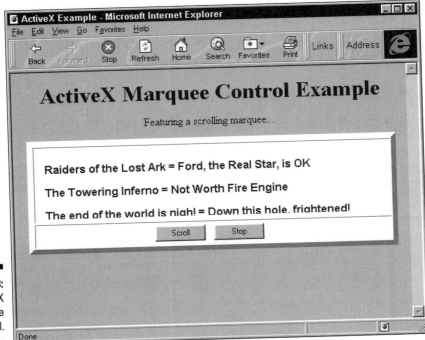

Figure 17-13:
The ActiveX
Marquee
control.

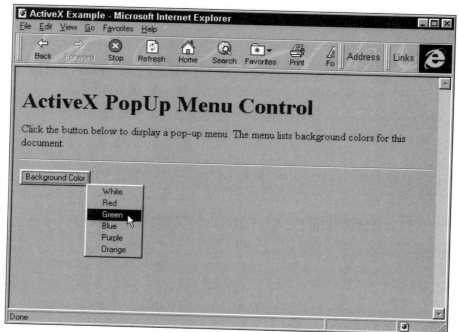

Figure 17-14:
The PopUp
Menu
control.

Following is the <OBJECT> tag for the PopUp Menu control:

```
<OBJECT
  ID="IEPOP1"
  WIDTH=0
  HEIGHT=0
  CLASSID="CLSID:7823A620-9DD9-11CF-A662-00AA00C066D2">
</OBJECT>
```

The WIDTH and HEIGHT attributes are set to 0 because this control works behind the scenes. It's not a control that the user interacts with directly. If the WIDTH and HEIGHT attributes are set to values other than 0, the control displays a blank area.

When this page loads, the following statements execute:

```
Dim MenuItems(6)
MenuItems(1)="White"
MenuItems(2)="Red"
```

```
MenuItems(3)="Green"
MenuItems(4)="Blue"
MenuItems(5)="Purple"
MenuItems(6)="Orange"
For i=1 to 6
    Call Iepop1.AddItem(MenuItems(i), i)
Next
```

The preceding block of code creates an array of six menu items. It then uses a For ... Next loop, which makes use of the AddItem method, to add the items to the control named Iepop1.

The page also has a button that, when clicked, executes the following event handler subroutine. This subroutine executes the PopUp method of the control:

```
Sub btnMenu_OnClick
    Iepop1.PopUp
End Sub
```

When the user makes a choice from the pop-up menu, a click event for the control is generated. Here's the event handler that takes the action. The click event passes an argument to the subroutine. The argument represents the menu choice.

```
Sub Iepop1_Click(ByVal x)
    Document.BGColor=MenuItems(x)
End Sub
```

You can probably think of many more uses for the ActiveX Popup Menu control.

The ActiveX ButtonMenu control

The ActiveX ButtonMenu control provides another way to present choices to a user. This control is interesting because it changes when the mouse pointer moves over it — the text on the button appears to pop out. The ActiveX ButtonMenu control is a relatively simple one. It has only two properties and six methods, and it responds to only two events. Unfortunately, you can't change the text color (which is always black) on the buttons.

Note: The Microsoft ButtonMenu control (btnmenu.ocx) is included on the companion disk. The example uses a CODEBASE parameter in the <OBJECT> tag, so this control is installed automatically when you access the example.

Figure 17-15 shows a page with three ButtonMenu controls. The first two have menu items, and the third doesn't. Selecting a menu item generates a Select event. Clicking the button generates a Click event. This page uses three controls, but you can use as many as you need.

Here's the <OBJECT> tag for a ButtonMenu object:

```
<OBJECT
  ID="BtnMenu1"
  CLASSID="CLSID:52DFAE60-CEBF-11CF-A3A9-00A0C9034920"
  CODEBASE="btnmenu.ocx#Version=4,70,0,1161"
  WIDTH=120
  HEIGHT=30>
</OBJECT>
```

You can, of course, set the WIDTH and HEIGHT attributes to any size you want (the width depends on the text that you assign to its Caption property).

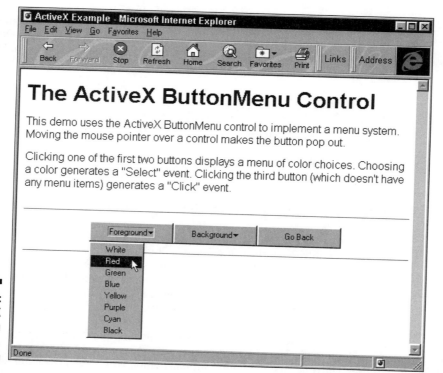

Figure 17-15:
The ActiveX
ButtonMenu
control.

If you examine the code behind this example, you find that I use a two-dimensional array to hold the menu item names and the color codes. I wrote the following event handler subroutines:

- ✔ **Window_Load():** This subroutine initializes the array and adds the items to the menus.
- ✔ **BtnMenu1_Select():** This subroutine executes when an item is selected from the first MenuButton.
- ✔ **BtnMenu2_Select():** This subroutine executes when an item is selected from the second MenuButton.
- ✔ **BtnMenu3_Click():** This subroutine executes when the third MenuButton is clicked.

The ActiveX Timer control

The ActiveX Timer control fires an event at a specified interval. Then you write a VBScript event handler subroutine to take action when the event occurs.

This example, shown in Figure 17-16, displays a message that shows the number of days, hours, minutes, and seconds until a specified date. An ActiveX Timer control updates the display every second. The countdown display uses a Label control to display the message.

Note: The companion disk includes the Microsoft ActiveX Timer control (ietimer.ocx). The example uses a CODEBASE parameter in the <OBJECT> tag, so this control is installed automatically when you access the example.

I wrote this code so that it can be easily added to any Web page. You provide the date. To make the screen more interactive, I add a button so the user can enter a new date.

You may think the VBScript code to determine the number of remaining days is fairly simple. I thought so, too, until I tried to write such a routine. To see the code I developed, view the source document on the companion disk.

Another ActiveX Timer control example

Figure 17-17 shows an example of a page that has a phony page hit counter, which is intended to be a humorous addition to a Web page. I use six ActiveX Label controls for the digits and place each one in a cell of a single-row table. The Timer control executes a subroutine that increments a variable and then updates the Caption properties of the Label objects. I also add randomness so that the increments aren't equal; the page appears as though it gets dozens of hits per minute.

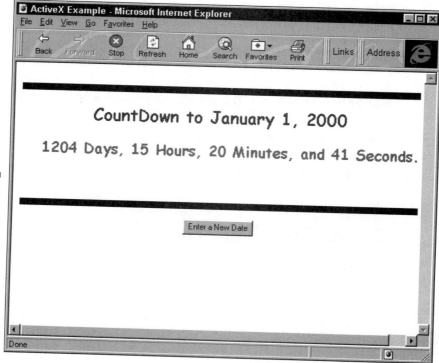

Figure 17-16:
It won't be
long
now.... This
example
uses a Timer
control to
update the
message
every
second.

The timer has an interval of 200 milliseconds, which means that the event is fired five times per second.

Here's a listing of the subroutine that handles the Timer event. The Num variable holds the number displayed in the counter. The six labels are updated only 30 percent of the time, which is controlled by the Rnd function. The Mid function extracts the appropriate digit from Num and assigns it to the Caption property for the appropriate Label control:

```
Sub Timer1_Timer
'    Update 30 percent of the time to make it look real
    If Rnd() <.3 Then
        Num=Num+1
        Label1.Caption = Mid(Num,1,1)
        Label2.Caption = Mid(Num,2,1)
        Label3.Caption = Mid(Num,3,1)
        Label4.Caption = Mid(Num,4,1)
```

```
        Label5.Caption = Mid(Num,5,1)
        Label6.Caption = Mid(Num,6,1)
    End If
End Sub
```

Figure 17-17:
A page hit
counter?
Not really.
This is a
simulated
counter, just
for fun.

Just in case you're wondering, you can't create a Web page hit counter using only VBScript. I haven't seen an ActiveX control that performs this function either.

Yet another ActiveX Timer control example

You've probably encountered Web pages that display a scrolling message in the browser's status bar. Most of these sites use JavaScript to do the scrolling. However, this technique is much easier to do with VBScript, thanks to the ActiveX Timer control. Figure 17-18 shows an example.

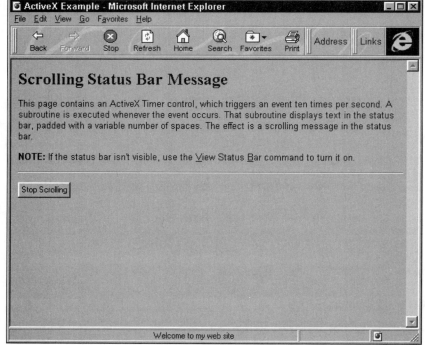

Figure 17-18:
This
example
displays a
scrolling
message
in the
status bar.

Following is the code that does the scrolling. The ScrollText variable holds the text to scroll, padded with space characters. I use the String function to add 128 spaces to the left of the text. The StatusTimer_Timer subroutine executes whenever the ActiveX timer control, named StatusTimer, generates an event ten times per second. The ScrollText variable is reduced by one character and is sent to the status bar using the Window.Status method. The final If-Then statement checks the length of ScrollText. If it's 0, then the process starts all over again.

```
Dim ScrollText
Text="Welcome to my Web site."
ScrollText= String(128," ") & Text
Sub StatusTimer_Timer()
    ScrollText=Right(ScrollText,(Len(Scrolltext)-1))
    Window.Status=ScrollText
    If Len(ScrollText)=0 Then ScrollText= String(128," ") &
            "Welcome to my Web site"
End Sub
```

Using ActiveX controls in HTML forms

The final example in this chapter demonstrates how to use ActiveX controls in an HTML form that is submitted to a server. This example is a modified version of the example that I present in Chapter 13. I replace all the HTML intrinsic controls, except the Reset and Submit buttons, with ActiveX controls. Refer to Figure 17-19 for an example.

Figure 17-19:
This form contains ActiveX controls. The values need to be transferred to HTML intrinsic controls before the form is submitted.

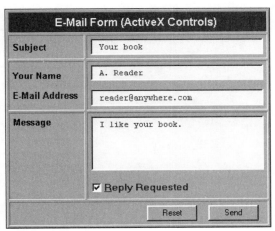

Because HTML forms can only submit the values of HTML intrinsic controls, using ActiveX controls in a form requires an additional step: You need to assign the values of the ActiveX controls to HTML intrinsic controls before the form is submitted. The HTML hidden intrinsic control is perfect for doing so because it doesn't appear in the form — it's invisible.

I use the following HTML code to generate hidden controls on the form. The names of these hidden controls correspond to the names of the ActiveX controls, except that each control name is preceded by H_:

```
<INPUT TYPE=Hidden NAME="H_Subject">
<INPUT TYPE=Hidden NAME="H_From">
<INPUT TYPE=Hidden NAME="H_ReturnMail">
<INPUT TYPE=Hidden NAME="H_Message">
<INPUT TYPE=Hidden NAME="H_SendReply">
```

After the form's data is validated, I used the following VBScript code to transfer the values of the ActiveX controls to the HTML hidden controls:

```
Form1.H_MAILTO_SUBJECT.Value = Form1.Subject.Value
Form1.H_From.Value = Form1.From.Value
Form1.H_ReturnMail.Value = Form1.ReturnMail.Value
Form1.H_Message.Value = Form1.Message.Value
Form1.H_SendReply.Value = Form1.SendReply.Value
```

Chapter 18

The Coolest Control: The HTML Layout Control

● ●

In This Chapter

▶ Introducing the HTML Layout control

▶ Using the ActiveX Control Pad to create Layout controls

▶ Demonstrating key elements of the Layout control by example

● ●

C hapters 16 and 17 introduce you to ActiveX controls, present examples, and demonstrate the basics of the Microsoft HTML Control Pad, a free product that makes inserting ActiveX objects into your HTML document easy. This chapter continues the saga by covering the HTML Layout control, a special ActiveX control that contains other ActiveX controls.

The HTML Layout control

The HTML Layout control has one *major* attraction: It gives you precise control over the appearance of an HTML document. As you may be aware, an HTML document can look drastically different depending on the browser that displays it. If you've every developed a great-looking Web page, you may have been shocked when you saw it displayed in a different browser. I've experienced such a shock on more than one occasion.

The upside of the HTML Layout control

Think of the HTML Layout control as a two-dimensional backdrop for other ActiveX controls. When you add an ActiveX control to a Layout control, you can specify the precise position of that control. Because you can control the exact size of each ActiveX control, every visitor to your site sees your page exactly as you designed it — assuming, of course, that their browser supports ActiveX controls.

An HTML Layout control works just like any other HTML object. You can center the control using the `<CENTER>` tag, place the control inside of a table, and even use multiple Layout controls in a single document.

The downside of the HTML Layout control

If the HTML Layout control is so great, why not use it for everything and scrap HTML altogether? As you find out in this chapter, the HTML Layout control has quite a bit of overhead. Consequently, a page that contains this control takes longer to display. Also, if someone uses a browser that doesn't support this control, they see only the HTML content of the page and miss out on everything contained in the Layout control.

An Introductory Example

Figure 18-1 shows a document that contains an HTML Layout control. The Layout control in this example contains five other ActiveX controls, which are Image controls.

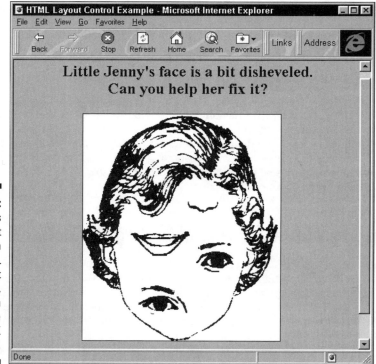

Figure 18-1: This document contains an HTML Layout control, which contains five ActiveX controls.

Using the example

This page looks similar to a standard HTML document that contains graphics. But if you load it into Internet Explorer 3.0, you find that the page is much different from a standard HTML document. You can click the graphic objects and actually move them around on-screen. Try doing that with HTML! Figure 18-2 shows the same page after body parts are rearranged.

Figure 18-2: After moving the Image controls, Jenny's face is fixed.

Looking at the ⟨OBJECT⟩ tag

As I indicate in this chapter, an HTML Layout control is an ActiveX object. Here's the ⟨OBJECT⟩ tag that I used to insert this object:

```
<OBJECT
  CLASSID="CLSID:812AE312-8B8E-11CF-93C8-00AA00C08FDF"
  ID="Layout1"
  STYLE="LEFT:0;TOP:0">
  <PARAM NAME="ALXPATH" REF VALUE="layout1.alx">
</OBJECT>
```

About ALX files

The preceding ⟨OBJECT⟩ tag may seem rather simple for this moderately complex example, but this ⟨OBJECT⟩ tag is for the HTML Layout control itself. This control holds other controls, which are defined in the layout1.alx file.

Can't view the ALX file?

Hopefully, you have lots of practice using the Internet Explorer View⇨Source command to view HTML source documents, including the VBScript code contained in the documents. If you attempt to use this command when the document contains an HTML Layout control, you see the containing HTML document, but you *don't* see the ALX file, which is probably what you want to see.

Does this mean that you can't view these ALX files? Nope. You just need to know where to find them. When Internet Explorer loads a document, it stores the document in its *cache* on your hard drive. So, if you revisit the document before the

cached version expires, the document can be retrieved from the cache and displayed almost instantaneously — it doesn't have to be retrieved from the server.

ALX files also are stored in the cache on your hard drive. All you need to do is locate the file and load it into your text editor to see it. You can find out the name of the ALX file by looking at the HTML Layout control <OBJECT> tag in the HTML document. The easiest way to locate the file is to use the Windows Find File command (which is on the Windows Start menu) and search your hard drive for all *.ALX files.

Every HTML Layout control must have an associated *ALX file*. An ALX file is an HTML file that contains the objects contained in the HTML Layout control. The layout1.alx file used in this example contains

- ✔ <OBJECT> tags for five ActiveX Image objects: the face, two eyes, the nose, and the mouth.
- ✔ VBScript code that enables the dragging action.

Here's the <OBJECT> tag for the ActiveX Image object that displays the nose.

```
<OBJECT
  ID="ImageNose"
  CLASSID="CLSID:D4A97620-8E8F-11CF-93CD-00AA00C08FDF"
 STYLE="TOP:105pt;LEFT:117pt;WIDTH:40pt;HEIGHT:14pt;ZINDEX:4;">
  <PARAM NAME="PicturePath" VALUE="nose.gif">
  <PARAM NAME="AutoSize" VALUE="-1">
  <PARAM NAME="BorderStyle" VALUE="0">
  <PARAM NAME="Size" VALUE="1411;494">
  <PARAM NAME="VariousPropertyBits" VALUE="19">
</OBJECT>
```

For the record, here's the MouseMove event handler subroutine for the ImageNose object. This subroutine executes when the user moves the mouse over the nose. If the left mouse button is pressed when this movement occurs, the subroutine changes the Left and Top properties of the object, which display the image in a different position:

```
Sub ImageNose_MouseMove(Button, Shift, x, y)
    If Button=1 Then
        ImageNose.Left=x+ImageNose.Left-(ImageNose.Width / 2)
        ImageNose.Top=y+ImageNose.Top-(ImageNose.Height / 2)
    End If
End Sub
```

The properties and events for the Image control are well documented in the ActiveX Control Pad's online Help file.

Hands-On: Creating a Layout

In this section, I describe the basics of creating a layout using the ActiveX Control Pad. I introduce the Control Pad in Chapter 16, so you may want to refer to that chapter if the ActiveX Control Pad is new to you.

In the sections that follow, I describe how to:

- ✔ Create a new HTML file using the ActiveX Control Pad
- ✔ Insert an ActiveX Layout control in the HTML document
- ✔ Add ActiveX controls to the Layout control
- ✔ Write VBScript to perform actions with the ActiveX controls

More specifically, the upcoming example displays an image of a house and uses three HotSpot ActiveX controls, which are invisible controls useful for tracking mouse movements. When the mouse moves over one of the HotSpot controls, a message in a Label control displays and remains visible until the mouse pointer is moved out of the HotSpot control.

Figure 18-3 shows how this HTML Layout looks. You may want to try this out for yourself, using the document on this book's disk. When the mouse pointer is over the chimney, the appropriate Label becomes visible. The HotSpot control is a rectangle that roughly corresponds to the shape of the chimney.

1. Creating the HTML File

To create a new HTML file, start the ActiveX Control Pad and choose the File⇨New HTML command. The Control Pad displays the file, which contains a few standard lines of HTML, in a new window.

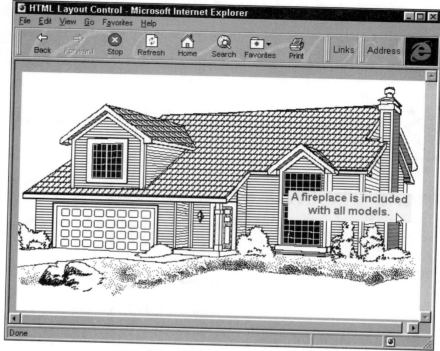

Figure 18-3:
This HTML
Layout uses
HotSpot
controls and
Label
controls to
describe the
house's
features.

2. Inserting a Layout control

To insert a Layout control into the HTML document:

1. **Position the cursor between the** `<BODY>` **and the** `</BODY>` **tags**

2. **Choose the Edit⇨Insert HTML Layout command.**

   You are prompted for a filename and location for the ALX file.

3. **Specify the directory, enter a filename, and click the Open button.**

   You will be asked if you want to create the file. Reply Yes.

   The Control Pad inserts the `<OBJECT>` tag, as shown in Figure 18-4.

3. Saving the HTML file

If you're following along in this chapter, now is a good time to save the HTML file. Press Ctrl+S and enter a name for the file.

Remember: Every project that uses an HTML Layout control consists of at least two files: an HTML file and an ALX file.

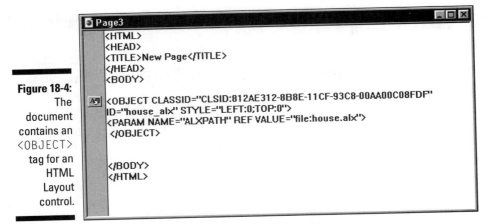

Figure 18-4:
The document contains an `<OBJECT>` tag for an HTML Layout control.

```
Page3
<HTML>
<HEAD>
<TITLE>New Page</TITLE>
</HEAD>
<BODY>

<OBJECT CLASSID="CLSID:812AE312-8B8E-11CF-93C8-00AA00C08FDF"
ID="house_alx" STYLE="LEFT:0;TOP:0">
<PARAM NAME="ALXPATH" REF VALUE="file:house.alx">
</OBJECT>


</BODY>
</HTML>
```

4. Editing the HTML Layout

The ActiveX Control Pad provides a WYSIWYG environment for editing HTML Layouts. To edit the Layout created in the previous section, click the icon in the left margin of the Control Pad's document window.

Your screen looks similar to Figure 18-5. The empty Layout control appears in a window, and the floating Toolbox appears in another window.

Note: The window that contains the HTML document, which contains the Layout control, remains open. You can arrange these windows any way you want. Use Ctrl+F6 to toggle between the windows.

5. Adding the Image control

To add an Image control to the Layout:

1. **Locate the Image control icon in the Toolbox.**

   If the Toolbox is not displayed, choose the View➪Toolbox command.

   Move the mouse over the icons in the Toolbox, and a ToolTip displays the name of the control.

2. **Click the Image control icon and then click and drag in the Layout window to place the control.**

   The exact size of the control doesn't matter.

   When you add the control to the Layout window, the control is empty and is selected automatically. The control appears with eight handles.

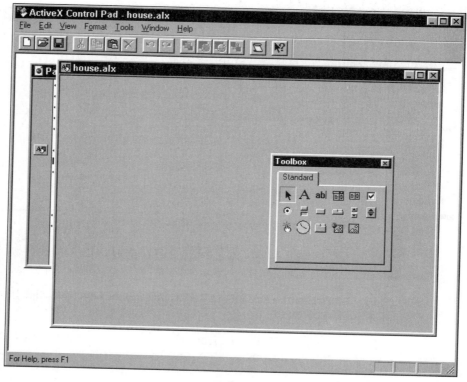

Figure 18-5:
Getting
ready to add
controls to
an HTML
Layout
control.

3. **If the Properties dialog box does not display, double-click the Image object or choose the View⟹Properties command.**

4. **Select the PicturePath property in the Properties dialog box and enter the name of the graphic file.**

   This example uses a GIF file named house.gif.

5. **Press Enter.**

   The image appears in the Image control.

6. **In the Properties dialog box, select the AutoSize property and set it to True.**

   The Image control adjusts its size to accommodate the size of the image.

7. **Click and drag the image so that it appears in the upper-left corner of the Layout window.**

   You also can accomplish this by setting the image's Top and Left properties to 0.

8. **Resize the Layout window so that it's at least as large as the image.**

Figure 18-6 shows how my screen looks as I create this example.

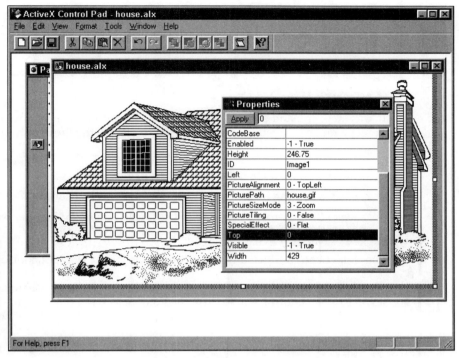

6. Adding a Label control

In this step, you insert an ActiveX Label control (the first of three). This control displays the message that appears when the mouse pointer moves over the chimney.

1. **In the Toolbox, click the Label control.**

   If the Toolbox is not displayed, choose the View⇨Toolbox command.

2. **Click and drag in the Layout window to draw the control.**

   Place the label somewhere near the chimney. You can always reposition the label later.

3. **In the Properties dialog box, enter the following text for the Caption property:** A fireplace is included with all models.

4. **Set the Label's Visible property to False.**

   When you change the Visible property, the control still appears on-screen. However, when the page loads in a browser, the label is invisible.

5. **Adjust the other properties to your liking.**

For example, you may want to change the font, increase the font size, change the foreground and background colors, or change the text alignment.

7. Adding a HotSpot control

In this step, you add the first of three HotSpot controls. This control is able to detect a mouse movement, which is used to display the previously created label.

1. **In the Toolbox, click the HotSpot control.**
2. **Click and drag in the Layout window to draw the control.**

   Make the control correspond to the house's chimney. In other words, this control is tall and relatively narrow.

You don't need to adjust any of the properties for the HotSpot control.

The HotSpot control is invisible and can be difficult to locate when unselected. If you lose the control, you can use the Edit⇨Select All command to select all objects in the Layout. This command helps you locate the HotSpot control.

8. Writing the VBScript

The next step is to create the VBScript code that does the work. Specifically, the code changes the Label control's Visible property to True when the mouse pointer is within the HotSpot control. The code also sets the Label control's Visible property to False when the mouse pointer moves out of the HotSpot control.

Note: In this example, I use the Script Wizard (described in Chapter 17) to create the VBScript code. You can write the code manually by editing the ALX file using any text editor.

The HotSpot control responds to events, two of which are relevant for this project.

✓ **MouseEnter:** The mouse pointer entering the HotSpot control triggers this event.

✓ **MouseExit:** The mouse pointer exiting the HotSpot control triggers this event.

The following steps describe how to create the VBScript code with the Script Wizard.

1. **Select the Tools⇨Script Wizard command.**

   The Script Wizard window appears.

2. **At the bottom of the Script Wizard window, make sure that the Code View option is selected.**

3. **In the left panel, click the + symbol next to the HotSpot1 control and then select the MouseEnter event from the list.**

   The Script Wizard creates a subroutine named HotSpot1_MouseEnter, which appears in the code window.

4. **In the code window, enter the following VBScript statement:**

   ```
   Label1.Visible=True
   ```

5. **In the left panel, select the MouseExit event for the HotSpot1 control.**

   The Script Wizard creates a subroutine named HotSpot1_MouseExit, which appears in the code window.

6. **In the code window, enter the following VBScript statement:**

   ```
   Label1.Visible=False
   ```

7. **Click OK to close the Script Wizard.**

Figure 18-7 shows the HotSpot_MouseExit subroutine that displays in the Script Wizard.

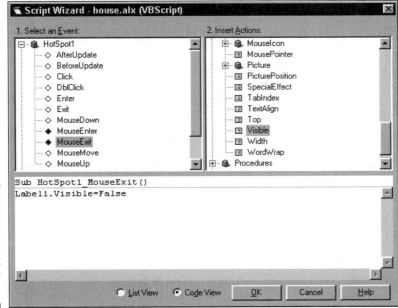

Figure 18-7:
Using the Script Wizard to create event handler subroutines.

9. Testing the subroutine

Now you can test the subroutine. Even though most of the work has gone into the ALX file, you load the HTML file into the browser. In the HTML file, the `<OBJECT>` tag for the Layout control causes the ALX file to open.

1. **Press Ctrl+S to save the ALX file.**

2. **Load the HTML file into your browser.**

3. **Move the mouse over the chimney.**

    The Label control becomes visible.

4. **Move the mouse pointer away from the chimney.**

    The Label control becomes invisible.

10. Finishing off the subroutine

You can add more HotSpot-Label combinations. The example on this book's disk contains three HotSpots. The procedures for adding more HotSpots and Labels are exactly the same as outlined in the previous example.

The layout may look cluttered when you add more controls. Simply make sure that the HotSpot controls don't overlap with each other. Otherwise, two Label controls are visible at once.

Discovering More about the HTML Layout Control

If working with Layout controls seems foreign to you, don't worry. The controls get much easier to use with practice. Although this book doesn't provide in-depth coverage of the HTML Layout controls, here are general tips on ways to improve your Layout control skills:

✔ **Read through the online Help for the ActiveX Control Pad.** The Help file contains lots of useful information and helps familiarize you with the Control Pad.

✔ **Look at other developers' work.** More and more sites are using the Layout control. Browsing these sites gives you ideas that you can adapt. Don't forget that you can view the ALX files that are downloaded from other sites.

✔ **View the examples on this book's disk.** In the next section, I present a few examples.

Layout Control Examples

In this section, I describe a few examples that I developed. These examples use the HTML Layout control.

Watch the bouncing balls

My bouncing balls example is very simple, yet it really demonstrates a key advantage of the Layout control: the ability to reposition objects on a Web page. Refer to Figure 18-8 for a look at my bouncing balls example.

The Layout control has three Image controls, three Timer controls, and one CommandButton control. The CommandButton toggles the Enabled property of the Timer controls and lets the user start and stop the balls. Each timer has a different interval so that the balls bounce at different speeds.

Following is one of the event handlers, which executes whenever a Timer event occurs. This routine sets the Top and Left properties of the Image control to a random number between 0 and 350. Changing the position of the image gives the appearance that the ball is bouncing randomly.

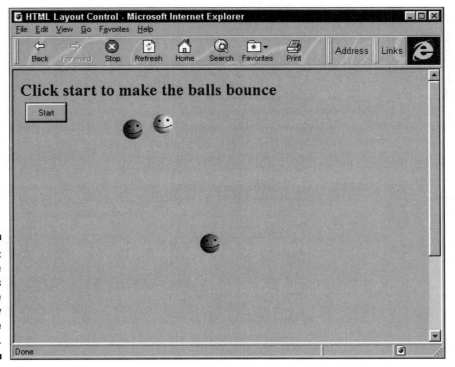

Figure 18-8:
These three balls bounce randomly around the window.

```
Sub IeTimer1_Timer()
    Image1.Top=Rnd()*350
    Image1.Left=Rnd()*350
End Sub
```

Rolling the dice

Figure 18-9 shows an example that uses an HTML Layout control to roll dice. Clicking the button rolls five dice. The label at the top displays the sum of the dice. The table at the bottom keeps a tally of the number of times each dice value appears. Use this information to determine whether the dice are loaded.

This Layout control contains the following ActiveX objects:

- ✔ **A Label control:** This control displays the sum of the dice rolled. VBScript code updates the control after the dice are rolled.

- ✔ **Five Image controls:** VBScript changes the PicturePath property, which determines the image that is displayed.

- ✔ **A CommandButton control:** When a user clicks the button, the dice roll, generating five random numbers between one and six.

The table that you see in Figure 18-9 is not in the Layout control. The table is created in the containing HTML document. This table contains six additional Label controls that keep track of the number of times each dice value appears.

Figure 18-9:
This HTML document contains an HTML Layout control.

This example demonstrates an important concept: The ALX file contains the VBScript code, but this code is able to modify the Label objects that are contained in the HTML document. You can modify the Label objects by using the Parent property to obtain the Document object that contains the Layout control. The following VBScript statement, which is contained in the ALX file, sets the Caption property of a Label object in the containing HTML document.

```
Parent.Label1.Caption = "0"
```

Using ListBox controls

This final example demonstrates how to use the ActiveX ListBox control. This control is similar to an HTML intrinsic select control, but is much more versatile. You can control formatting, display data in multiple columns, and add and delete items from lists.

Figure 18-10 shows the Online Fruit Stand, which is done entirely in an HTML Layout control. The user selects an item from the list box on the left and then copies it to the shopping cart list on the right by clicking the Order button. A Label control keeps a running tally of the total cost. Items can also be removed from the shopping cart by selecting the item and clicking the Remove button.

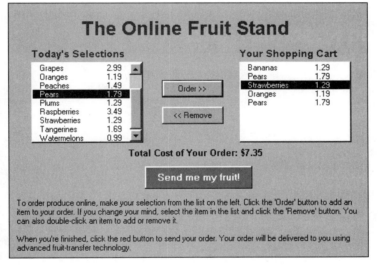

Figure 18-10: The Online Fruit Stand consists of an HTML Layout control and other ActiveX objects.

Part VI
Putting It All Together

The 5th Wave   By Rich Tennant

"IT SAYS HERE IF I SUBSCRIBE TO THIS MAGAZINE, THEY'LL SEND ME A FREE DESK-TOP CALCULATOR. DESKTOP CALCULATOR?!! WHOOAA — WHERE HAVE I BEEN?!!"

In this part . . .

This part consists of four chapters, each of which describes a particular VBScript application. You find out the details behind these useful pages to adapt to your own needs. Even if a particular topic doesn't appeal to you, I recommend that you still read about it. Many of the techniques may come in handy in a completely different situation.

Chapter 19

Creating Column Charts with VBScript

In This Chapter

▶ Introducing a technique for creating an attractive column chart using standard HTML
▶ Extending the technique by using VBScript to write the HTML
▶ Creating a chart on the fly using VBScript

*V*BScript has absolutely no graphics or charting capabilities, but with a few clever techniques, you can push the envelope and create attractive column charts using VBScript. In this chapter, you find out the tricks involved in creating column charts — and you may be surprised how easy you can create them.

What is a Column Chart?

A column chart is a common type of chart that represents values as vertical columns. Figure 19-1 shows an example of a simple column chart that I created in an Excel spreadsheet. This chart shows a company's sales volume by month. Higher columns mean more sales in that month. Pretty simple, eh?

Using graphic files

If you need to display a column chart in a Web page, you probably think you should create the chart using a graphics program or a spreadsheet and then convert the image to a GIF or JPG file. Then you can use the <IMG> tag to insert the graphic into your HTML document. Although this technique certainly works, it's a lot of trouble and is of no use at all if the data is being generated by the user or by VBScript.

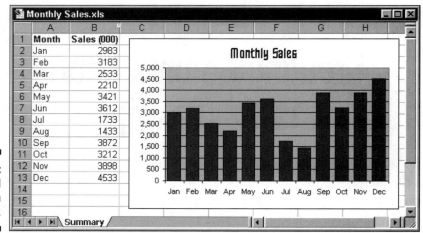

Figure 19-1:
I created
this chart in
Excel.

Another approach for charting applications is to use an ActiveX control. Several such controls exist, including one from Microsoft.

A cool chart-making technique

Actually, you can create simple column charts using straight HTML. Figure 19-2 shows such a chart. The best part is that when you create these charts, you use only a single GIF file, which is a mere 85 bytes in size (yes, *bytes!*)

Here's the HTML that produces this chart.

```
<HTML>
<BODY>
<CENTER>
<H1>Monthly Sales</H1>
<TABLE BORDER=5 RULES=none CELLPADDING=4>
<TR VALIGN=Bottom ALIGN=Center>
<TD><IMG SRC=bluevert.gif WIDTH=30 HEIGHT=145><BR>Jan</TD>
<TD><IMG SRC=bluevert.gif WIDTH=30 HEIGHT=131><BR>Feb</TD>
<TD><IMG SRC=bluevert.gif WIDTH=30 HEIGHT=121><BR>Mar</TD>
<TD><IMG SRC=bluevert.gif WIDTH=30 HEIGHT=159><BR>Apr</TD>
<TD><IMG SRC=bluevert.gif WIDTH=30 HEIGHT=164><BR>May</TD>
<TD><IMG SRC=bluevert.gif WIDTH=30 HEIGHT=111><BR>Jun</TD>
<TD><IMG SRC=bluevert.gif WIDTH=30 HEIGHT= 99><BR>Jul</TD>
<TD><IMG SRC=bluevert.gif WIDTH=30 HEIGHT=128><BR>Aug</TD>
<TD><IMG SRC=bluevert.gif WIDTH=30 HEIGHT=142><BR>Sep</TD>
<TD><IMG SRC=bluevert.gif WIDTH=30 HEIGHT=155><BR>Oct</TD>
<TD><IMG SRC=bluevert.gif WIDTH=30 HEIGHT=182><BR>Nov</TD>
```

```
<TD><IMG SRC=bluevert.gif WIDTH=30 HEIGHT=165><BR>Dec</TD>
</TR>
</TABLE>
</CENTER>
</BODY>
</HTML>
```

This chart is actually a table with 1 row and 12 columns. Each cell of the table contains an `<IMG>` tag that points to the tiny GIF file, which is 20 pixels wide by 1 pixel high. The `HEIGHT` attribute for the image makes the column appear in various heights. Each cell also contains the month name, separated from the image by a `<BR>` tag, which causes the cell to appear below the column.

Creating a Chart with VBScript

If you understand the column chart technique that I describe in the previous section, you may realize where I'm headed. Because VBScript can write information to a document, VBScript code that automates the creation of such charts should be possible. Automating the creation of such charts is indeed possible, as you see in Figure 19-3. I created the chart in this figure by using VBScript.

This document is available on the companion disk.

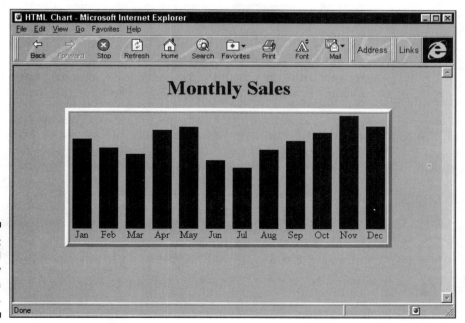

Figure 19-2:
I created this chart by using plain HTML.

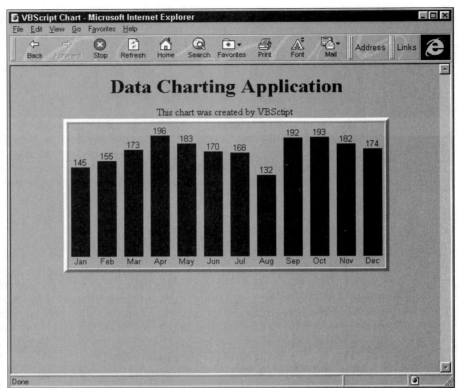

Figure 19-3:
VBScript
generates
the HTML
that creates
this chart.

The code behind the magic

The data for the chart in Figure 19-3 is stored in a 12-element array named Data. In addition, another 12-element array (named Months) holds the month names.

Following is the part of the HTML document that generates the table.

```
<TABLE BORDER=5 RULES=none CELLPADDING=4>
<TR VALIGN=Bottom ALIGN=Center>
<SCRIPT LANGUAGE=VBScript>
For i = 1 To 12
    Document.Write "<TD><FONT Face=Arial Size=2>"
    Document.Write Data(i)
    Document.Write "<BR>"
    Document.Write "<IMG SRC=bluevert.gif WIDTH=30 HEIGHT="
```

```
    Document.Write Data(i) & ">"
    Document.Write "<BR>" & Months(i)
    Document.Write "</TD>"
Next
</SCRIPT>
</TR>
</TABLE>
```

How the code works

The preceding code may look a bit daunting, but is really quite simple. The first two lines are standard HTML. These lines begin the table with the <TABLE> tag and begin a table row with the <TR> tag. Then the VBScript kicks in to write the HTML that defines the cells. Notice that I add a new twist: The data value appears at the top of the graphic in each column.

Here's the first <TD> tag that's generated by the script.

```
<TD><FONT Face=Arial Size=2>145<BR>
<IMG SRC=bluevert.gif WIDTH=30 HEIGHT=145><BR>Jan</TD>
```

The Script generates 11 additional <TD> tags, one for each of the other months.

Using VBScript to create the chart has a major advantage over hard coding the data with HTML. To update the chart, you change only the values in the Data array. Of course, these values can be generated automatically, which begins the next topic: Creating a Chart in a Frame.

Creating a Chart in a Frame

To make chart generation interactive, the chart needs to be in a floating frame. Why? Because after a document is loaded, the document cannot be changed. If the document contains a floating frame, however, you can change the information that displays in the frame. You can make this change by using VBScript code to generate the HTML and then sending the HTML code to the document in the frame using the Document.Write method.

Creating the floating frame

I use the following HTML to insert a floating frame named ChartFrame.

```
<IFRAME
  SRC="chart.htm"
  NAME=ChartFrame
  WIDTH=520
  HEIGHT=340
  SCROLLING=No
  FRAMEBORDER=No>
</IFRAME>
```

The chart.htm file is simply an empty file that initially loads into the frame.

Creating the chart

I also insert a button named CreateChart. Clicking this button executes an event handler script called CreateChart_OnClick. Here's the listing for that subroutine:

```
Sub CreateChart_OnClick()
  Data(0)=100
  For i=1 to 12
    Data(i)=Abs(Int(Data(i-1) + (Rnd()*30) -(Rnd()*20)))
  Next
  Content="<CENTER><H1><FONT COLOR=DarkBlue FACE=Arial>"
  Content=Content & "Monthly Sales</FONT></H1>"
  Content=Content & "<TABLE BORDER=5RULES=none CELLPADDING=4>"
  Content=Content & "<TR VALIGN=Bottom ALIGN=Center>"
  For i = 1 to 12
    Content=Content & "<TD><FONT Face=Arial Size=2>"
    Content=Content & Data(i)
    Content=Content & "<BR>"
    Content=Content & "<IMG SRC=bluevert.gif WIDTH=30HEIGHT="
    Content=Content & Data(i) & ">"
    Content=Content & "<BR>" & Months(i)
    Content=Content & "</TD>"
  Next
  Content=Content & "</TR></TABLE>"
  Frames(0).Document.Write Content
  Frames(0).Document.Close
End Sub
```

The routine starts by assigning random data to the elements of the Data array. The technique I use to generate the random values is a bit more complex than simply assigning a random number. In my technique, each value uses the previous value as a starting point and then adds a random number to that value. The result is a more orderly sequence of random numbers, which looks more real.

I use a variable named Content to hold the generated HTML code. The HTML code is progressively added to the Content variable. Finally, the Content variable, which contains the code for a complete HTML document, is written to the document in the floating frame.

Trying out the chart example

Figure 19-4 shows an example of a chart created by this procedure. If you try out this page and click the button to generate new charts, you find that the height of the charts varies significantly. Some charts are tall, and some are small. You need a way to *scale* the data so that the chart is always the same height.

Scaling the chart

Here's the code I developed to scale the data. I declared a 12-item array called ScaledData to hold the new data. I inserted this block of code right after the For-Next loop that generates the random data.

```
' Scale the data so the table is always the same size
MaxHt=200
MaxData=Data(I)
' Determine the maximum value
For i = 1 to 12
    if Data(i) > MaxData then MaxData = Data(i)
Next
' Scale the data
For i = 1 to 12
    ScaledData(i) = (Data(i)/MaxData) * MaxHt
Next
```

The variable MaxHt holds a value of 200, which is changed to create taller or shorter charts. The first For-Next loop determines the maximum value in the Data array and assigns this value to the MaxData variable. In the second For-Next loop, a simple formula assigned values to the ScaledData array. Each value is divided by the maximum value (MaxData), and the result is multiplied by the maximum height (MaxHt).

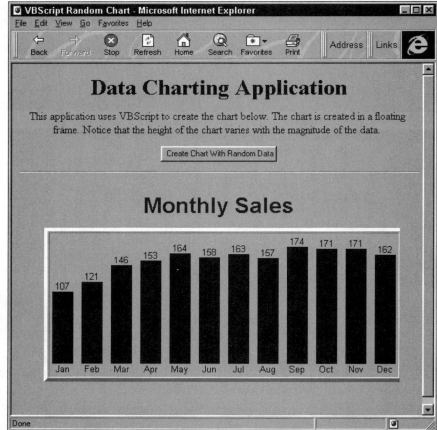

The only other modification is to change the statement that generates the data in the chart table. Rather than use values of the Data array for the height of the column, the code uses values of the ScaledData array.

If you try out the example after making this addition, you can find out that the chart is always the same height, regardless of the range of values in the Data array.

Getting Even Fancier

I close this chapter with a final example that adds a few bells and whistles to the charting application. As you can see in Figure 19-5, this example uses two select controls to let the user select

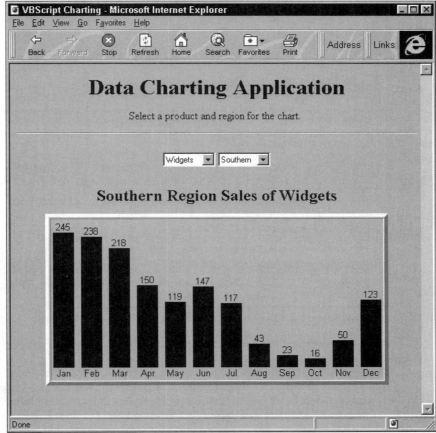

Figure 19-5:
In this example, the user can use the select controls to specify which data to chart

🖝 Which product to show (Widgets or Sprockets).

🖝 Which sales region to show (Northern, Southern, Western, or Eastern).

Declaring the variables

Following is the declarations section of the VBScript:

```
Dim P1(), P2() ,Regions(), Months()
Dim ProdNames(2)
Dim NumRegions,NumMonths
NumRegions=4
NumMonths=12
ReDim P1(NumMonths,NumRegions)
```

(continued)

(continued)
```
ReDim P2(NumMonths,NumRegions)
ReDim Regions(NumRegions)
ReDim Months(NumMonths)
```

Table 19-1 describes the arrays used in this application.

Table 19-1	The Arrays Used
Array	*Description*
P1	A two-dimensional array that holds data for Widget sales. For example, P1(2,1) holds February Widget sales for the first sales region.
P2	A two-dimensional array that holds data for Sprocket sales. For example, P2(3,4) holds March Sprocket sales for the fourth sales region.
Regions	A one-dimensional array that holds the region names. For example, Regions(1) holds *Northern*.
Months	A one-dimensional array that holds the month names. For example, Months(12) holds *Dec*.
ProdNames	A one-dimensional array that holds the product names. For example, ProdNames(1) holds *Widgets*.

Notice that I use variables to store the number of regions (NumRegions) and the number of Months (NumMonths). I then use these variables to redimension the arrays, using the ReDim statement. This technique makes maintaining the code easy — adding a new region is a relatively simple matter.

Generating the select controls

The two select controls let the user specify which data to plot. The first select control, named ProductSelect, holds the product names. The second select control, named RegionSelect, holds the region names. I use VBScript to generate the HTML that creates these two controls. This technique helps make the code easier to maintain. If a product or region name changes, for example, you can assign the new name to a VBScript variable.

```
Document.Write "<FORM NAME=Form1>"
Document.Write "<SELECT Name=ProductSelect>"
Document.Write "<Option>" & ProdNames(1)
Document.Write "<Option>" & ProdNames(2)
```

```
Document.Write "</SELECT>"
Document.Write "<SELECT Name=RegionSelect>"
For i=1 to NumRegions
    Document.Write "<Option>" & Regions(i)
Next
Document.Write "</SELECT>"
Document.Write "</FORM>"
```

Generating the chart

When the user makes a selection from either of the select controls, the appropriate OnChange event is triggered. Following are the event handler routines for these two select controls. As you can see, these subroutines simply call the DrawChart subroutine.

```
Sub RegionSelect_OnChange()
    Call DrawChart()
End Sub

Sub ProductSelect_OnChange()
    Call DrawChart()
End Sub
```

The DrawChart subroutine uses the same basic chart-making concepts that I present earlier in this chapter. But this subroutine is a little more complex because it needs to know which data to plot. At the beginning of the DrawChart subroutine, I use the following statements:

```
ProductIndex= Document.Form1.ProductSelect.selectedIndex +1
RegionIndex = Document.Form1.RegionSelect.selectedIndex +1
ChartTitle= Regions(RegionIndex) & _
    " Region Sales of " & ProdNames(ProductIndex)
```

The Product Index variable holds the index number for the product that is selected. Because these index numbers begin with 0, I increment this number by one. The RegionIndex variable holds the index number of the selected region. The ChartTitle variable holds a string that describes the data being plotted. For example, if the user selects Widgets from the ProductSelect control and Southern from the RegionSelect control, ChartTitle holds the following string: Northern Region Sales of Widgets.

The DrawChart routine then transfers the appropriate data to an array named Data. Here's the code that transfers the data:

```
For i = 1 To 12
    If ProductIndex=1 Then Data(i)=P1(i,RegionIndex)
    If ProductIndex=2 Then Data(i)=P2(i,RegionIndex)
Next
```

This For-Next loop simply fills up the Data array with the data from either the P1 array (Widgets) or the P2 array (Sprockets).

The remainder of the routine uses the same techniques that I describe previously in this chapter: The data is scaled, HTML code is generated, and the HTML is sent to the floating frame.

Adapting These Techniques

This chapter provides a realistic demonstration of how to create an attractive column chart using HTML and VBScript, with the assistance of a tiny GIF file. These examples demonstrate how to use VBScript to generate HTML on the fly and send it to a floating frame. This technique is useful because it provides an excellent way to create an interactive Web page that's free of delays caused by loading a new document.

You can easily adapt this technique for your own needs — many variations are possible. For example, you may want to display the chart horizontally (a bar chart rather than a column chart). Or, you may want to use a different GIF file for the chart.

Chapter 20
Calculating Mortgage Payments

. . . .

In This Chapter

▶ Developing a useful financial application

▶ Creating forms for data input and for displaying calculated results

▶ Using VBScript to write HTML code that is sent to a document in a frame

. . . .

*I*f you're involved in the mortgage industry, or if you are shopping for a house, you may know that many mortgage loan options are available. Look around, and you can find a wide variety of stand-alone programs and spreadsheet templates that make calculating mortgage loan payments, based on various loan parameters, easy to do. Most programs also generate amortization schedules, which show you how much of each loan payment applies to interest and how much applies to reducing the principal.

Note: Even if you have no interest in mortgage loans, you may find the techniques in this chapter useful.

Project Goals

The example in this chapter demonstrates how to use VBScript to calculate mortgage loan information and display the information directly on a Web page.

The goals for this project are to:

✔ **Allow the user to provide the following information about a mortgage loan:** The purchase price of the property, the down payment expressed as a percentage of the purchase price, the length of the loan expressed in months, and the annual interest rate.

✔ **Use VBScript to calculate and display the following information:** The down payment amount, the loan amount, and the monthly payment amount.

✔ **Allow the user to request a complete amortization schedule for the loan.** This schedule shows month-by-month loan payment details.

✔ **Make the application attractive and easy to use.**

The Game Plan

Using the HTML Layout control for this project is tempting, but this project lends itself quite well to plain old HTML forms. In general, using the simplest solution is best. In this case, using standard forms rather than ActiveX controls is the simplest approach. And, as you can find out in this chapter, you can use these HTML intrinsic elements and still have an attractive page.

For details on the HTML intrinsic controls, refer to Chapter 12. I discuss HTML forms in Chapter 13.

This project consists of two distinct sets of information:

✔ Loan information provided by the user

✔ Data calculated by VBScript

The page uses two forms and needs a button that executes the VBScript subroutine that calculates the results. Another button is provided to create the amortization schedule on demand. The amortization schedule is generated by VBScript and displayed in a floating frame.

Creating the Forms

Figure 20-1 shows the page layout that I came up with. This page actually contains three tables:

✔ The table on the left contains a form with five HTML intrinsic controls: a text control, two select controls, and two radio controls.

✔ The table on the right contains a form with four HTML intrinsic text controls.

✔ The third table contains two cells that hold the other two tables.

In other words, this example uses tables within a table, which is how I'm able to get the tables to appear next to each other. Refer to the sidebar "Nesting tables," later in this chapter for more information.

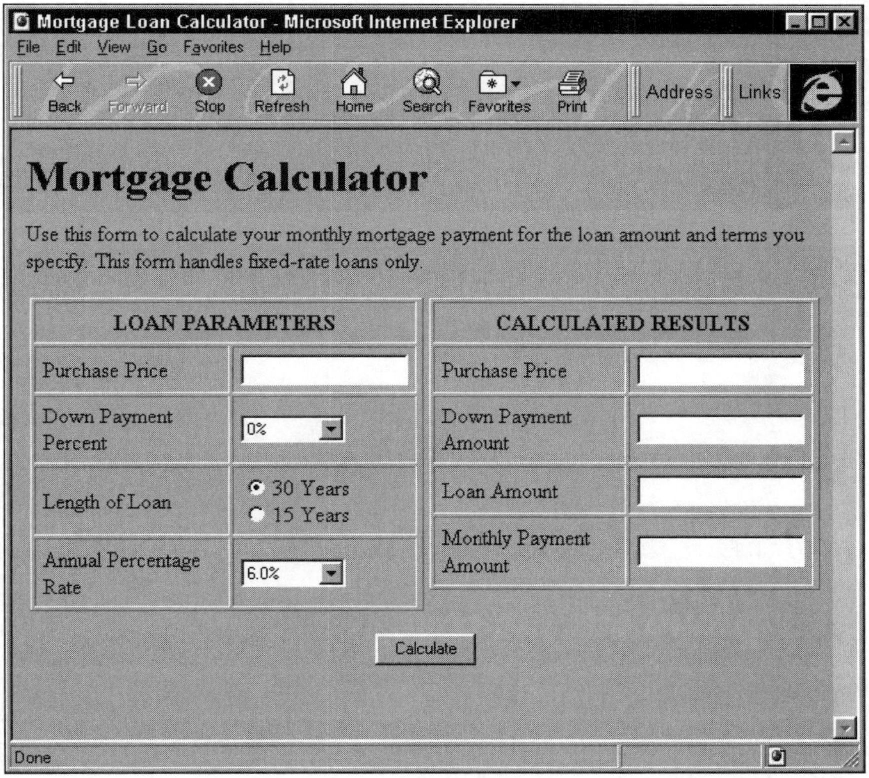

Figure 20-1:
This page
uses three
tables. Two
tables are
contained
within
another
table.

The data input form

The data input form, named InputForm, contains the five HTML intrinsic
controls listed in Table 20-1.

Table 20-1	Controls in the Data Input Form
Type	*Name*
Text	PurchasePrice
Select	PercentDown
Radio	Term
Radio	Term
Select	InterestRate

> ## Nesting tables
>
> Displaying tables within another table may seem rather confusing, but it's a useful technique that allows information to be displayed in a manner that is otherwise impossible.
>
> The example in this chapter uses a table with two cells, and each cell contains another table. This table design allows the two inner tables to be displayed side by side. Here's a "skeleton" listing of how the tables are set up:
>
> ```
> <TABLE>
>   <TD>
>     <TABLE>
>     </TABLE>
>   </TD>
>   <TD>
>     <TABLE>
>     </TABLE>
>   </TD>
> </TABLE>
> ```
>
> When setting up such tables, you may want to develop the innermost tables first and then add the tags to create the outer table, with each of the existing tables occupying a cell. This technique can be extended. In this example, the outermost table consists of only one row. However, you can have multiple rows, if you want.

The results form

The results form, named ResultsForm, contains four HTML text controls, listed in Table 20-2.

Table 20-2	Controls in the Results Form
Type	*Name*
Text	PurchasePrice2
Text	DownAmount
Text	LoanAmount
Text	MonthlyPayment

Calculating the Results

The page also contains a button control named Calc. Clicking this button executes its event handler subroutine, which is named Calc_OnClick. This subroutine:

- ✔ Performs simple data validation.
- ✔ Makes calculations.
- ✔ Places the results of the calculations in the Results form.

The On_Click subroutine

Here's the complete listing of the Calc_OnClick subroutine:

```
Sub Calc_OnClick()
'    Validate the purchase price
     vPrice = Document.InputForm.PurchasePrice.Value
     If Not IsNumeric(vPrice) Then
         Msg="The Purchase Price field is invalid. "
         Msg=Msg & "Please correct it and try again."
         MsgBox Msg ,16,"Mortgage Calculator"
         Exit Sub
     End If
'    Reproduce the purchase price in Results forms
     Document.ResultsForm.PurchasePrice2.Value = vPrice
'    Determine the down payment percent
     vPctDown = Document.InputForm.PercentDown.Options _
         (Document.InputForm.PercentDown.selectedIndex).Text
     vPctDown = (Left(vPctDown,Len(vPctDown)-1)) * .01
'    Calculate the down payment amount
     vDownAmt = vPctDown * vPrice
     Document.ResultsForm.DownAmount.Value = VDownAmt
'    Calculate the loan amount
     vLoanAmount = (1-vPctDown) * vPrice
     Document.ResultsForm.LoanAmount.Value = vLoanAmount
'    Determine the loan term
     If Document.InputForm.Elements(2).Checked Then _
         vTerm=360 Else vTerm=180
'    Determine the APR
     vAPR = Document.InputForm.InterestRate.Options _
         (Document.InputForm.InterestRate.selectedIndex).Text
```

(continued)

(continued)

```
vAPR = (Left(vAPR,Len(vAPR)-1)) *.01
'    Calculate the monthly payment
    vPayment=PMT(vAPR/12, vTerm, vLoanAmount)
    Document.ResultsForm.MonthlyPayment.Value = vPayment
End Sub
```

How the subroutine works

This subroutine is rather lengthy, but it's quite straightforward, if you look at it step by step. Here's what's going on:

1. **The purchase price entered by the user is assigned to a variable, vPrice.**

   If the value is not numeric, the user is warned, and the subroutine ends with no further action.

2. **The purchase price entered by the user is reproduced in the Results form.**

   This step is redundant, but the reproduced purchase price makes the Results form contain all the relevant information.

3. **The percent down payment is retrieved from the drop-down box and is assigned to the vPctDown variable.**

   Two statement are needed to perform this step.

4. **The down payment amount is calculated, assigned to a variable (vDownAmt), and entered in the Results form.**

5. **The loan amount is calculated, assigned to a variable (vLoanAmt), and entered in the Results form.**

6. **The interest rate is retrieved from the drop-down box and is assigned to the vAPR variable.**

7. **The monthly payment is calculated, assigned to a variable (vPayment), and entered into the Results form.**

Calculating the monthly payment

You may have noticed that I use the PMT function to calculate the monthly loan payment. I developed this custom function because VBScript doesn't have a built-in function to do the calculation.

Here's a listing of the PMT function. By the way, I'm not really a financial genius. I found the formula in a finance book.

```
Function PMT(rate,nper,princ)
    PMT = princ * rate / (1 - ((rate + 1) ^ -nper))
End Function
```

This function takes three arguments:

- ✔ **princ:** The loan principal amount
- ✔ **rate:** The annual interest rate
- ✔ **nper:** The number of payment periods (term)

Note: Spreadsheet users may notice that my PMT function works very much like the function provided with spreadsheet products such as Excel and 1-2-3.

Figure 20-2 shows this Web page in use. The page works fine, with one problem: The numbers displayed in the Results form are not very attractive (for example, the loan payment amount is 1386.81504463202). The numbers are much more readable when they include dollars signs, commas, and only two decimal places. In other words, these numbers need to be formatted. Tackling this problem is next.

Formatting the numbers

VBScript doesn't have a way to format numbers, but you may recall from Chapter 15 that I developed a function that displays numbers in dollars and cents format. This function is called FormatDollar, and it takes one argument: the number to be formatted. It returns a well-formatted string that includes a dollar sign and commas that separate thousands. It also is rounded to two decimal places.

For this example, I copied the FormatDollar function to the document and then modified the assignment statements so that they call the function. For example, I changed this statement:

```
Document.ResultsForm.DownAmount.Value = VDownAmt
```

to:

```
Document.ResultsForm.DownAmount.Value =FormatDollar(VDownAmt)
```

Figure 20-3 shows how the page looks after this function displays the results. Much better, don't you agree?

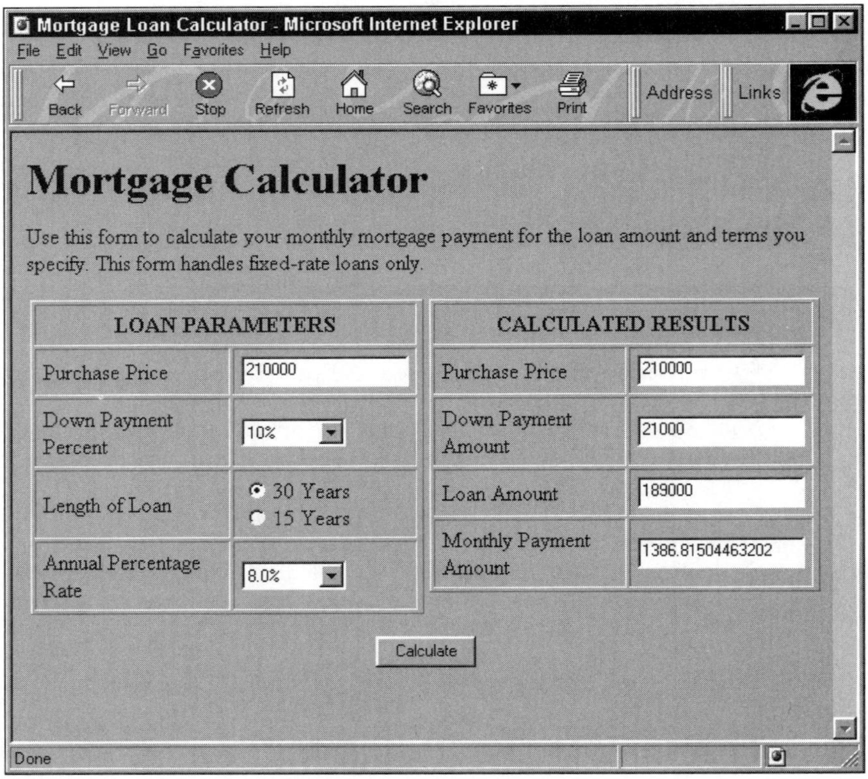

Figure 20-2:
Trying
out the
Mortgage
Calculator.

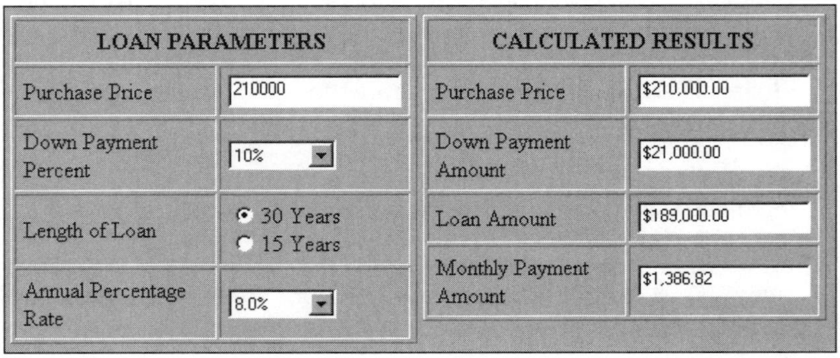

Figure 20-3:
Using the
FormatDollar
function
makes the
results look
much better.

Amortizing the Loan

The final part of this project involves generating an amortization schedule. An amortization schedule shows, on a month-by-month basis, the amount of each loan payment that is applied to interest, the amount applied to the loan principal, and the balance of the loan.

At the beginning of the loan, most of the payment goes to interest. But toward the end of the loan, when the loan balance gets lower, the situation is reversed, and most of the payment is applied to reducing the principal.

This phase of the project has two components:

- ✔ Calculating the amortization schedule
- ✔ Showing the schedule to the user

The amortization schedule is generated on the fly, using the loan information provided by the user. Whenever new information needs to be generated, consider using a floating frame to show the information — an ideal solution for this phase.

Inserting a floating frame

A good place to put the floating frame is directly below the button. Here's the HTML code that inserts a floating frame:

```
<IFRAME
   SRC="amortize.htm"
   NAME=Amortize
   WIDTH=600
   HEIGHT=400
   SCROLLING=Yes
   FRAMEBORDER=1>
</IFRAME>
```

This floating frame loads the amortize.htm document, which is essentially an empty HTML document. Because the amortization schedule doesn't fit into the frame, I set the SCROLLING attribute to Yes. This attribute allows the user to scroll up or down through the document in the frame.

Adding another button

The page also allows the user to request the amortization schedule, with the addition of another button. I placed the button next to the Calc button and named it Amortize.

Figure 20-4 shows how the page looks after adding the button and the floating frame.

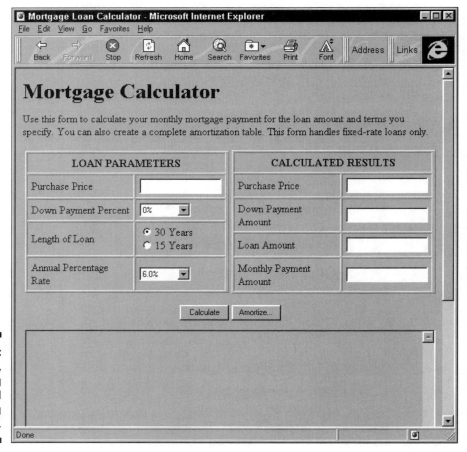

Figure 20-4:
The page, after adding a button and a floating frame.

Calculating the amortization schedule

The amortization schedule is best presented in a table. Calculating the amortization schedule consists of performing calculations for each month and then constructing HTML code that is eventually sent to the document in the floating frame.

Note: Because the Amortize_OnClick routine uses the variables that are calculated in the Calc_OnClick routine, I make those variables available by declaring them outside of any procedure. The following code provides an example:

```
Dim vTerm
Dim vPayment
Dim vLoanAmount
Dim vAPR
```

The Amortize_OnClick subroutine

When the Amortize button is clicked, it executes the Amortize_OnClick subroutine, as seen in the following code.

```
Sub Amortize_OnClick()
'    Validate the purchase price
     vPrice= Document.InputForm.PurchasePrice.Value
     If Not IsNumeric(vPrice) then
         Msg="The Purchase Price field is invalid. "
         Msg=Msg & "Please correct it and try again."
         MsgBox Msg,16,"Mortgage Calculator"
         Exit Sub
     End If
     Call Calc_OnClick()
     Content="<BODY BGCOLOR=" & Document.BGColor & "><CENTER>"
     Content=Content & "<H1>Amortization Schedule</H1>"
     Content=Content & "<TABLE BORDER=2 CELLPADDING=9
             CELLSPACING=3>"
     Content=Content & "<TR><TD>Month</TD><TD>Payment</TD>"
     Content=Content & "<TD>To Interest</TD><TD>To Principal</
             TD>"
     Content=Content & "<TD>Balance</TD></TR>"
     vBalance=vLoanAmount
     For i=1 to vTerm
         Content=Content & "<TR ALIGN=Right><TD>" & i & "</
                 TD>"
         Content=Content & "<TD>" & FormatDollars(vPayment) &
```

(continued)

(continued)

```
"</TD>"
        vInterest=(vAPR/12)* vBalance
        Content=Content & "<TD>" & FormatDollars(vInterest) &
            "</TD>"
        vPrincipal=vPayment-vInterest
        Content=Content & "<TD>" &
            FormatDollars(vPrincipal) & "</TD>"
        vBalance=vBalance-vPrincipal
        Content=Content & "<TD>" & FormatDollars(vBalance) &
            "</TD>"
        Content=Content & "</TR>"
    Next
    Frames(0).Document.Write Content
    Frames(0).Document.Close
End Sub
```

How the subroutine works

The Amortize_OnClick subroutine looks complicated, but if you examine it closely, you can understand how it works. Here's a play-by-play analysis of what's going on in this subroutine.

1. **The purchase price entered by the user is assigned to a variable, vPrice.**

   If the value is not numeric, the user is warned, and the subroutine ends with no further action. This code is the same verification code used in the Calc_OnClick subroutine.

2. **This routine executes the Calc_OnClick subroutine, just in case the user doesn't calculate the loan before requesting the amortization schedule.**

3. **The Contents variable is a string that holds the HTML code as it is being constructed.**

   It uses six statements to add the initial HTML that defines the `<BODY>` tag, the `<TABLE>` tag, and the table headers.

4. **The current loan balance is assigned to the vBalance variable.**

   Initially, this variable is the value contained in vLoanAmount.

5. **A For-Next loop cycles through each month.**

   The number of months is determined by vTerm. Within this loop, the Interest, Principal, and new Balance are calculated, and HTML code is generated to insert those values in table cells. Notice that I use the FormatDollars function to format the data placed in the table.

6. **The Contents string is sent to the document in the floating frame.**

Figure 20-5 shows an example of part of the amortization schedule.

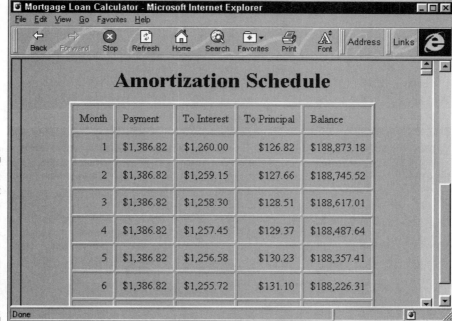

Figure 20-5:
VBScript
calculates
the
amortization
schedule
and sends
the results
to a floating
frame.

Testing the subroutine

When I tested this subroutine, I was surprised at how long it took to create and display the amortization schedule. Even on my relatively fast system, the delay bordered on intolerable. A *lot* was happening behind the scenes, though. For example, a 30-year amortization schedule results in 360 months of calculations, and the FormatDollars function is called 1,440 times! This fairly lengthy function accounts for a lot of the time.

Because of the lengthy calculation time, I added the following statements at the beginning of the subroutine, which displays the message box shown in Figure 20-6. The message box lets the user know that the display isn't instantaneous.

Figure 20-6:
Calculating
an
amortization
schedule
takes time.

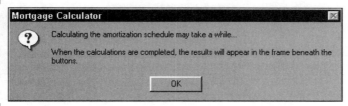

```
Msg="Calculating the amortization schedule may take a while"
Msg=Msg & Chr(13) & Chr(13)
Msg=Msg & "When the calculations are completed, the results "
Msg=Msg & "will appear in the frame beneath the buttons."
Msgbox Msg,32,"Mortgage Calculator"
```

A change of plans

In an effort to speed up the results, I made one final change to this application. Rather than calculate a *monthly* amortization schedule, I changed the code to create an annual amortization schedule. You can open the document and view the code to see how I did it. After making this change, only a slight delay occurs before the frame is filled with the calculated results.

Figure 20-7 shows part of the annual amortization schedule as it appears in the floating frame.

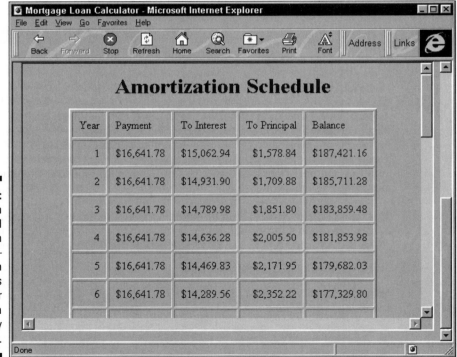

Figure 20-7: Part of an annual amortization schedule — which calculates much faster than a monthly version.

Chapter 21

Creating a Calendar Application

● ●

In This Chapter

▶ Step-by-step procedures for developing a useful calendar application

▶ Examples of using ActiveX controls

▶ Using floating frames to display information

▶ Using VBScript to generate HTML code

● ●

*I*n this chapter, you get another taste of how to develop a useful HTML page that uses VBScript. You work on a project that displays a calendar for any month. The project also sets up links so that clicking a date loads another document into a frame.

Project Background

This project involves a fictitious company, Tantalizing Tours, that provides guided tours for a fictitious vacation spot, the Callipygian Islands. Tantalizing Tours provides four different tours, but because it's a small company, it doesn't provide the tours on a regular schedule. The company has decided to set up a World Wide Web site so that potential tourists can find out when a particular tour is scheduled.

Tantalizing Tours wants a potential customer to be able to view a calendar that lists the days on which a tour is scheduled. The company also wants the customer to be able to find out the tour details by clicking a date. Finally, Tantalizing Tours wants to update the information, add new tours, and make scheduling changes very easily.

This project presents several challenges:

✔ How to display a calendar in a Web page

✔ How to display a calendar that changes months

✔ How to make certain days in the month contain links to other documents

✔ How to make the whole document easily modifiable

The Game Plan

With a relatively complex project like this one, devising a general plan before diving in is best, which is just what I do. I tackle this project in four stages:

1. **Develop a way to let the user specify a month.**

2. **Display a calendar for the user-specified month.**

3. **Incorporate the links for days that have a tour scheduled.**

4. **Make the page look good.**

Specifying a Month and Year

Because the calendar must work for any month and year, the first step is to develop an interface for the user. The simplest approach is to let the user type in a month and year, which is not very user-friendly and is prone to errors. A better solution requires more sophisticated user interface elements — like ActiveX controls.

Refer to Part V for information about using ActiveX controls.

Inserting the ActiveX controls

My solution uses two ActiveX SpinButton controls and two ActiveX Label controls. Here's the code that adds a Label and a SpinButton to handle the month. The code to add controls for the year is not listed, but is very similar. The only difference is that the Spin2 control uses different values for the Min and Max parameters.

```
<CENTER>
<OBJECT ID="Label1" WIDTH=80 HEIGHT=24
   CLASSID="CLSID:978C9E23-D4B0-11CE-BF2D-00AA003F40D0">
   <PARAM NAME="BackColor" VALUE="16777215">
   <PARAM NAME="Size" VALUE="2117;635">
   <PARAM NAME="SpecialEffect" VALUE="1">
   <PARAM NAME="FontName" VALUE="Arial">
   <PARAM NAME="FontEffects" VALUE="1073741825">
   <PARAM NAME="FontHeight" VALUE="200">
   <PARAM NAME="FontCharSet" VALUE="0">
   <PARAM NAME="FontPitchAndFamily" VALUE="2">
```

```
  <PARAM NAME="FontWeight" VALUE="700">
</OBJECT>
<OBJECT ID="Spin1" WIDTH=16 HEIGHT=24
CLASSID="CLSID:79176FB0-B7F2-11CE-97EF-00AA006D2776">
  <PARAM NAME="Size" VALUE="423;706">
  <PARAM NAME="Min" VALUE="0">
  <PARAM NAME="Max" VALUE="13">
  <PARAM NAME="SmallChange" VALUE="1">
</OBJECT>
</CENTER>
```

Figure 21-1 shows how the controls look. Not bad. Now you need to write code to connect the SpinButtons to the Labels.

Creating an array of month names

Before writing the event handler code, you may want to display the month name, rather than the month number, in the Label controls. To display the month name, insert the following code to define the month names. This block of code is outside of any procedures, so the MonthNames array can be used in any subroutine.

```
Dim MonthNames(12)
MonthNames(1)="January"
MonthNames(2)="February"
MonthNames(3)="March"
MonthNames(4)="April"
MonthNames(5)="May"
MonthNames(6)="June"
MonthNames(7)="July"
MonthNames(8)="August"
MonthNames(9)="September"
MonthNames(10)="October"
MonthNames(11)="November"
MonthNames(12)="December"
```

Adding a Window_OnLoad subroutine

Next, you can add a subroutine that executes when the page loads. This subroutine initializes the Label controls and SpinButton controls to the current month and year.

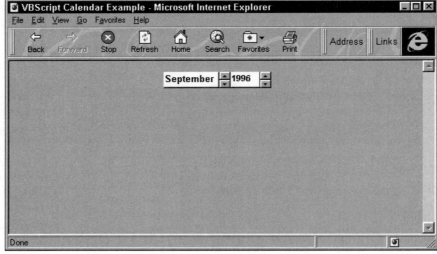

Figure 21-1:
These
controls
allow the
user to
specify a
month and
date for the
calendar.

```
Sub Window_OnLoad()
    NowMonth=Month(Now())
    NowYear=Year(Now())
    Spin1.Value=NowMonth
    Spin2.Value=NowYear
    Label1.Caption=MonthNames(Spin1.Value)
    Label2.Caption=Spin2.Value
End Sub
```

The event handlers

Here's the event handler subroutine that executes when the user clicks the up arrow of the Spin1 control to move to the next month:

```
Sub Spin1_SpinUp()
    If Spin1.Value=13 Then
        Spin1.Value=1
        Spin2.Value=Spin2.Value+1
    End if
    Label1.Caption=MonthNames(Spin1.Value)
    Label2.Caption=Spin2.Value
End Sub
```

Notice that this code includes a nice twist. If the current month is December, the SpinButton's value goes to one (January), and the year is incremented by one.

The subroutine to handle switching to the previous month is similar. Here's the code that executes when the user clicks the down arrow of the Spin1 control.

```
Sub Spin1_SpinDown()
    If Spin1.Value=0 then
        Spin1.Value=12
        Spin2.Value=Spin2.Value-1
    End If
    Label1.Caption=MonthNames(Spin1.Value)
    Label2.Caption=Spin2.Value
End Sub
```

Finally, here are the two subroutines that handle the Spin2 control, which holds the year. These routines are much simpler than the Spin1 control routines.

```
Sub Spin2_SpinUp()
    Label2.Caption=Spin2.Value
End Sub

Sub Spin2_SpinDown()
    Label2.Caption=Spin2.Value
End Sub
```

Testing the controls

To test the project, load the document and try out the controls. You can see that everything works as it should. Clicking the spinners changes the captions of the Label controls.

Developing the Calendar

The objective for the second phase of the project is to display a calendar for the month and year specified by the user.

One solution is to simply develop a separate HTML document for each month and year, which is a lot of work and causes delays while a new document loads.

A better solution involves using a floating frame. A good solution is to write VBScript code that generates the HTML code to display a calendar and then using Document.Write to send this code to the frame to create a calendar. The exact HTML code that's generated depends on the month and year, which are stored in the ActiveX SpinButton controls.

Adding a floating frame

Here's the HTML code that inserts a floating frame into the document. I broke the code into several lines so that the attributes are easier to read.

```
<IFRAME
  SRC="calframe.htm"
  NAME=CalFrame
  WIDTH=440
  HEIGHT=310
  SCROLLING=No
  FRAMEBORDER=0>
</IFRAME>
```

The source for this frame is calframe.htm, which is an empty document.

Figure 21-2 shows how this frame looks. For this figure, I set the FRAMEBORDER to 1 so that you can see where the frame is positioned. If the FRAMEBORDER is set to 0, the floating frame blends in perfectly with the document.

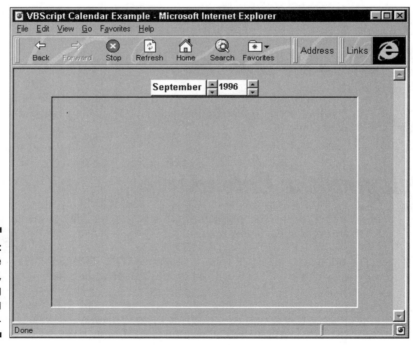

Figure 21-2:
The document, after adding a floating frame.

Sending HTML to the frame

Now comes the challenging part: writing a VBScript subroutine that generates HTML code that displays a calendar and sends that code to the document in the floating frame. This part of the project took me a while, but I eventually got it working.

To create a calendar for a particular month, you need to know two things:

- ✔ The day of the week for the first day
- ✔ The number of days in the month

Here are two VBscript statements that determine this information (*y* is a variable that holds the year, and *m* is a variable that holds the month number).

```
FirstDay = WeekDay(Dateserial(y,m,1))
DaysInMonth= Day(Dateserial(y,m+1,1)-1)
```

I pictured the calendar as a 7-column by 6-row table and then conceived of a 42-element array of consecutive numbers that are inserted in the table, by rows. All that's needed is the column in which to start — which happens to be the week day for the first day of the month. The following statement assigns a value from one to seven to the FirstDay (1 = Sunday, 2 = Monday, and so on).

```
FirstDay = WeekDay(Dateserial(y,m,1))
```

Here's a subroutine I developed, called GenerateCalendar, which has two arguments: the month and the year:

```
Sub GenerateCalendar(m,y)
    Dim Days(42)
    FirstDay = WeekDay(Dateserial(y,m,1))
    DaysInMonth= Day(Dateserial(y,m+1,1)-1)
    LastDay = DaysInMonth + FirstDay -1
'   Initialize the array with blanks
    For i = 1 to 42
        Days(i)= " "
    Next
'   Insert the days in the array
    TheDay = 0
    For i = FirstDay To LastDay
        TheDay = TheDay + 1
```

(continued)

(continued)

```
    Days(i) = TheDay
  Next
' Generate the HTML
Content=""
Content=Content & "<BODY><CENTER>"
Content=Content & "<TABLE BORDER=9 CELLPADDING=5 COLS=7>"
Content=Content & "<TH COLSPAN=7><FONT SIZE=5>"
Content=Content & MonthNames(m) & " " & y & "</TH>"
Content=Content & "<TR><TH WIDTH=60>Sun</TH>"
Content=Content & "<TH WIDTH=60>Mon</TH>"
Content=Content & "<TH WIDTH=60>Tue</TH>"
Content=Content & "<TH WIDTH=60>Wed</TH>"
Content=Content & "<TH WIDTH=60>Thu</TH>"
Content=Content & "<TH WIDTH=60>Fri</TH>"
Content=Content & "<TH WIDTH=60>Sat</TH></TR>"
TheDay = 1
For Row=1 To 6
    Content=Content & "<TR ALIGN=CENTER>"
    For Col=1 to 7
        Content=Content & "<TD>" & Days(TheDay) & "<TD>"
        TheDay=TheDay+1
    Next
    Content=Content & "</TR>"
Next
Content=Content & "</TABLE>"
'   Send it to the frame
Frames(0).Document.Write Content
Frames(0).Document.Close
End Sub
```

You don't need to understand this subroutine to use it, but it's really not as complex as it may look. If you follow the code carefully, you can probably understand it.

The HTML code that generates the calendar is stored in a variable named Content. The code continually adds text to this variable until it eventually contains everything you need to create a calendar in a table. Note the use of a nested For-Next loop, which loops through each column for each row. As a final step, I use Document.Write to write the Content variable to the document in the frame.

This code works for any month (m) and year (y) that you provide.

Calling the GenerateCalendar subroutine

The next step is to figure out how to call the GenerateCalendar subroutine. The routine needs to be called

- ✔ When the document loads using the current month and year as arguments.
- ✔ When the user changes the month using the values of the SpinButton controls as arguments.
- ✔ When the user changes the year using the values of the SpinButton controls as arguments.

Here's a statement I added to the Window_OnLoad subroutine and the SpinButton control event handler routines:

```
Call GenerateCalendar(Spin1.Value,Spin2.Value)
```

Testing it again

Figure 21-3 proves that the subroutine does what it's supposed to do. Load this document and give it a spin (pun intended). When the document loads, a calendar for the current month displays in the frame. Clicking the SpinButton controls changes the calendar appropriately.

Figure 21-3:
It works!

You can expect a slight delay while the GenerateCalendar subroutine executes because a lot of work is being done. On a reasonably fast system, however, the calendar displays almost immediately.

Adding the Links

Ready for another challenge? As you may recall, this project requires that the user click dates to see a description of the tours for that particular day. Another requirement is that the document is easy to update.

Creating an array

Rather than hard code tour dates into the subroutine, a better idea is to store the dates in an array, which can be easily modified. I devised a rather clever solution: Use the date as the name of the HTML document that holds the tour description. Here's my code:

```
Dim TourDoc(), TourDates()
Dim NumTours
NumTours=6
ReDim TourDoc(NumTours)
ReDim TourDates(NumTours)
TourDoc(1)="010397.htm"
TourDoc(2)="011497.htm"
TourDoc(3)="012397.htm"
TourDoc(4)="020997.htm"
TourDoc(5)="021997.htm"
TourDoc(6)="022797.htm"
For i = 1 to NumTours
    m = Left(TourDoc(i),2)
    d = Mid(TourDoc(i),3,2)
    y = Mid(TourDoc(i),5,2)
    TourDates(i)=DateSerial(y,m,d)
Next
```

The preceding code is inserted at the top of the document, outside of any procedures.

In this example, six tours are scheduled, and each tour is described in a document that is named according to the tour date using the following format: mmddyy.htm. For example, the tour scheduled for January 3, 1997, is described in the document named 010397.htm.

The TourDoc array holds the HTML document names. I then use a For-Next loop to fill the TourDates array with dates that are extracted from the filenames stored in the TourDoc array.

The advantage to this technique is that the document is *very* easy to update. Here's what you do:

1. **Set the value for the NumTours variable to correspond to the number of tours.**

2. **Enter filenames for the TourDoc array.**

Obviously, the Web server must have an HTML document that corresponds to each file referenced in the TourDoc array.

Displaying the tour information

Because details for each tour are contained in a separate document, the next challenge is how to display the document. Here are two options for displaying the document:

✔ Open the document in a new window.

✔ Open the document in a frame.

The second choice is preferable because it reduces the amount of on-screen clutter. Following is the code that adds a second floating frame to the document (the first floating frame holds the calendar). The second frame displays the tour information documents.

```
<IFRAME
  SRC="infoframe.htm"
  NAME=InfoFrame
  WIDTH=440
  HEIGHT=210
  SCROLLING=No
  FRAMEBORDER=0>
</IFRAME>
```

Creating the links

Now comes the fun part:

✔ Determining which date has a tour

✔ Writing the HTML code to create a link within the calendar display for that day

Following is the original code that inserts the dates into the 43-element Days array:

```
'   Insert the days in the array
    TheDay = 0
    For i = FirstDay To LastDay
        TheDay = TheDay + 1
        Days(i) = TheDay
    Next
```

Modifications to the code follow.

```
'   Insert the days in the array
    TheDay = 0
    For i = FirstDay to LastDay
        TheDay = TheDay + 1
        Days(i) = TheDay
        For t=1 to NumTours
            If Year(TourDates(t))= y Then
                If Month(TourDates(t))= m Then
                    If Day(TourDates(t)) = TheDay Then
                        Days(i)="<A HREF=" & TourDoc(t)
                        Days(i)=Days(i) & " TARGET=InfoFrame"&">"
                        Days(i)=Days(i) & TheDay & "</A>"
                    End If
                End If
            End If
        Next
    Next
```

The new code includes an additional For-Next loop that checks every member of the TourDates array. If the year, the month, and the day all match the date, then the Days array is assigned HTML code that generates a link. Notice that I use a TARGET attribute that specifies the floating frame as the target for the document.

Trying out the code

Load the revised document, and you'll find that the document works as it should. The example has six links, which are in January and February 1997. Figure 21-4 shows the calendar for January 1997, which has links for the 3rd, 14th, and 23rd.

January 1997						
Sun	Mon	Tue	Wed	Thu	Fri	Sat
			1	2	<u>3</u>	4
5	6	7	8	9	10	11
12	13	<u>14</u>	15	16	17	18
19	20	21	22	<u>23</u>	24	25
26	27	28	29	30	31	

Figure 21-4:
Three of
these dates
have tour
schedules
and appear
with links.

Making It Look Good

The final phase of this project involves adding text and making cosmetic enhancements. You can load the document and view the code for the details. Here's a list of the modifications I make.

- ✔ I add text to the page to describe it.
- ✔ I add a background color.
- ✔ I change the background color of the calendar table.
- ✔ I insert the ActiveX controls into a table.

Figure 21-5 shows the final version of this product.

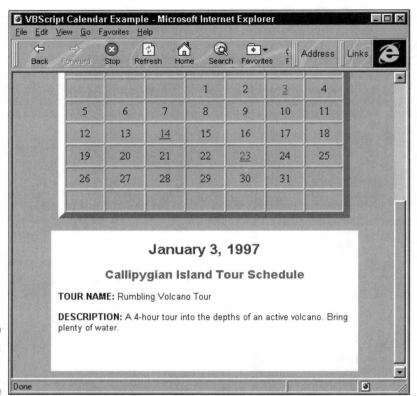

Figure 21-5:
The finished
product.

Chapter 22
Administering an Online Quiz

· ·

In This Chapter

▶ Step-by-step procedures for developing a useful online quiz application

▶ How to adapt the quiz application to your own needs

· ·

*O*n my Web surfing adventures, I frequently encounter a site that has a brief quiz. These quizzes can be commercial, educational, and just for fun. Regardless of the purpose, the quizzes I see have one feature in common: They're implemented using HTML intrinsic controls, which makes them ugly and boring. Even worse, the quiz responses are sent back to the server, which causes a delay in retrieving the results.

In this chapter, I present a method to create attractive and easy-to-use Web page quizzes. This example solves all the problems: it's not ugly or boring, and the user gets immediate feedback because VBScript tallies the answers.

Project Goals

This project involves creating an online quiz that can be taken by a visitor to a Web site. The goals of this project are to make sure that:

- ✔ The application is very general in nature so that it's easily adapted or modified.
- ✔ The quiz accommodates any number of quiz items.
- ✔ The quiz allows quiz items that have from two to five options. (This covers True/False items as well as five option multiple choice items.)
- ✔ The quiz items are presented one item at a time.
- ✔ The user is allowed to skip ahead and backtrack through the items.
- ✔ The application provides feedback to the user when the quiz is finished.
- ✔ The quiz is easy to use and attractive to the eye.

Note: The example that I develop in this chapter is a ten-item quiz about guitars. Adapting this example to any other topic is easy.

The Game Plan

You can approach such a project in a number of ways, but using an HTML Layout Control and ActiveX controls seems like the way to go. The advantages of using the Layout Control include

- ✔ Precise control over the positioning of the items.
- ✔ The ability to hide and unhide items. For example, if a particular quiz item has only two options, the unused options are not displayed.
- ✔ Control over fonts, sizes, and colors.

Project Components

This project is relatively complex, so I broke it into the following steps:

1. **Determine the best way to store the data.**

   In this case, the data consists of the quiz items, the options for each item, and the correct answer.

2. **Determine the best way to present the quiz items to the user.**

   This presentation needs to include a method to go back and forth among the items.

3. **Figure out how to keep score.**

4. **Make the application look good.**

Storing the Data

I use several arrays to store the quiz item data and keep track of other information. Here are the arrays:

- ✔ **ItemText:** This one-dimensional array holds the quiz items.
- ✔ **Answers:** This one-dimensional array stores the index number of the correct answer.
- ✔ **Responses:** This one-dimensional array stores the index number of the user's response to each item. Initially, each element in this array is set to 0, which means that the item has not been answered.
- ✔ **Options:** This two-dimensional array holds the options for each item. The first dimension corresponds to the quiz item number, and the second dimension corresponds to the option number. For example, the second option for the first quiz item is referred to as Options(1,2).

Following is an example of VBScript code that assigns values for the second quiz item. The quiz item is stored in ItemText, the two options are stored in ItemOps, and the index number for the correct answer is stored in Answers. Each item in the quiz is defined in a similar manner, although quiz items can have more than two options.

```
ItemText(2)="Acoustic guitar bodies are always made of wood."
ItemOps(2,1)="True"
ItemOps(2,2)="False"
Answers(2)=2
```

Presenting the Items

I used the ActiveX Control Pad to create the HTML file, which is shown in the following. This file contains one HTML Layout Control named QuizLayout. The Layout Control uses the guitar.alx file, which contains all the other ActiveX controls and the VBScript code.

```
<HTML>
<TITLE>Take a Guitar Quiz</TITLE>
<BODY BGCOLOR=FFFFFF BACKGROUND=guitar.gif>
<CENTER>
<H1><FONT COLOR=Navy>Test Your Knowledge of Guitars
</FONT></H1>
<TABLE BORDER=10>
<TD>
<OBJECT CLASSID="CLSID:812AE312-8B8E-11CF-93C8-00AA00C08FDF"
   ID="QuizLayout" STYLE="LEFT:0;TOP:0">
   <PARAM NAME="ALXPATH" REF VALUE="guitar.alx">
</OBJECT>
</TD>
</TABLE>
</CENTER>
</BODY>
</HTML>
```

Figure 22-1 shows how my final layout looks in the browser.

Table 22-1 gives descriptions of the ActiveX controls.

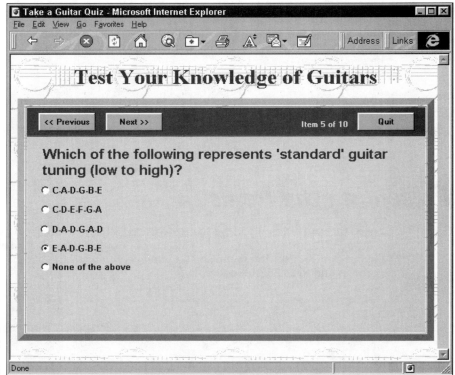

Figure 22-1:
One item
from a quiz,
displayed
using the
HTML
Layout
control.

Table 22-1	**ActiveX Controls and Their Functions**	
Button	**Control**	**Function**
Previous	An ActiveX CommandButton control named btnPrevious.	The user clicks this button to move to the previous item. If the current item is the first item, the button is disabled (grayed).
Next	An ActiveX CommandButton control named btnNext.	The user clicks this button to move to the next item. If the current item is the last item, the button is disabled (grayed).
Item counter	An ActiveX Label control named LabelStatus.	This displays the current item number and the total number of quiz items.

Button	Control	Function
Quit	An ActiveX CommandButton control named btnQuit.	When the user clicks this button, VBScript code displays the score. When all items have been answered, the caption on this button reads *Show Score* and the background color of the button changes to bright red.
Item text	An ActiveX Label control named QuizItem.	Displays the text for the current item.
Options	Options consist of six ActiveX OptionButton controls, named Option0, Option1, and so on, to Option5.	The Option0 control, which represents a nonanswer, is always hidden and is selected by default. If a quiz item has fewer than five options, the unused options are hidden.
Button background	The colored background behind the three buttons at the top is a CommandButton control named btnButtonFrame.	The Button background exists for cosmetic purposes only.
Start	An ActiveX CommandButton control named btnStartQuiz (this button is not visible in Figure 22-1).	This button fills the entire Layout Control area when the document is loaded and is hidden when it is clicked.

To make it easier to refer to the options in the VBScript code, I created an array of object variables for the five OptionButton controls. Here's the code I used:

```
Dim Options(5)
Set Options(0)=Option0
Set Options(1)=Option1
Set Options(2)=Option2
Set Options(3)=Option3
Set Options(4)=Option4
Set Options(5)=Option5
```

How the Application Works

The best way to understand how this application works is to examine the guitar.alx file, which contains the VBScript code. Following is a summary of how the application works.

1. **When the document loads, the ItemLayout_OnLoad subroutine executes.**

   ItemLayout is the name of the HTML Layout control. This subroutine initializes the data.

2. **When the document loads, the user sees only the large button, btnStartQuiz that describes the quiz.**

   Figure 22-2 shows how this button looks. Clicking the button executes the btnStartQuiz_Click subroutine.

3. **The btnStartQuiz_Click subroutine hides the btnStartQuiz button and unhides all the other controls.**

   The subroutine sets a public variable, CurrentItem, to 0. CurrentItem keeps track of which quiz item is currently displayed. The btnStartQuiz_Click subroutine ends by calling the btnNext_Click subroutine.

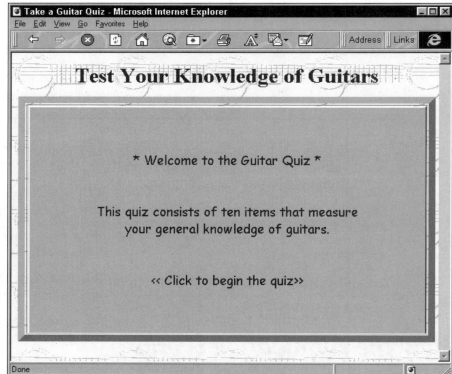

Figure 22-2:
A large button displays when the document opens. Clicking the button starts the quiz.

4. **The btnNext_Click subroutine increments the CurrentItem variable and loads the next quiz item, if one exists.**

   The subroutine then calls the DisplayItem subroutine, which takes one argument: the quiz item number. The btnPrevious_Click subroutine works in a similar manner, except that it decrements the CurrentItem variable.

5. **The DisplayItem subroutine does a lot of work.**

   It changes the caption of the QuizItem label, changes the caption of the Option controls, and redraws the controls so that they are nicely spaced, which is necessary because the number of characters in the labels vary. This subroutine also determines whether to enable the Previous and Next buttons.

6. **When the user clicks an Option button to respond to a quiz item, the Option button's event handler executes.**

   For example, if the user responds to the second option, the Option2_Click subroutine executes. This routine stores the response in the Responses array and then checks to see whether all items have been answered. If the items have been answered, the caption of the Quit button changes to *Show Score*.

7. **If the user clicks the Quit button before all items have been answered, the btnQuit_Click subroutine displays a message like the one shown in Figure 22-3.**

   If all of the items have been answered, the user sees a message like the one shown in Figure 22-4.

Figure 22-3:
The user sees a message similar to this one, if all items have not been answered.

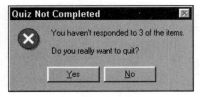

Figure 22-4:
If all items are answered, the user sees the score.

Creating Your Own Quiz

Adapting this quiz to any topic is easy. The quiz can handle any number of quiz items, and each quiz item can have between two and five response options. Here's how to adapt this quiz.

1. **Modify the HTML file.**

   For example, you can change the <TITLE>, the background color or graphic, and the <H1> heading.

2. **Change the message that displays on the btnStartQuiz button.**

   Make the message descriptive, according to the topic of your quiz. To do so, edit the guitar.alx file. (You can change the name of this file, but make sure that you also change the name in the <OBJECT> tag in the HTML file.)

3. **In the ALX file, set the NumItems variable equal to the number of quiz items that you have.**

4. **In the ALX file, enter the data for each quiz item.**

   Change the ItemText, ItemOps, and Answers variables for each item.

5. **In the ALX file, modify the btnQuit_Click subroutine to display messages of your choice.**

That's it! Good luck on the quiz.

Part VII
The Part of Tens

In this part . . .

All the books in the ...*For Dummies* series have chapters that include lists. This book is no exception. The next three chapters contain my own Top Ten lists, which deal with frequently-asked questions, VBScript resources on the Net, and how you can become a VBScript guru. My lists may not be as funny as David Letterman's, but they're definitely more informative.

Chapter 23

Top Ten VBScript
Questions and Answers

In This Chapter

▶ Is VBScript the same as Visual Basic?

▶ Where can I get a copy of the VBScript programming language?

▶ How does VBScript compare to JavaScript and Java?

▶ What are the typical uses for VBScript?

▶ If I use VBScript in my Web document, is the number of people who can access my site limited?

▶ If a user accesses my Web site with a VBScript compatible browser, can the user automatically load a different VBScript enhanced page?

▶ How can I prevent my competitors from viewing my VBScript code?

▶ When a user loads my page, how do I execute a program that's on the user's local drive?

▶ How can you view the source code for a document contained in a frame?

▶ Can I set up a Web page hit counter using VBScript?

*I*n this chapter, I answer the most frequently asked questions about VBScript.

Is VBScript the same as Visual Basic?

No. VBScript is a subset of Visual Basic. It lacks many of the features of Visual Basic and implements other features differently. The two languages are very similar, however, so if you know Visual Basic, you may have little trouble adapting to VBScript.

VBScript is designed to be a small and lightweight interpreted language. Consequently, it does not use strict types for variable (all variables are variants). Also, because VBScript is intended to be a safe subset of the language, it does not include file I/O or direct access to the underlying operating system.

Where can I get a copy of the VBScript programming language?

Don't worry if you can't find VBScript at your local software store. Unlike programming languages such as Visual Basic, C++, or Delphi, VBScript doesn't exist as a stand-alone product. VBScript code is embedded in HTML documents, and, unlike most programming languages, no VBScript development environment exists. The VBScript code springs to life when the HTML document is loaded into a browser that can understand VBScript.

How does VBScript compare to JavaScript and Java?

VBScript is almost functionally equivalent to JavaScript, but most people find that VBScript is much easier to learn and use. Both VBScript and JavaScript are scripting languages, and the source code is embedded directly in the HTML document. Neither language can produce a stand-alone application. Java, on the other hand, is a full-scale programming language that generates applets (which are used in Web documents) as well as stand-alone applications. Despite the commonality in their names, Java and JavaScript have very little in common. A Java applet is similar to an ActiveX control.

What are the typical uses for VBScript?

Web page developers use VBScript for a variety of purposes, including:

- Performing client-side validation of data entered into a form.
- Controlling ActiveX objects
- Getting input from users without using a form.
- Displaying pop-up messages.
- Creating highly interactive Web pages by writing information to frames.
- Reading and writing cookies. A *cookie* is information stored on the user's local drive. A cookie can be read only by the Web site that created the cookie.
- Creating HTML code on the fly.
- Performing special effects, such as a background that fades from one color to another.

If I use VBScript in my Web document, is the number of people who can access my site limited?

To get the full impact of your enhanced VBScript site, visitors need to use a browser that supports VBScript. If a browser does not support VBScript, the page is still viewable, but the parts that rely on VBScript do not function.

If a user accesses my Web site with a VBScript compatible browser, can the browser automatically load a different VBScript enhanced page?

Yes. The easiest way to determine if a browser supports VBScript is to use VBScript! Enter the following code at the top of your HTML document. If the browser understands VBScript, the index.htm document in the vbs subdirectory is loaded into the browser window. If the browser doesn't understand VBScript, the document continues loading as usual.

```
<SCRIPT LANGUAGE=VBScript>
<!—
Window.Location.Href = "vbs/index.htm"
—>
</SCRIPT>
```

I use VBScript on my Web site to perform proprietary calculations. How can I prevent my competitors from viewing my VBScript code?

You can't. Every line of VBScript ever written on a publicly accessible Web page is available for anyone in the world to view.

When a user loads my page, how do I execute a program that's on the user's local drive?

You can't. For security reasons, VBScript cannot access files on a user's system. VBScript can't read them, write them, or execute them, which are all good things. You don't want VBScript to execute a command like the following, do you?

```
format c:
```

When I visit a site that uses VBScript, I like to look at the source code. But if the site uses frames, I find that the View↪Source command only shows the top level frame. What gives?

You can view the source code in the document in any frame. The trick is to right-click on the frame and then choose View Source from the shortcut menu.

Can I set up a Web page hit counter using VBScript?

No. VBScript is very powerful, but keeping track of the number of times your page has been loaded is not possible using VBScript alone.

Chapter 24

Top Ten VBScript Resources on the Net

....

In This Chapter

▶ A list of useful Web sites that contain information about VBScript

▶ How to subscribe to a VBScript mailing list

▶ Information about several newsgroups that may be of interest

....

*1*n this chapter, I list ten of my favorite Internet resources that focus on VBScript. Many of these resources also deal with ActiveX controls.

And here's the standard Internet disclaimer: These sites were all running when I wrote this chapter, but I do not guarantee that they are still running as you read this chapter. In other words, the Net is a dynamic entity.

The Microsoft VBScript Site

For the latest information on VBScript, don't overlook the Microsoft site. Following are a few URLs that may be of interest to you.

VBScript Home Page:

```
http://www.microsoft.com/vbscript/
```

VBScript Online Documentation:

```
http://www.microsoft.com/vbscript/us/vbsmain/vbsdocs.htm
```

Internet Explorer Object Model Documentation:

```
http://www.microsoft.com/intdev/sdk/docs/scriptom/
```

Gallery of ActiveX Controls:

```
http://www.microsoft.com/activex/controls/
```

Microsoft ActiveX Control Pad:

```
http://www.microsoft.com/workshop/author/cpad/
```

The VBScript Mailing List

The VBScript mailing list covers all aspects of VBScript. If you aren't familiar with Internet mailing lists, here's how they work: Subscribers to the mailing list send e-mail to the list server. The list server distributes the message to all other subscribers. To subscribe to the VBScript Mailing List, which is free, send an e-mail message to:

```
listadmin@lists.msn.com
```

In the body of the message, enter the following, substituting your name with *your name*:

```
SUBSCRIBE VBScript your name
```

The list server responds with a message that provides complete information about using the mailing list.

VBScript Newsgroups

The Internet provides access to thousands of newsgroups. A *newsgroup* is sort of like a bulletin board devoted to a particular topic. Most Internet newsgroups are part of Usenet. However, Microsoft maintains a number of newsgroups that are available only from the Microsoft news server. To access any of these Microsoft newsgroups, you need to set up your news reader software to access the following news server site:

```
msnews@microsoft.com
```

After you connect to this site, look for the following newsgroups:

```
microsoft.public.internetexplorer.scripting
```

```
microsoft.public.activex.controlpad_html_layout_control
```

```
microsoft.public.internetexplorer.win95
```

```
microsoft.public.internetexplorer.beta.win95
```

VBScript Central

This site bills itself as "your one-stop clearinghouse for information on Microsoft's VBScript product." Among other things, you can find an extensive collection of links to other Web sites that incorporate VBScript. Go to

```
http://www.inquiry.com/vbscentral/
```

The VBScript / ActiveX Demo Page

This is my very own Web site, which I created to give me a reason to find out about this new technology. The site has become amazingly popular, and I receive rave reviews all the time. Check it out at

```
http://www.j-walk.com/vbscript/
```

Scribe: The VBScript Writers Resource

This site features a comprehensive list of links to other sites that use VBScript. Although I find this site to be very tedious to navigate, it contains good information. The URL is

```
http://www.km-cd.com/scribe/
```

ActiveX Journal for HTML Writers

You can subscribe to this an online magazine for a fee. As I write this book, the magazine is just getting started, but I am quite impressed with the quality and quantity of information provided. You can find articles about VBScript and sample applications that use VBScript. Nonsubscribers can get to many parts of the site, but need to subscribe to get the whole enchilada. The URL is

```
http://www.folkarts.com/journals/activex/
```

ActiveX Resource Center

Although this site is devoted primarily to ActiveX technology, it does contain information about VBScript. The URL is

```
http://www.active-x.com/
```

ACTIVEX.COM

This site, from the CNET Computer Network, is an excellent place to find new ActiveX controls. The URL is

```
http://www.activex.com
```

Web Search Engines

New VBScript sites arrive on the Web on a daily basis. Don't overlook the standard Web search engines for locating VBScript information. Following are my favorite search engines. If you haven't used these engines before, take a few minutes to read the instructions available at each site.

AltaVista:

```
http://www.altavista.digital.com
```

HotBot:

```
http://www.hotbot.com
```

Infoseek:

```
http://guide-p.infoseek.com
```

Lycos:

```
http://www.lycos.com
```

Chapter 25

Top Ten Ways to Become a VBScript Guru

In This Chapter

▶ A list of ways that can help you master VBScript

*Y*ou've reached the final chapter in the saga. (Were you surprised by the ending?) If you've explored the other chapters in the book, you know enough to develop some useful VBScript applications.

But this book is only an introduction. For those who hunger for more, I've put together a list of items that may help you progress even further.

Browse the Web

The absolute best source for discovering more about VBScript is — you guessed it — the Web. Chapter 25 lists URLs that provide good starting places for your adventures. More VBScript-related sites pop up all the time.

Look at a Lot of VBScript Code

Programming in VBScript offers a tremendous advantage over programming in other programming languages: You can look at the source code for every VBScript program you ever encounter. Be on the lookout for sites that use VBScript and examine the code by using the View⇨Source command.

Communicate with Others

Although VBScript is currently the new kid on the block, it already has a following. You may find developing contacts and keeping touch with others who do what you do to be helpful. A good source of contacts is the VBScript mailing list, which I describe in Chapter 25. The only downside to subscribing to the mailing list is that your mailbox is always jammed with messages that can be good, bad, and downright ugly.

Borrow and Adapt Others' Ideas

If you find a site that uses VBScript in an unusual or interesting way, save a copy of the HTML document to your hard drive. Even if you don't have an immediate need for the technique, it may come in handy later.

While we're on the subject of borrowing code, check with the person who wrote the code to make sure that duplicating it is okay. They'll probably be flattered.

Study the Documentation

Yes, VBScript has documentation. If you have free time, surf on over to the Microsoft site and browse through the docs. Chances are good that you can discover something new. The URL is

```
http://www.microsoft.com/vbscript/us/vbsmain/vbsdocs.htm
```

Study the Examples in This Book

I spent more time developing the examples for this book than I did actually writing the text. I've found that most people (perhaps yourself included) would rather examine a well thought out example than read dozens of pages of explanatory text. Please don't let my time investment go to waste. Even if a particular example is not of immediate interest, you can find a few tricks by looking at the code.

Think like a Web Site Visitor, Not a Designer

When people develop Web pages, it's far too easy to forget the entire point of the page. The point of the page is to communicate with visitors to the site. You may find switching hats occasionally to be beneficial. Better yet, enlist a few impartial friends to check out your site and watch them as they work their way through it. Your friends' actions can often provide excellent ideas for future development. As you may know, future development often involves VBScript.

Think Modular

When you write a VBScript subroutine or function, give special consideration to the fact that the code may be reusable. Do what you can to make a routine generally useful so that when the need arises, you can simply copy your old code rather than rewrite it.

Experiment

When I begin a new VBScript project, I almost always begin by designing a number of small experiments to help me thoroughly understand a concept. Usually, this experimentation continues throughout the project. These experiments are performed outside of the main application, which lets me focus exclusively on the concept at hand without being distracted by the main application. Eventually, my experiments result in a good understanding of the concept, and I'm able to incorporate my understanding into the application with confidence.

Experiment More

Enough said.

Index

• A •

Abs function, 98
accessor property, 72
ActiveX Control Pad, 256–268
  Control editor, 257–258
  document creation, 259
  document viewing, 263
  downloading, 16
  HTML Layout editor, 258
  HTML text editor, 256–257
  HTML text insertion, 263
  label properties, 261
  script testing, 266
  Script Wizard, 258
  SpinButton control, 262
ActiveX controls, 7, 13, 241–294
  animation, 244
  ButtonMenu, 271–273
  Calendar application, 324–325
  calendars, 245
  charts, 244
  color changes, 243–244
  commercial, 243
  Control Pad, 256–268
  described, 241
  document viewers, 245
  downloading, 17, 248
  element editing after loading page into
    browser, 242–243
  examples, 268–278
  fm20.dll file, 245
  forms, 277–278
  freeware, 243
  HotSpot, 288
  HTML forms, 277–278
  HTML Layout, 279–294
  Image, 285–287
  Internet Explorer support, 37
  Internet resources, 351–354
  Label, 242, 287–288, 324–325
  ListBox, 293
  maps, 244
  Marquee, 269
  methods, 267–268
  Microsoft controls, 245–247
  MS Forms 2.0, 245–246
  object <OBJECT> HTML tag, 254–255
  online quiz application, 340–341
  param <PARAM> HTML tag, 255
  PopUp Menu, 269–271
  properties, 267–268
  pros/cons, 250–252
  real-time data acquisition, 245
  ScrollBar, 242–243
  security, 249–250
  shareware, 243
  SpinButton, 262, 324–325
  Timer, 273–276
  types, 243–245
  understanding, 247–250
  user interface, 244
  video, 244
  viewing hidden controls, 288
  versus intrinsic controls, 185
ActiveX Journal for HTML Writers, online
  magazine, 353
ActiveX objects, 59–59
ActiveX Resource Center, 354
ACTIVEX.COM file, 354
Address box, URL location display, 42–43
Age variable, 113

alert dialog box, Internet Explorer, 26
Alert statements, 155–156
alphabet radio buttons, 193–194
alx file extension, 281–283
amortization, loan, 317–322
anchor <A> HTML tag, 42
Anchor object, 58–59, 67
anchors, HTML documents, 42
animation
  ActiveX controls, 244
  floating frames, 221–222, 225
Answers array, online quiz application, 338
apostrophe character, comments, 52
applications
  Calendar, 323–336
  Mortgage Payments, 309–322
  online quiz, 337–344
arguments
  function, 131–132
  Pmt function, 315
  subroutines 83, 85–88
arrays, 101–106
  Answers, 338
  Calendar application, 325, 332–333
  column charts, 306
  declaring, 101–102
  described, 101
  Dim statement declarations, 101–102
  dynamic, 103
  elements, 103–104
  For-Next loop, 123–125
  ItemText, 338
  LinkArray, 124–125
  MonthNames, 325
  multidimensional, 102–103
  Nums, 124
  online quiz application, 338–339
  Options, 338
  Responses, 338
  ScaledData, 303
  scope, 104–106

sorting, 236–237
  TourDates, 333
  TourDoc, 333
Asc function, 134–135
assignment statements
  expressions, 97–98
  variables, 96–101
Atn function, 138
attributes
  CLASSID, 255
  CODEBASE, 255
  HEIGHT, 255
  ID, 255
  LANGUAGE, 50
  MULTIPLE, 180
  SIZE, 180
  WIDTH, 50, 255
audio greetings, 233
author
  e-mail address, 9
  Spreadsheet Page (The) Web site, 2

• *B* •

backwards loop, 123
Bebak, Arthur, 5
blur, controls, 171
book, study examples, 356
borderless frames, 220–221
bouncing balls, HTML Layout control,
    291–292
browsers
  ActiveX control processing steps, 248
  compatibility, 349
  control, 7
  frame document loading, 216
  hiding scripts from display, 50–51
  HTML tag nonsupport display, 50–51
  Microsoft versus Netscape, 16
  script-aware, 51
  VBScript compatibility issues, 15, 54–55,
    232–233

bugs, 149–160
  identifying, 153–154
  prevention tips, 157–159
  troubleshooting, 31
built-in functions, 131–141
button clicks, MsgBox function code
      returns, 147
Button control, 163–168
ButtonMenu, ActiveX control, 271–273
buttons
  adding to HTML documents, 25
  captions, 166–167
  subroutines, 26–28

• C •

cache, hard drive, 282
CalcRoot function, 89–90
calculations
  monthly payments, 314–315
  Mortgage Payment application results,
      313–316
  performing, 7
Calendar application, 323–336
  ActiveX controls, 324–325
  arrays, 325, 332–333
  code testing, 334–335
  control testing, 327, 331–332
  development, 327–332
  event handlers, 326–327
  floating frames, 328–330
  game plan, 324
  generating, 331
  links, 332–335
  MonthName array, 325
  project background, 323
  subroutines, 325–326, 331
  tour information, 333
  user interface, 324–327
calendars, ActiveX controls, 245
Call keyword, 87–88

calls, subroutines, 87–88
captions, buttons, 166–167
CardType function, 233–234
cascading style sheets, Internet Explorer,
      36–37
case, code scripts, 52–53
cents format, 227–228
characters
  apostrophe, 52
  colon, 119
  concatenation operator, 156
  dot notation, 60
  equal sign operator, 71
  parentheses, 83, 100–101, 131
  quotes, 52–53
chart.htm file, 301–302
charts
  ActiveX controls, 244
  frame, 301–304
Check Box control, 164, 178–179
child-parent relationship, objects, 62–63
Chr function, 133
CLASSID attribute, object <OBJECT>
      HTML tag, 255
click events, Button controls, 165–166
client-side data validation
  data selections, 196
  forms, 189, 196–202
  OnSubmit event, 197–198
client-side image maps, 7
code
  alphabet radio buttons, 193
  array sorting, 236–237
  audio greetings, 233
  background fade-in, 235–236
  button click returns, 147
  column charts, 300–301
  comments, 51–52
  consistent indentation, 158
  credit card number validation, 233–234
  date list generation, 195–196

code *(continued)*
  date/time display, 230–232
  debugging, 153–157
  developing in small bits, 157
  error correction (bugs), 149–160
  forcing line breaks, 133–134
  frame examples, 206–214
  hex to decimal conversion, 232
  If-Then, 78
  indents, 53
  line spacing, 53
  lottery numbers, 237–238
  make reusable, 357
  MsgBox function, 146
  noncase sensitive, 52–53
  number formatting functions, 227–229
  number list generation, 194–195
  object references, 59–60
  quotes characters capitalization effects,
    52–53
  scrolling status bar message, 234–235
  special effects, 235–236
  statements, splitting between lines, 53–54
  syntax error messages, 150–151
  testing, 158–159
  text control, 168–169
  variable declaration forcing, 157–158
  VBScript-compatible browser detection,
    232–233
  writing, 51–54
CODEBASE, object <OBJECT> HTML tag, 255
codebase, URL, 248
collections
  Anchor object, 67
  Element object, 68
  Form object, 67
  Frame object, 66
  Link object, 67
  object groups, 59
colon character, multistatement-per-
    line, 119

colors
  changing with ActiveX ScrollBar control,
    243–244
  frames, 213–214
column charts, 297–308
  arrays, 306
  creating, 298–308
  described, 297
  frames, 301–304
  generating, 307–308
  graphic files, 297–298
  HTML techniques, 298–299
  scaling, 303–304
  select controls, 306–307
  variable declarations, 305–306
commands
  Edit➪Insert ActiveX Control, 257, 260
  Edit➪Insert HTML Layout, ActiveX
    Control Pad, 284
  Edit➪Select All, ActiveX Control Pad, 288
  File➪New HTML, ActiveX Control Pad,
    259, 283
  File➪Open, 27
  File➪Open, Internet Explorer, 24
  Help➪About Internet Explorer, Internet
    Explorer, 35
  Open in New Window, Internet
    Explorer, 38
  Tools➪Script Wizard, ActiveX Control
    Pad, 264, 289
  View➪Options, Internet Explorer, 233,
    249
  View➪Options, Windows, 18
  View➪Properties, ActiveX Control Pad,
    286
  View➪Refresh, Internet Explorer, 27
  View➪Source, Internet Explorer, 54, 174,
    282, 349
  View➪Toolbox, ActiveX Control Pad, 285
comment HTML tags <!– and –>, 50–51

comments
  apostrophe character, 52
  code, 51–52
common operators, 98–99
communication, with VBScript users, 355–356
companion disk
  credit card number validation, 233–234
  document object properties, 73
  event handling example, 76–78
  frame references, 209–211
  sample HTML document, 20–21
  URL hyperlinks, 16
  VBScript Function Reference, 132, 148
components
  ActiveX controls, 241–252
  book, 2–4
concatenation operator character, 156
conditional expressions, If-Then structure, 113–114
conditions, If-Then structure, 113–114
Control editor, ActiveX Control Pad, 257–258
control structures
  backwards loop, 123
  Do Until loop, 126–127
  Do While loop, 127–128
  Do-Loop Until loop, 128
  Do-Loop While loop, 128–129
  For-Next loop, 121–123
  If-Then structure, 112–114
  If-Then-Else, 115–117
  loops, 121–129
  nested Select Case, 119–120
  Select Case, 117–120
controls
  ActiveX, 241–294
  form, 188
  form elements, 42
  form references, 189–193
  HTML intrinsic, 163–184

intrinsic, 25
intrinsic versus ActiveX, 185
select, 306–307
viewing hidden, 288
conversion functions, 133–137
cookies, 7
copying/pasting functions, 228
Cos function, 138
Counter variable, 156
credit cards, number validation, 233–234
CubeRoot function, 83
currency formats, 227–228

• D •

data input form, Mortgage Payment application, 311–312
data types, 97
Date function, 136–137
dates
  displaying, 230–232
  list generation, 195–196
DayName function, 230
debugging
  Alert statements, 155–156
  code examinations, 155
  described, 153–154
decimal values, hex conversions, 232
declarations
  forcing variables, 107–109, 157–158
  multiple variables, 106
  variable, 305–306
deferred scripts, 47–48
desktop, dragging-dropping graphics to, 39
dialog box, displaying with MsgBox-InputBox functions, 132, 144–148
dice, HTML Layout control, 292
Dim statement, array declarations, 101–102
Do Until loop, 126–127
Do While loop, 127–128

Document objects, 58, 67
document viewers, ActiveX controls, 245
documentation, studying, 356
documents
 ActiveX Control Pad creation, 259
 frame loading, 214–216
 HTML, 15, 20–21
dollars format, 227–228
DollarText function, 229
Do-Loop Until loop, 128
Do-Loop While loop, 128–129
dot notation character, object links, 60
downloading, 15–17
 ActiveX Control Pad, 16
 ActiveX Controls, 17, 248
 Internet Explorer 3.0, 16, 36
 SitePad, 18–19
dweeb, 1
dynamic arrays, 103

• E •

Edit⇨Insert ActiveX Control command,
 257, 260
Edit⇨Insert HTML Layout, ActiveX
 Control Pad command, 284
Edit⇨Select All, ActiveX Control Pad
 command, 288
editors, HTML, 17–19
Element object, 58–59, 68
elements, array, 103–104
e-mail addresses, author, 9
embedded scripts, HTML documents,
 45–48
End Function statement, 83
End Sub statement, 82–83
equal sign operator, object property
 values, 71
error corrections, 149–160
error messages, avoiding, 154–155

event handlers
 Calendar application, 326–327
 subroutines, 83–85, 166–168
events
 click, 165–168
 handling, 76–78
 MouseEnter, 288
 MouseExit, 288
 object 75–78
 OnBlur, 171–172
 OnClick, 76–78, 165–168
 OnFocus, 171–172
 OnSubmit, 197–198
examples, study, 356
experiment with new projects, 357
expressions
 Abs function, 98
 assignment statement, 97–98
 conditional, 113–114
 defined, 97
 operator order of precedence, 100–101
 operators, 98–101
 Rnd function, 98
 Sqr function, 98
 variables, 97–98

• F •

FadeText function, 236
fields, text controls, 168–172
file extensions
 alx, 281–283
 ocx, 246
File⇨New HTML, ActiveX Control Pad
 command, 259, 283
File⇨Open command, 24, 27
files
 ALX, 281–283
 cache, 282
 chart.htm, 301–302
 dragging/dropping, 27

fm20.dll, 245
graphics, 297–298
guitar.alx, 339
left.htm, 206–207
loader.htm, 210–211
makeframes.htm, 61
right.htm, 207
saving, 284–285
survey.htm, 63–65
vbs/index.htm, 232–233
VBSCRIPT.DLL, 15
Fix function, 135–136
flashing message, floating frames, 222–224
floating frames, 217–225
 animation effects, 221–222, 225
 Calendar application, 328–330
 column charts, 301–304
 dynamic page updates, 217–219
 flashing message, 222–224
 IE, 37
 Mortgage Payment application, 317
 object model, 63–65
 variables, 156–157
flow control, 111–130
 control structures, 111–113
 loops, 121–129
 top-to-bottom, 111
fm20.dll file, 245
focus, controls, 171
form <FORM> HTML tag, 42, 169, 187–188
Form object, 58–59, 67
FormatDollars function, 227–228, 315–316
FormatPct function, 228–229
formless user input, 7
forms, 185–204
 ActiveX controls, 277–278
 alphabet radio buttons, 193–194
 client-side data validation, 189, 196–202
 client-side input validation, 7
 control references, 189–193
 controls, 188

credit card number validation, 233–234
 data input, 311–312
 date list, 195–196
 defining, 186–188
 elements, 42
 HTML documents, 42
 index number control reference, 191–192
 intrinsic versus ActiveX controls, 185
 link list controls, 202–203
 Mortgage Payment application, 310–312
 number list, 194–195
 object variable control references,
  192–193
 references, 189–193
 results calculations, 312–316
 server-side validation, 188–189
 table nesting, 312
 validating, 188–189
For-Next loop, 121–126
frame <FRAME> HTML tag, 63–65
Frame objects, 63, 66
frames, 7, 205–226
 borderless, 220–221
 code examples, 206–214
 color changes, 213–214
 column chart, 301–304
 document loading, 214–216
 floating, 37, 63–65, 217–225
 IE, 40
 Mortgage Payment application, 317
 object hierarchy, 205
 references, 208–209
 source codes, 349
 URL loading, 212–213
 vertical, 206–207
frameset <FRAMESET> HTML tag, 61
freeware, ActiveX controls, 243
FriendlyDate function, 231
FriendlyNow function, 231
FriendlyTime function, 231
Function keyword, 83

functions
Abs, 98
arguments, 132
Asc, 134–135
Atn, 138
built-in, 131–141
CalcRoot, 89–90
CardType, 233–234
Chr, 133
conversion, 133–137
copying/pasting, 228
Cos, 138
CubeRoot, 83
Date, 136–137
DayName, 230
described, 81
DollarText, 229
FadeText, 236
Fix, 135–136
FormatDollars, 227–228, 315–316
FormatPct, 228–229
FriendlyDate, 231
FriendlyNow, 231
FriendlyTime, 231
Function keyword, 83
Hex, 89, 135, 232
Hex2Dec, 232
HTML document placement, 91–92
InputBox, 7, 103, 132, 147–148
Instr, 142–143
Int, 135–136
IsDate, 143
IsNumeric, 144
Lcase, 141
Left, 140–141
Len, 31, 135, 142
math, 138–139
Mid, 135, 140
MonthName, 231
MsgBox, 132, 144–147

naming conventions, 82
Now, 21, 230–232
number formatting, 227–230
parentheses character with arguments, 131–132
PMT, 315
random number, 138–139
Randomize, 135, 138–139
ReverseText, 90
Right, 140–141
Rnd, 98, 135, 138–139
Sin, 138
spelling conventions, 131
Sqr, 98
string, 140–143
Tan, 138
Time, 114, 136–137
trigonometric, 138
troubleshooting, 92–93
Ubound, 103–104
Ucase, 141
UI (user interface), 132, 144–148
variant, 143–144
VBScript Function Reference, 132
WavyText, 236
Weekday, 116, 137–138
Year, 96

• *G* •

games, 7
geek, 1
GoBack event handler, 167–168
GoForward event handler, 167–168
Gookin, Dan, 5
graphics
column charts, 297–298
dragging-dropping to desktop, 39
greetings, audio time of day, 233
guitar.alx file, 339

guru
  adapt others' ideas, 356
  browse the web, 355
  communicate with other users, 355–356
  experiment with new projects, 357
  look at a lot of VBScript code, 355
  make code reusable, 357
  study documentation, 356
  study examples in book, 356
  think like a visitor, 356

• *H* •

handlers, event, 76–78
hard drive, cache, 282
HEIGHT attribute, object <OBJECT> HTML
    tag, 255
Help⇨About Internet Explorer, Internet
    Explorer command, 35
hex conversions, decimal values, 232
Hex function, 89, 135, 232
Hex2Dec function, 232
hexadecimal numbers, 27–28, 30
Hidden control, 164, 183
hierarchy
  frames, 205
  object model, 58
  parent-child object relationships, 62–63
history list, Internet Explorer, 43
History objects, 66
hit counter, set up with VBScript, 349
hosting VBScript, 15
HotSpot, ActiveX control, 288
hotspots, adding to layouts, 288
HTML, on the fly creation, 7
HTML documents, 20–21
  ActiveX Control Pad creation, 259
  anchors, 42
  buttons, adding, 25
  chart.htm, 301–302
  components, 40–42

copying/pasting functions, 228
creating, 24
deferred scripts, 47–48
embedding VBScript code, 15
forms, 42
frame loading, 214–216
left.htm, 206–207
Layout control insertion, 284
links, 41
links.htm, 61
loader.htm, 210–211
main.htm, 61
makeframes.htm, 61
procedures, 47–48
procedures placement, 91–92
right.htm, 207
scripts, embedding, 45–48
scripts, inserting, 26–31
scripts, placement, 49
subroutines, 26–28
survey.htm, 63–65
troubleshooting bugs, 31
vbs/index.htm, 232–233
viewing, 263
HTML editor, adding to toolbar, 18–19
HTML forms, 185–204
HTML intrinsic controls, 163–184
HTML Layout control ActiveX, 279–294
  alx file extension, 281–283
  bouncing balls, 291–292
  described, 279
  examples, 280–283, 291–293
  features, 290
  inserting, 284
  layout creation, 283–290
  object <OBJECT> HTML tag, 281
  Online Fruit Stand, 293
  pros/cons, 279–280
  rolling the dice, 292
HTML Layout editor, ActiveX
    Control Pad, 258

HTML tags
  anchor <A>, 42
  browser non-support display, 50–51
  comment tags <!– and –>, 50–51
  form <FORM>, 42, 169, 187–188
  frame <FRAME>, 63–65
  frameset <FRAMESET>, 61
  input <INPUT>, 87, 188
  marquee <MARQUEE>, 222–224
  object <OBJECT>, 254–255, 281
  opening/closing, 49
  param <PARAM>, 255
  script <SCRIPT>, 45–51, 108–109
  script blocks, 49
  select <SELECT>, 188
  textarea <TEXTAREA>, 188
HTML text, ActiveX Control Pad
    insertion, 263
HTML text editors, ActiveX Control Pad,
    256–257
hyperlinks, loading URL into different
    frames, 213

• I •

icons, used in book, 8
ID attribute, object <OBJECT> HTML tag, 255
ideas, adapt other users, 356
Internet Explorer 3.0, 35–44
  accessing Web site included with book, 8
  ActiveX support, 37
  Address box, 42–43
  components, 36–38
  development history, 2
  documents, 38, 40–42
  downloading, 16
  dragging-dropping graphics to desktop, 39
  fast text display, 38
  floating frames, 37, 217–225
  frames, 40
  full-screen mode, 39
  history list, 43
  HTML standards compatibility, 38
  IntelliMouse support, 40
  keyboard shortcuts, 39
  kiosk mode, 39
  loading HTML documents, 24
  marquee, scrolling, 37
  multimedia, enhancements, 37
  multitasking, 38
  object relationships, 60–63
  progressive rendering, 38
  security, features, 38
  shortcut menus, 38–39
  style sheets, cascading, 36–37
  tables, features, 37
  toolbars, 39
  upgrading, 36
  URL location display, 42–43
  VBScript support, 38
  VBSCRIPT.DLL file, 15
  version numbers, 35–36
  versus Netscape Navigator, 38
  Web site search, 39
  window, 40
If-Then structure, 78, 112–114
If-Then-Else structure, 115–117
image maps, client-side, 7
images, adding to layouts, 285–287
immediate scripts, 45–47, 91–92
indents
  code, 53
  consistent, 158
index numbers, form control reference,
    191–192
input <INPUT> HTML tag, 87, 188
input field, text controls, 168–172
InputBox function, 7, 103, 132, 147–148
Insert ActiveX Control dialog box, 260
Instr function, 142–143
Int function, 135–136

IntelliMouse, 40
interactive games, 7
intrinsic controls, 25, 163–184
  Button, 163–168
  Check Box, 178–179
  form <FORM> HTML tags, 169
  forms, 188
  Hidden, 183
  link list, 202–203
  LostFocus, 171
  OnBlur events, 171–172
  OnFocus events, 171–172
  Password, 173–174
  Radio Button, 174–178
  Reset, 168
  Select, 179–183, 195–196
  Submit, 168
  text, 168–172
  Textarea, 172–173
  versus ActiveX controls, 185
IsDate function, 143
IsNumeric function, 144
items
  multiple selections, 182–183
  selecting, 179–183
ItemText array, online quiz application, 338

• J •

James, Steve, 3, 5
Java, compared to VBScript, 348
JavaScript
  blur, 171
  versus VBScript, 55–56, 348

• K •

keyboard shortcuts, Internet Explorer, 39
keys, F5 (Reload), 25, 27
keywords
  Call, 87–88
  Function, 83
  Set, 107, 192–193
  Sub, 82–83
kiosk mode, 39

• L •

label controls, 260
Label, ActiveX control, 242, 287–288, 324–325
labels, layout, 288
LANGUAGE attribute, HTML tags, 50
layouts
  creating, 283–290
  editing, 285
  hotspots, 288
  Image, ActiveX control, 285–287
  labels, 287–288
  saving, 284–285
  subroutine testing, 290
Lcase function, 141
Left function, 140–141
left.htm HTML document, 206–207
Len function, 31, 135, 142
Levine, John R., 5
line breaks, forcing, 133–134
line spacing, code, 53
link lists, form controls, 202–203
Link object, 58–59, 67
LinkArray array, 124–125
links
  Calendar application, 332–335
  dot notation, 60
  HTML documents, 41
links.htm document, 61
ListBox, ActiveX control, 293
lists, link, 202–203
loader.htm HTML document, 210–211
loan amortization, 317–322
Location objects, 66
logical flaws, program bugs, 151, 153
logical operators, 99, 133

LoopIndex variable, 156
loops, 121–129
  backwards, 123
  Do Until, 126–127
  Do While, 127–128
  Do-Loop Until, 128
  Do-Loop While, 128–129
  For-Next, 121–126
  nested For-Next, 125–126
  when to use, 129
LostFocus events, 171–172
lottery number generator, 237–238

• *M* •

mailing lists, 352
main.htm document, 61
makeframes.htm document, 61
maps
  ActiveX controls, 244
  client-side image, 7
Mark, Steve, 229
marquee <MARQUEE> HTML tag, 222–224
Marquee, ActiveX control, 269
marquees, scrolling, 37
math functions, 138–139
mathematical operators, 99
MaxData variable, 303
MaxHt variable, 303
menus, shortcut, Internet Explorer, 38–39
message box, creating with MsgBox
    function, 144–147
message flasher, floating frames, 222–224
messages
  avoiding errors, 154–155
  Cannot assign to a variable, 82, 96
  displaying in dialog box, 7, 144
  Expected identifier, 82
  Expected statement, 82
  MsgButton event handler display, 166
  scrolling status bar, 234–235
  syntax error, 150–151

methods
  ActiveX controls, 267–268
  Alert, 74–75
  Back, 75
  Confirm, 75
  described, 74
  object, 73–75
  SetTimeOut, 221
  Write, 74
Microsoft ActiveX controls, 245–247
Microsoft HTML Control Pad, 13
Microsoft IntelliMouse, 40
Microsoft Internet Explorer 3.0, 13
Microsoft VBScript site, 351–352
Microsoft Word, with Internet Assistant,
    as HTML editor, 18
Mid function, 135, 140
Mod operator, 98
modes, kiosk, 39
monthly payments, calculations, 314–315
MonthName arrays, 325
MonthName function, 231
Mortgage Payment application, 309–322
  data input form, 311–312
  floating frames, 317
  forms, 310–312
  loan amortization, 317–322
  monthly payment calculations, 314–315
  number formatting, 315–316
  project goals, 309–310
  results calculations, 313–316
  results form, 312
  subroutine testing, 321–322
  table nesting, 312
MouseEnter event, 288
MouseExit event, 288
MS Forms 2.0, ActiveX controls, 245–246
Msg variable, 119
MsgBox function, 132, 144–147
MsgButton event handler, message
    display, 166
multidimensional arrays, 102–103

MULTIPLE attribute, Select control, 180
multiple instructions
  If-Then structure, 114
  If-Then-Else, 115–117
multistatement-per-line colon
      character, 119
multitasking, 38

• *N* •

Name variable, 127–128
naming conventions, functions, 82
Navigator objects, 66
negative step value, backwards loop, 123
nerd, 1
nested
  For-Next loop, 125–126
  loops, 125–126
  objects, 62
  Select Case structures, 119–120
Netscape Navigator
  VBScript plug-in, 54
  versus Internet Explorer, 38
newsgroups, VBScript resources, 352–353
Not logical operator, 113
notations, dot, 60
Notepad, as HTML editor, 17
Now function, 21, 230–232
nper argument, Pmt function, 315
number formatting functions, 227–230
numbers
  formatting, 315–316
  hexadecimal, 27–28, 30
  index, 191–192
  list generation, 194–195
  random, 237–238
  version, 35
numeric values, 229
Nums array, 124
NumValues variable, 103

• *O* •

object <OBJECT> HTML tag, 254–255, 281
object model, 57–59
  floating frames, 63–65
  hierarchy, 58
  HTML intrinsic controls, 164
object variables, 106–107, 192–193
objects
  accessor property, 72
  ActiveX controls, 59, 241–252
  Anchor, 58–59, 67
  collection groups, 59
  concepts, 62
  defined, 57
  described, 65–65
  Document, 58, 67
  dot notation links, 60
  Element, 58–59, 68
  events, 75–78
  Form, 58–59, 67
  Frame, 66
  fully qualified reference, 72
  hierarchy, 58
  History, 66
  importance of, 65
  Link, 58–59, 67
  Location, 66
  methods, 73–75
  Navigator, 66
  nested, 62
  parent-child relationship, 62–63
  pointing to, 71–73
  properties, 70–73
  property references, 70
  property values, 70–71
  references, 59–60
  relationships, 60–63
  Scripts, 67
  variables, 106–107
  Window, 58, 66

ocx file extension, 246
On Error Resume Next statement, error message avoidance, 154
OnBlur events, 171–172
onClick events, 165–168
OnFocus events, 171–172
Online Fruit Stand, HTML Layout control, 293
online magazines, ActiveX Journal for HTML writers, online magazine, 353
online quiz application, 337–344
ActiveX controls, 340–341
adaptations, 344
components, 338
data storage, 338–339
described, 341–343
game plan, 338
item presentation, 339–341
project goals, 337
OnSubmit event, 197–198
OOP (object-oriented programming), 57
Open in New Window, Internet Explorer command, 38
operators
common, 98–99
concatenation, 156
equal sign character, 71
expressions, 98–101
logical, 99, 113
mathematical, 99
Mod, 98
order of precedence, 100–101
parentheses characters, 100–101
Option Explicit statement, 108–109
Options array, online quiz application, 338
Options dialog box, Internet Explorer, 249
order of precedence, operators, 100–101
output fields, text controls, 168–172

• P •

pages
element editing after page is loaded into browser, 242–243
floating frame updating, 217–219
param <PARAM> HTML tags, 255
parent-child relationship, objects, 62–63
parentheses characters
function arguments, 131–132
operator order of precedence, 100–101
subroutines, 83
parsing, Textarea control, 173
Password control, 164, 173–174
percentages format, 228–229
plug-ins, VBScript/Netscape Navigator, 54
PMT function, 315
pointers, object, 71–73
PopUp Menu, ActiveX control, 269–271
princ argument, PMT function, 315
procedures
deferred scripts, 47–48
HTML document placement, 91–92
multiple variable declarations, 106
program bugs, 149–160
debugging, 153–154
identifying, 153–154
logical flaws, 151, 153
prevention tips, 157–159
runtime errors, 151–153
programmers, described, 1–2
programming language, VBScript, 348
programming, described, 1–2
programs
execute on users local drive, 349
flow control, 111–130
VBCompanion, 268
properties
accessor, 72
ActiveX controls, 267–268

Bgcolor, 70–71
objects, 70–73
read-only, 71
value editing, 70–71
public variable, 105
publications
American Heritage Dictionary, 57
Creating Web Pages For Dummies, 5
HTML For Dummies, 3, 5
Internet For Dummies, 5
PCs For Dummies, 5

• Q •

questions
access to Web site limited, 348
browser compatibility, 349
execute program on users local drive, 349
Java compared to VBScript, 348
JavaScript compared to VBScript, 348
protecting VBScript code, 349
uses for VBScript, 348
VBScript programming language, 348
VBScript, same as Visual Basic, 347
viewing source code, 349
Web page hit counter, 349
quiz, online, 337–344
quotes characters, with code case, 52–53

• R •

Radio Button control, 164, 174–178
random numbers
functions, 138–139
sorting, 237–238
Randomize function, 135, 138–139
rate argument, Pmt function, 315
readers, assumptions, 5

read-only property, 71
real-time data acquisition, ActiveX
controls, 245
ReDim statement, redimensioning
arrays, 103
references
form controls, 189–193
frame, 208–209
fully qualified, 72
object, 59–60, 70
Reload (F5) key, 25, 27
Reset controls, 164, 168
resources
ActiveX Journal for HTML writers, online
magazine, 353
ActiveX Resource Center, 354
ACTIVEX.COM, 354
Microsoft VBScript site, 351–352
newsgroups, 352–353
Scribe: The VBScript Writers
resource, 353
VBScript Central, 352
VBScript mailing list, 352
VBScript/ActiveX demo page, 353
Web search engines, 354
Responses array, online quiz
application, 338
responses, message box returns, 145
results form, Mortgage Payment
application, 312
ReverseText function, 90
RGB (Red-Green-Blue) color model, 30
Right function, 140–141
right.htm HTML document, 207
Rnd function, 98, 135, 138–139
rolling dice, HTML Layout control, 292
runtime errors, program bugs, 151–153

• S •

Save (Ctrl+S) keyboard shortcut, 27, 284
ScaledData array, 303
schedules, loan amortization, 319–321
scope arrays, 104–106
acope variable, 104–106, 158
Scribe: The VBScript Writers resource, 353
script <SCRIPT> HTML tag, 45–51
script blocks, HTML tags, 49, 108–109
Script Error dialog box, 152
Script objects, 67
Script Wizard, ActiveX Control Pad, 258, 264–267
script-aware browsers, 51
scripts
  apostrophe character with comments, 52
  deferred execution, 47–48
  editing, 29–30
  embedding, 45–48
  hiding with comment tags, 50–51
  immediate execution, 45–47, 91–92
  inserting, 26–32
  placing in documents, 49
  quotes characters capitalization effects, 52–53
  screen resolution, 27
  testing, 29, 266
  troubleshooting bugs 31
  writing tips, 27
ScrollBar, ActiveX control, 242–243
scrolling marquee, Internet Explorer, 37
scrolling status bar message, 234–235
search engines, 354
SearchButton event handler, opening new URL, 167
searches, Web sites, 39
security
  ActiveX controls, 249–250
  Internet Explorer, 38

select <SELECT> HTML tags, 188
Select Case structure, 117–120
Select control, 164, 179–183, 195–196
select controls, column charts, 306–307
selections, multiple items, 182–183
servers, code testing, 159
server-side validation, forms, 188–189
Set keyword, object variables, 107, 192–193
SetTimeOut method, 221
shareware, ActiveX controls, 243
shortcut menus, Internet Explorer, 38–39
Sin function, 138
SitePad, 18–19
SIZE attribute, Select control, 180
Smith, Bud, 5
software, downloading, 15–17
sorts
  arrays, 236–237
  lottery numbers, 237–238
sounds, playing, 233
source codes, viewing, 349
special effects, 7, 221–222, 225, 235–236
spelling conventions, functions, 131
SpinButton, ActiveX control, 262, 324–325
Sqr function, 98
statements
  Alert, 155–156
  Dim, 101–102
  End Function, 83
  End Sub, 82–83
  On Error Resume Next, 154
  Option Explicit, 108–109
  ReDim, 103
  splitting between lines, 53–54
  variable assignment, 96–101
status bar messages, scrolling, 234–235
step value, For-Next loop, 122–123
string functions, 140–143
structures, programming, 111–112
style sheets, cascading, 36–37
Sub keyword, 82–83

Submit control, 163, 168
subroutines, 26–28
  arguments, 83, 85–88
  Calendar application, 325–326, 331
  calling, 87–88
  deferred scripts, 47–48
  described, 81
  event handler, 83–85, 166–168
  HTML document placement, 91–92
  modifying, 27–28
  multiple, 28
  naming conventions, 82
  parentheses characters, 83
  Sub keyword, 82–83
  testing, 321–322
  tests, 290
  troubleshooting, 92–93
subsets, VBScript, 347
survey.htm document, 63–65
Switch (Alt+Tab) keyboard shortcut, 27
syntax errors, correcting, 149–151

• *T* •

tables, nesting, 312
Tan function, 138
ten top
  VBScript Q & A, 347–349
  VBScript resources on the Net, 351–354
tests
  Calendar application controls, 327,
    331–332
  code, 158–159
  subroutine, 290, 321–322
text controls, 168–172
text editor, 17–19
text editors, ActiveX Control Pad, 256–257
textarea <TEXTAREA> HTML tags, 188
Textarea control, 164, 172–173
Time function, 114, 136–137
time of day audio greetings, 233

time, displaying, 230–232
Timer, ActiveX control, 273–276
Tittel, Ed, 3, 5
toolbars
  adding HTML editor to, 18
  Internet Explorer, 39
Tools⇨Script Wizard, ActiveX Control Pad
    command, 264, 289
TourDates array, Calendar application, 333
TourDoc array, Calendar application, 333
trigonometric functions, 138
troubleshooting
  bugs, 31, 149–160
  debugging code, 153–157
  functions, 92–93
  logical flaws, 151–153
  program bugs, 151–153
  runtime errors, 151–153
  subroutines, 92–93
  syntax errors, 149–151

• *U* •

Ubound function, 103–104
Ucase function, 141
UI (user interface) function, 132, 144–148
URL (uniform resource locator)
  codebase, 248
  loading into different frames, 212–213
  opening new with SearchButton, 167
  toolbar location display, 42–43
user interface, ActiveX controls, 244
UserName variable, 84, 113
users, formless input, 7
uses, for VBScript, 348

• *V* •

validation
  credit card numbers, 233–234
  forms, 188–189

values
button captions, 166–167
decimal, 232
numeric, 229
object properties, 70–71
step, 122–123
variable, 96–101
variable scoping, 93
variables
Age, 113
arrays, 101–106
assignment statements, 96–101
combining with concatenation (&)
operator, 156
Counter, 156
data types, 97
declaration forcing, 107–109, 157–158
declarations, 305–306
described, 95
expressions, 97–98
floating frame, 156–157
LoopIndex, 156
MaxData, 303
MaxHt, 303
monitoring, 156–157
Msg, 119
multiple declaration, 106
Name, 127–128
naming conventions, 95–96
NumValues, 103
object, 106–107, 192–193
public, 105
scope, 104–106, 158
UserName, 84, 113
variants, 97
VisitorName, 148
X, 113
Y, 113
variant functions, 143–144
variants, variables, 97
VB (Visual Basic) programming language, 6

VBA (Visual Basic for Applications), 6
VBCompanion program, 268
vbs/index.htm HTML document, 232–233
VBScript (Visual Basic Scripting), 6
becoming a guru, 355–357
browser compatibility issues, 54–55
browser support, 15
code writing process, 20
control generation, 193–196
form generation, 193–196
hosting, 15
HTML form creation, 189
learning curve, 14, 24
uses, 6–7, 348
VBSCRIPT.DLL file, 15
version numbers, displaying, 35
versus JavaScript, 55–56
Web site support, 6
when to use/avoid, 55
VBScript Central, resource site, 353
VBScript code
look at for experience, 355
protecting from public view/use, 349
VBScript Function Reference, 132, 148
VBSCRIPT.DLL file, 15
VBScript/ActiveX demo page, 353
VBScript-compatible browser, detecting,
232–233
vertical frames, 206–207
video, ActiveX controls, 244
View⇨Options, Internet Explorer com-
mand, 233, 249
View⇨Options, Windows command, 18
View⇨Properties, ActiveX Control Pad
command, 286
View⇨Refresh, Internet Explorer com-
mand, 27
View⇨Source command, 174, 349
View⇨Source, Internet Explorer com-
mand, 54, 282

View⊃Toolbox, ActiveX Control Pad
        command, 285
viewers, document, 245
VisitorName variable, 148

• W •

WavyText function, 236
Web
  browse to become a guru, 355
  search engines, 354
Web pages
  element editing after page is loaded into
        browser, 242–243
  floating frame updating, 217–219
  set up hit counter, 349
  VBScript code, 349
Web sites
  access limited by VBScript, 348
  ActiveX Control Pad, 16–17
  ActiveX Journal for HTML writers, online
        magazine, 353
  ActiveX Resource Center, 354
  ACTIVEX.COM, 354
  AltaVista, 167
  Apex, 268
  history list, 43
  HTML editors, 19
  included with book, 8–9
  Internet Explorer 3.0, 16
  Microsoft, 36
  Microsoft Forms 2.0 ActiveX controls, 255
  resource sites, 351–354
  Scribe: The VBScript Writers resource, 353
  searching for, 39
  SitePad, 18–19
  Spreadsheet Page (The), 2
  think like a visitor to design, 356
  VBScript Central, 353
  VBScript/ActiveX demo page, 353

VBScript/Netscape Navigator plug-in, 54
Weekday function, 116, 137–138
WIDTH attribute, HTML tags, 50, 255
Window object, 58, 63, 66
Windows
  adding HTML editor to toolbar, 18
  Notepad, 17
  WordPad, 17
windows
  documents, opening new, 38
  Internet Explorer, 40
  Script Wizard, 265–266
  switching between, 27
Wizards, Script, 258, 264–267
WordPad, as HTML editor, 17
WWW (World Wide Web), 1
  Microsoft versus Netscape browsers, 16
WYSIWYG (what-you-see-is-what-you-get),
        18

• X •

X variable, 113

• Y •

Y variable, 113
Year function, 96
Young, Margaret Levine, 5

Notes

IDG BOOKS WORLDWIDE, INC.
END-USER LICENSE AGREEMENT

<u>Read This</u>. **You should carefully read these terms and conditions before opening the software packet(s) included with this book ("Book"). This is a license agreement ("Agreement") between you and IDG Books Worldwide, Inc. ("IDGB"). By opening the accompanying software packet(s), you acknowledge that you have read and accept the following terms and conditions. If you do not agree and do not want to be bound by such terms and conditions, promptly return the Book and the unopened software packet(s) to the place you obtained them for a full refund.**

1. <u>**License Grant**</u>. IDGB grants to you (either an individual or entity) a nonexclusive license to use one copy of the enclosed software program(s) (collectively, the "Software") solely for your own personal or business purposes on a single computer (whether a standard computer or a workstation component of a multiuser network). The Software is in use on a computer when it is loaded into temporary memory (i.e., RAM) or installed into permanent memory (e.g., hard disk, CD-ROM, or other storage device). IDGB reserves all rights not expressly granted herein.

2. <u>**Ownership**</u>. IDGB is the owner of all right, title, and interest, including copyright, in and to the compilation of the Software recorded on the disk(s)/CD-ROM. Copyright to the individual programs on the disk(s)/CD-ROM is owned by the author or other authorized copyright owner of each program. Ownership of the Software and all proprietary rights relating thereto remain with IDGB and its licensors.

3. <u>**Restrictions on Use and Transfer**</u>.

   (a) You may only (i) make one copy of the Software for backup or archival purposes, or (ii) transfer the Software to a single hard disk, provided that you keep the original for backup or archival purposes. You may not (i) rent or lease the Software, (ii) copy or reproduce the Software through a LAN or other network system or through any computer subscriber system or bulletin-board system, or (iii) modify, adapt, or create derivative works based on the Software.

   (b) You may not reverse engineer, decompile, or disassemble the Software. You may transfer the Software and user documentation on a permanent basis, provided that the transferee agrees to accept the terms and conditions of this Agreement and you retain no copies. If the Software is an update or has been updated, any transfer must include the most recent update and all prior versions.

4. <u>**Restrictions on Use of Individual Programs**</u>. You must follow the individual requirements and restrictions detailed for each individual program in the "About the Disk or CD" section of this Book. These limitations are contained in the individual license agreements recorded on the disk(s)/CD-ROM. These restrictions may include a requirement that after using the program for the period of time specified in its text, the user must pay a registration fee or discontinue use. By opening the Software packet(s), you will be agreeing to abide by the licenses and restrictions for these individual programs. None of the material on this disk(s) or listed in this Book may ever be distributed, in original or modified form, for commercial purposes.

5. <u>**Limited Warranty**</u>.

(a) IDGB warrants that the Software and disk(s)/CD-ROM are free from defects in materials and workmanship under normal use for a period of sixty (60) days from the date of purchase of this Book. If IDGB receives notification within the warranty period of defects in materials or workmanship, IDGB will replace the defective disk(s)/CD-ROM.

(b) **IDGB AND THE AUTHOR OF THE BOOK DISCLAIM ALL OTHER WARRANTIES, EXPRESS OR IMPLIED, INCLUDING WITHOUT LIMITATION IMPLIED WARRANTIES OF MERCHANTABILITY AND FITNESS FOR A PARTICULAR PURPOSE, WITH RESPECT TO THE SOFTWARE, THE PROGRAMS, THE SOURCE CODE CONTAINED THEREIN, AND/ OR THE TECHNIQUES DESCRIBED IN THIS BOOK. IDGB DOES NOT WARRANT THAT THE FUNCTIONS CONTAINED IN THE SOFTWARE WILL MEET YOUR REQUIREMENTS OR THAT THE OPERATION OF THE SOFTWARE WILL BE ERROR FREE.**

(c) This limited warranty gives you specific legal rights, and you may have other rights which vary from jurisdiction to jurisdiction.

6. <u>**Remedies**</u>.

(a) IDGB's entire liability and your exclusive remedy for defects in materials and workmanship shall be limited to replacement of the Software, which may be returned to IDGB with a copy of your receipt at the following address: Disk Fulfillment Department, Attn: VBScript For Dummies, IDG Books Worldwide, Inc., 7260 Shadeland Station, Ste. 100, Indianapolis, IN 46256, or call 1-800-762-2974. Please allow 3-4 weeks for delivery. This Limited Warranty is void if failure of the Software has resulted from accident, abuse, or misapplication. Any replacement Software will be warranted for the remainder of the original warranty period or thirty (30) days, whichever is longer.

(b) In no event shall IDGB or the author be liable for any damages whatsoever (including without limitation damages for loss of business profits, business interruption, loss of business information, or any other pecuniary loss) arising from the use of or inability to use the Book or the Software, even if IDGB has been advised of the possibility of such damages.

(c) Because some jurisdictions do not allow the exclusion or limitation of liability for consequential or incidental damages, the above limitation or exclusion may not apply to you.

7. <u>**U.S. Government Restricted Rights**</u>. Use, duplication, or disclosure of the Software by the U.S. Government is subject to restrictions stated in paragraph (c) (1) (ii) of the Rights in Technical Data and Computer Software clause of DFARS 252.227-7013, and in subparagraphs (a) through (d) of the Commercial Computer—Restricted Rights clause at FAR 52.227-19, and in similar clauses in the NASA FAR supplement, when applicable.

8. <u>**General**</u>. This Agreement constitutes the entire understanding of the parties and revokes and supersedes all prior agreements, oral or written, between them and may not be modified or amended except in a writing signed by both parties hereto which specifically refers to this Agreement. This Agreement shall take precedence over any other documents that may be in conflict herewith. If any one or more provisions contained in this Agreement are held by any court or tribunal to be invalid, illegal, or otherwise unenforceable, each and every other provision shall remain in full force and effect.

The VBScript For Dummies Sample Files

The companion diskette contains dozens of examples that are described in the book. The following sections describe how to install the files and how to access the examples.

Installing the Sample Files

To install the sample files, follow these steps:

1. **Insert the diskette into drive A or drive B.**
2. **Click the My Computer icon on the Windows desktop.**

   Windows displays a new folder window.
3. **Double-click the icon that represents the drive you used in step 1.**
4. **Click the folder icon labeled VBSBook.**
5. **Choose the Edit⇨Copy command.**
6. **Click the Up One Level icon in the folder window's toolbar.**

   (This icon displays a folder with an upward-pointing arrow.)
7. **Double-click the drive to which you want to install the files (for example, drive C).**
8. **Choose Edit⇨Paste command.**

   Windows copies the files and folders from the floppy disk to the drive you selected in Step 7.

Using the Sample Files

The examples are arranged as if they were files at a Web site. In other words, the "home page" is the index.htm document, which contains links to each of the chapters (the examples for each chapter are stored in a separate folder). Each chapter document contains links to the specific samples.

To view an example:

1. **Start by loading the index.htm file into Internet Explorer.**

   If you installed the files using the preceding instructions, index.htm will be located in the VBSBook folder. You can use Internet Explorer's File⇨Open command and click the Browse button to locate the index.htm file. Or, you can simply drag the index.htm file from a folder window into the Internet Explorer window.

   You may want to add the index.htm file to your list of favorites. When the index.htm document is displayed, choose the Favorites⇨Add to Favorites command. After doing so, you can quickly open the index.htm file by clicking the Favorites icon in Internet Explorer.

2. **When the index.htm document is displayed, click the hyperlink that represents the chapter in which the example is described.**

   Internet Explorer loads a new document that contains links to the examples for the chapter you selected.

3. **Click the hyperlink for the example that you're interested in.**

   Internet Explorer loads the example file.

4. **To return to the chapter page, click Internet Explorer's Back button.**

While you're viewing an example, you can examine the source document (including the VBScript code) by selecting the View⇨Source command.

If you have problems with the installation process, you can call the IDG Books Worldwide, Inc., Customer Support number: 800-762-2974 (outside the U.S.: 317-596-5261).

IDG BOOKS WORLDWIDE REGISTRATION CARD

RETURN THIS REGISTRATION CARD FOR FREE CATALOG

Title of this book: **VBScript For Dummies®**

My overall rating of this book: ❏ Very good [1] ❏ Good [2] ❏ Satisfactory [3] ❏ Fair [4] ❏ Poor [5]

How I first heard about this book:

❏ Found in bookstore; name: [6]

❏ Advertisement: [8]

❏ Word of mouth; heard about book from friend, co-worker, etc.: [10]

❏ Book review: [7]

❏ Catalog: [9]

❏ Other: [11]

What I liked most about this book:

What I would change, add, delete, etc., in future editions of this book:

Other comments:

Number of computer books I purchase in a year: ❏ 1 [12] ❏ 2-5 [13] ❏ 6-10 [14] ❏ More than 10 [15]

I would characterize my computer skills as: ❏ Beginner [16] ❏ Intermediate [17] ❏ Advanced [18] ❏ Professional [19]

I use ❏ DOS [20] ❏ Windows [21] ❏ OS/2 [22] ❏ Unix [23] ❏ Macintosh [24] ❏ Other: [25]_____
(please specify)

I would be interested in new books on the following subjects:
(please check all that apply, and use the spaces provided to identify specific software)

❏ Word processing: [26]

❏ Data bases: [28]

❏ File Utilities: [30]

❏ Networking: [32]

❏ Other: [34]

❏ Spreadsheets: [27]

❏ Desktop publishing: [29]

❏ Money management: [31]

❏ Programming languages: [33]

I use a PC at (please check all that apply): ❏ home [35] ❏ work [36] ❏ school [37] ❏ other: [38] _____

The disks I prefer to use are ❏ 5.25 [39] ❏ 3.5 [40] ❏ other: [41]_____

I have a CD ROM: ❏ yes [42] ❏ no [43]

I plan to buy or upgrade computer hardware this year: ❏ yes [44] ❏ no [45]

I plan to buy or upgrade computer software this year: ❏ yes [46] ❏ no [47]

Name: _____ Business title: [48] _____ Type of Business: [49] _____

Address (❏ home [50] ❏ work [51]/Company name: _____)

Street/Suite# _____

City [52]/State [53]/Zipcode [54]: _____ Country [55] _____

❏ **I liked this book!** You may quote me by name in future
IDG Books Worldwide promotional materials.

My daytime phone number is _____

IDG BOOKS
THE WORLD OF
COMPUTER
KNOWLEDGE